P9-EDP-299

CALIFORNIA - WESTERN AMERICANA   OP 87/8

Santa Clara
County
Free Library

REFERENCE

 5816

California-
Where the Twain
Did Meet

California-
Where the Twain
Did Meet

ANNE LOFTIS

519581

Macmillan Publishing Co., Inc.
NEW YORK
Collier Macmillan Publishers
LONDON

SANTA CLARA COUNTY LIBRARY
3 3305 00207 5467

Santa Clara County Free Library
San Jose, California

Copyright © 1973 by Anne Loftis

All rights reserved. No part of this book may be
reproduced or transmitted in any form or by
any means, electronic or mechanical, including
photocopying, recording or by any information
storage and retrieval system, without permission
in writing from the Publisher.

Macmillan Publishing Co., Inc.
Collier-Macmillan Canada Ltd.

Library of Congress Catalog Card Number:
72-11278

First Printing

Printed in the United States of America

FOR

J. CLYDE LOFTIS

AND

JOHN LOFTIS

Contents

✿ ★ ✿

Preface

❧ ★ ❧

THIS IS THE STORY of the conflict of people of different races and nationalities, of diverse skills and ambitions, in California, where the relationship of the first inhabitants, the Indians, with their conquerors, the Spaniards, set a pattern for future interaction between groups. Because of its geographical isolation, California was late in becoming a focal point for settlement by people from other parts of the world. The discovery of gold in the foothills of the Sierra Nevada in 1848 started the extraordinary population boom that has continued for nearly a century and a quarter.

Whether they came seeking gold or desiring a benign climate, whether they came to make a living or to flee the oppressions and conventions of older communities, the new arrivals tended to look on California as a place where they could express themselves with freedom. Daring and improvisation were rewarded on the frontier.

There was a danger, however, that unrestrained individualism might degenerate into anarchy. In order to create some form and order in a chaotic society, early leaders passed hastily conceived laws and practiced extralegal forms of justice, taking it upon themselves to decide which groups should be banished from the new Arcadia. This

heritage of freedom and initiative, with its counterpart of
vigilante reaction, survives in the state today in the politics
which have been quixotic to the point of schizophrenia and
in the proliferation of utopian ideas and bizarre living patterns which invite threats of repression in the next swing
of the pendulum.

Carelessness is another frontier legacy in California.
Successive waves of immigrants have tapped the wealth
of minerals, forests, and open land with spendthrift abandon. Early visitors to the state noted the despoilment of
rivers—silted with gravel and earth in the wake of hydraulic mining—a forecast of present-day concern over
the destruction of hillsides and trees, the pollution of water
and air. Until recently there was no thought that these ravages were not a necessary concomitant of "the career of
civilization," of which an early Californian boasted, "Its
progress has been an ovation—steady, august, and resist-
less." [1]

Human beings were also sacrificed to what another
California governor called "the stimulus of American
energy." [2] In the rush to develop the new country, the people who got in the way, such as the Indians, were simply
trampled down. In the nineteenth and early twentieth centuries certain groups of men, usually with darker skins,
were regarded as tools for the creation of other men's
wealth. The crops were harvested, railroads were built,
sloughs were drained, and levees were constructed by gangs
of faceless laborers—Orientals, Mexicans, East Indians from
the Punjab—all of whom were prevented from following
the paths to success open to white immigrants. Though
black people did not arrive in significant numbers until
World War II, perhaps in no other state has race prejudice
been so virulent against so many different groups as in
California.

Today the dark-skinned immigrants are finding some
encouragement toward realizing the opportunities open

from the beginning to Anglos; or rather, to most Anglos most of the time, for the Dust Bowl migrants of the Depression era were not welcomed when they came to pick fruit at a dollar a day. Economics have been as important a factor as race in the relationship of various groups.

California has long been a place of bewildering changes. When Richard Henry Dana returned to San Francisco in 1859 and reflected on the transformation of the crude port he had visited twenty-four years before, he exclaimed, "I could scarcely keep my hold on reality." What would an observer of the sleepy "cow town" of Mexican days say about the megapolis of Los Angeles, where the motion picture industry created a twentieth-century Gold Rush?

The social changes have been equally dramatic. The descendants of many foreign immigrants who arrived penniless now control wealth and power in the state. The children of the dark-skinned races have joined together to proclaim their common concerns. The anger of the younger generation has exploded at Watts and Berkeley, setting a pattern for race riots and student unrest in other parts of the nation. "Things tend to happen first in California," said the embattled chancellor of the state college system.

In approaching the subject from an ethnic viewpoint, this book subjects California history to a different focus. Some of the events which form the basis of economic and political studies of the state are omitted or barely mentioned here. Other occurrences are given more emphasis than they would have in another context. It should also be noted that in isolating the story of the people of California we may lose sight of their regional and national ties. For all its vaunted uniqueness, the Golden State shows much similarity to its neighbors in the Southwest in the history of Indian-white and Chicano-Anglo relationships. European-American and Asian-Caucasian encounters resemble those in the other Pacific Coast states, while the black-white confrontations of recent years conform in many ways to a nationwide pattern. California has only the advantage of containing an immense variety of races and nationalities in sufficient numbers to make their study significant.

I FIRST BECAME interested in ethnic groups in California through reading the books and articles of Carey McWilliams. His powerful landmark studies combine a feeling for people with an unsentimental grasp of economic and political realities. I found the same characteristics in the writings of Dr. Paul S. Taylor, University of California economist. At closer hand, the late Elsa Alsberg, executive director of the Palo Alto Fair Play Council, gave me the benefit of her lifetime of work with immigrants and people of various races. My father, the late Allan Nevins, impressed on me the value of social history, and searched his library for books to educate me for this project.

I received valuable help from the staffs of the Stanford University Library and the Bancroft Library of the University of California at Berkeley. I thank Dr. Franz Lassner, director of archives, and his assistants at the Hoover Institution on War, Revolution and Peace, and Dr. Willa Baum and her staff at the Regional Oral History Office of the Bancroft Library. Father Arthur Spearman, S. J., the archivist at the University of Santa Clara, made valuable suggestions and put his manuscripts at my disposal, as did Ronald J. Mahoney, head of special collections, and Mary Ann Fox, librarian for ethnic studies at the California State University, Fresno. I thank Mrs. Joseph Wilson of the Bibliothèque of the Alliance Française in San Francisco, and Mrs. M. K. Swingle of the California Historical Association Library. Professor Doyce Nunis drew my attention to theses on California ethnic groups written at the University of Southern California. Dr. William Mason, curator of archives of the History Division of the Los Angeles County Museum of Natural History, suggested points for investigation. Mary Powell Flanders of Oakland loaned me her great-grandfather's diary of his immigration to California from Wales, which she has edited and enriched with contemporary reports on the Gold Rush migration from the London *Times*. I received much help from the staff of the International Institute in San Francisco, and from Grace McDonald, editor of the *California Farmer Consumer Reporter*.

I was fortunate in finding intelligent and resourceful research assistants: Joan Ewing, who translated articles from Spanish; Barbara Kinsman, who hunted material in Southern California; Sylvia Vane, who searched out legislative and court documents and provided source materials from her anthropological studies; and Peter and Susan Vogel, who collected information in the San Francisco area. Jean Simpson, who typed the manuscript, corrected stylistic weaknesses. Dr. Walter Warren, director of the California History Center at De Anza College, read an intermediate draft and made valuable suggestions.

Helen June Mitchell, the librarian in Livingston, California, made contact for me with people from half a dozen immigrant groups in her area of the San Joaquin Valley. Dr. Paul Barnes of Walnut Grove, and his wife Lucy, put me in touch with Chinese and Japanese residents of the Sacramento Delta. Jefferson Mulkey, a native of Modoc County, sent me to relatives and friends in northeastern California.

I thank the following people for lending material or suggesting interviews: Joseph Barnes, Bruce Bliven, Maydene Burtt, Eugenia Buss, George Chu, Margo Courtois, Leola Cullinan, Dr. Nathaniel Handy, Patricia Kepler, David Kherdian, Frances and James Kirihara, Elizabeth Lanz, Ping K. Lee, Mr. and Mrs. C. H. Loehlin, Devon and Luella McFarland, Marlys Maier, Margo Manley, Rachelle Marshall, Tosh Matsuoka, Lee Nelson, Mary R. Nevins, Leona Nichols, Woesha North, David Podbielski, the Reverend Louis Riley, Lynne Rinehart, Frank Rodrigues, Dr. Irwin Roth, Imogen and G. S. Sahi, Tosh Sakai, George Sakogawa, Hildegard Sander, Thelma Shiplet, Alice Smith, the Reverend Walter Smith, B. S. Teja, Simon Toulouse, and Kathy Vinokur; also Donna and Thomas Ambrogi, Mary and Stephen Brayton, Lilia Chung, Rosemary Cooper-rider, Prof. Richard T. La Piere, and Margaret Paulekas.

Finally, I thank my husband for the greatest influence.

ANNE LOFTIS

Portola Valley, California

1. Gov. John Bigler to Redick McKee, April 9, 1852, *Appendix to the Statutes of the Legislature, 1852,* p. 714.
2. Leland Stanford at the ground-breaking ceremony for the Central Pacific Railroad at Sacramento, February 22, 1863.

California–
Where the Twain
Did Meet

I

Indians and White Men on the Frontier

⚜ ★ ⚜

THE CLASH OF OLD and new world cultures began late in California—in the mid-eighteenth century—when a small colonizing expedition of Spaniards from Mexico invaded the territory of Indians who had been in exclusive possession of the land for thousands of years. The brief two-century period of European and American domination, which began at that time, is but a small fraction of the long span of human history in the area.

The events of the early history of California are obscure since the natives had no written languages to record them. Our evidence comes mainly from twentieth-century archeological and anthropological discoveries and from the oral traditions of the people handed down from one generation to the next up to the present day. Some information can be gleaned as well from the chronicles of the first white men to come in contact with the Indians, though their accounts must be interpreted in the light of their attitudes and intentions toward members of another race.

The native Californians, like all American aboriginals, were descended from Asians, who, it is surmised, crossed from Siberia to Alaska and moved southward in a migra-

1

tion that took place so far in the distant past that no memory of it appears in their folklore or mythology. The West Coast of North America was a favorable environment for human beings, and many settled there. At the time the Spaniards arrived, California had a population estimated at between 125,000 and 400,000 people.[1]

The Indians lived in small groups with different languages and dialects, widely scattered throughout the varied climate zones of the region which today comprises 158,693 square miles. In the heavily forested areas of the north they clothed themselves in fur and built houses of boughs and bark to withstand the cold in winter, though it was customary for the bands to move out of the mountains into the more temperate valleys when heavy snows fell. They hunted game with bows and arrows, knives, and occasionally fire, as an alternative to the chase, encircling an area with flames to drive the animals out of cover or using various ruses to lure them into the open. They caught salmon in the rivers with nets, hooks, or harpoons. The tribes along the coast hunted otter in boats and gathered shellfish. The desert dwellers made ingenious use of the sparse vegetation and animal life to supply themselves with food, medicine, and shelter. Mesquite pods were a staple of diet in the desert, while acorns—ground, leached, and cooked —were a principal food in the less dry regions where oak trees grew.

There was some trade between neighboring peoples which made possible a wider variety of natural resources than were available in the area claimed by each group. Clans lived within a known territory, migrating for seasonal variety or food gathering, but respecting the boundaries of neighbors. This peaceful co-existence depended on adequate natural resources. Wars of annihilation between groups are supposed to have occurred in the wake of famine caused by severe drought or some other disaster that destroyed the food supply.

The Mojave and other Colorado River peoples were culturally distinct from the rest of the California Indians. They were more aggressive. They also developed a flood-basin agriculture, dropping seeds into the mud left by the receding river water, a technique similar to that practiced by the ancient Egyptians. Most of the California natives were food gatherers rather than cultivators, though they devised methods of increasing the productivity of indigenous plants by fallowing, pruning, and burning.[2] It has been said that before the coming of the white man, the California Indians lived with little disturbance to each other or to their surroundings because they had achieved "a Malthusian equilibrium." [3] Though they sometimes resorted to abortion and infanticide to limit their numbers, they did not in general need to develop agriculture to augment the food supply or engage in hostilities to protect their territory.

Since they did not continually engage in warfare, they had little political organization. Social hierarchy was not a part of community structure except among villages of the Northwest, where interest in wealth and property led to the enslavement of debtors. There was no individual land ownership, but money, in the form of shell beads, was valued by most groups.

Individuals were esteemed on the basis of age and leadership positions so that, in general, the elders spoke for the group and meted out discipline or punishment to lawbreakers. Marriage was usually arranged between individuals of different clans but in the same tribe, with the wives, sometimes more than one, purchased by the husband for shell money or deer skins. Unsatisfactory marriages could be dissolved by separation. Children were carefully instructed in the skills appropriate to their sex, the girls becoming adept at food gathering, cooking, and basket-making, while the boys were taught by their fathers to make weapons and to hunt. They were also trained in the rules of conduct toward other members of the clan and impressed with the danger of straying beyond the country occupied by their group.

Adolescents underwent initiation rites to mark their transition into adulthood. Birth, death, and puberty, as well as important community occasions such as harvests, were celebrated with elaborate rituals, often accompanied by singing and dancing. Sick people and women after child-birth were frequently sweated, and the *temescal,* or sweat-house, was also a community gathering place for men. Like the ritual burning of the houses and possessions of the dead, it served a hygienic purpose, not least in cutting down the number of fleas that infested the settlements. The people revered the shamans, or wise men, who were both healers and religious leaders and who knew the secrets of poisoning enemies since they understood the properties of noxious plants. They also assisted in interpreting the elaborate myths which were handed down orally from one generation to another.

The religious rites, which varied from group to group, were complex and of great importance to the psychic well-being of the people. The legends concerned the mysteries of the past and the future. Central in many cults was the be-lief that the creation of the universe, followed by a primor-dial flood, had occurred in their own tribal country many years before. Some groups believed in a prehuman race, while others, inspired by the cycles of the earth, sun, and moon, saw evidence of man's perpetual renewal. Yet the rigors of daily existence called for the enforcement of stringent taboos. Some of these were commonsense rules, while others were propitiatory gestures to deities governing the unknown, performed in order to ward off famine and other calamities. A pervasive sense of the precariousness of life seems to have haunted the California native people, even though they appeared to the whites as carefree hedon-ists.

Strangers Arrive

Friendly meetings took place between the first Californians and the crews of European ships which occasionally landed along the coast beginning in the mid-sixteenth century. The Indians wavered between fear and curiosity at the sight of the strange, heavily clothed men who arrived in vessels that skimmed across the sea like birds but were larger than whales. The light skin color of these voyagers, some of whom had reddish hair and blue eyes, was so startling that some of the people believed the sailors were not men but gods; others thought they were the ghosts of their ancestors returned from the dead. The white men, in turn, were often shocked by the near-nakedness of the Indians or the ceremonial painting of their faces. Some found their appearance pleasing, admiring their lithe bodies and well-defined musculature.

The Indians sometimes hid their wives and children from the eyes of the strangers, but they generally offered the sort of friendship that the Coast Miwok villagers extended to the Spanish crew that explored San Francisco Bay six years after the San Diego Mission was founded. When some sailors rowed a small boat toward the shore, the native men left their huts and came close to the water to stare at them. One of the chiefs made a long speech while the rest threw down their arms to show their peaceful intentions. For several days they made speeches from the shore, inviting the Spaniards to come and accept presents of seeds, grass skirts, and hair ornaments. They appeared to be more at ease than the party of Europeans who took the gifts when the Indians were absent, leaving in their place trinkets of glass, beads, and earrings.

After several days of this sort of oblique approach, the two races met together, the Indians weaponless and seated to show their good will. Finally the Spaniards and the chiefs sampled each other's food and exchanged visits, the crew venturing to the native village, or *rancheria*, as they called it, and the Indians paddling out in their balsa craft to board the ship.[4]

In this series of encounters, as in earlier meetings between European explorers and natives, both races were merely onlookers into each other's culture. The missionaries and soldiers of the 1769 expedition from Mexico, however, arrived with the intention of carrying out a plan patterned on experience with Indians in other parts of New Spain. Wherever they founded colonies, which extended from Peru to Central America, the *conquistadores* incorporated the original inhabitants into the Hispanic system. Though some of the Indian civilizations were highly developed, the Spaniards imposed their own government and religion with ruthless disregard for the cultural values of the vanquished.

Under an *encomienda* plan, a Spanish warrior who had assisted in expelling the Moors from Granada was given Indian serfs on his arrival in the New World. The Indians who formed the *peon* class often labored under conditions very close to slavery, as they had earlier in their own hierarchical systems under Aztec, Inca, and Maya rulers. The Spaniards felt no repugnance toward people with dark skin, so unions with Indian women took place freely along class lines, the knights choosing native princesses, while their guards took the female servants to live with them. Thus the Indians gradually became Spanish by conversion to Catholicism, by language, and by blood.

Many of the soldiers and artisans who accompanied the expedition of 1769 were *mestizos* (part Spanish, part Indian). Some were mulattos, since black slaves had been imported from Africa to the New World in response to criticism over the decline of the Indians in servitude, and the blacks had been absorbed into the native population. California was colonized by a people who had achieved a racial homogeneity within a class structure. The leaders, however, were men born in Spain, and Spanish birth continued to be a requisite for high office until Mexico and California declared their independence from the mother country.

In joining a religious and a military expedition, the Franciscan Father Junipero Serra, and the soldier Don Gaspar de Portolá, were following a pattern that had been successful in northern Mexico, Baja California, and elsewhere. The mission, guarded by the *presidio*, was an instrument for "reducing the Indians to civilization," and at the same time, for carrying the flag of Spain to new frontiers. It was intended that these northern settlements would discourage the covetous designs of other nations whose ships were beginning to appear along the coast.

The new missions were to be supplied from established ones in Baja California. Cattle to start new herds were driven ahead of the settlers who came by land. Precious seeds to plant new gardens were carried by ship, as were church ornaments to adorn the chapels that were to be built. Christian Indians were brought along to assist in the conversion of a new flock.

By the first of July 1769, the scurvy-racked crews of two ships and the surviving members of two overland parties had assembled in a place they called San Diego, which had been discovered by Juan Rodríguez Cabrillo over two hundred years earlier. The "sacred expedition" was half depleted by the deaths of many who had set out from La Paz and Loreto and by the loss of a third ship. While the invalids languished in a tent hospital, Father Serra bravely founded the first mission, San Diego de Alcalá, in a temporary hut two days after Portolá set out, with as many of his *soldados de cuera* as could march, to hunt for the Bay of Monterey. The natives who furnished guides and food for this northward-bound exploring party were described as being "very docile and tractable." [5]

Meanwhile, the Franciscans, guarded by a few half-ill

soldiers, solicited the friendship of the local Indians, whom they called Dieguenos. The narrative of Francisco Palóu, interpreting information received in a letter from Father Serra, illustrates how great was the misunderstanding between the two groups. The fear of contagion and the dread of being poisoned led the Indians to refuse gifts of food. They accepted the cloth presented to them, but angered the missionaries by helping themselves to more than was offered. "They went so far that not even the ship's sails were safe; for one night, having paddled out to it in their tule rafts, they were surprised in the act of cutting out a piece of one; and on another occasion cutting off a hawser so as to make off with it," Palóu wrote. When they began arming themselves, the small company of Europeans was convinced that the Dieguenos had "decided to tempt fortune, kill us all off and make away with the spoils."

The Spanish soldiers opened fire with their muskets; the Indians discharged their arrows. After the battle in which there were casualties on both sides, the Dieguenos brought their wounded to be treated by the Spanish surgeon and from that time on came to the mission unarmed, "filled . . . with fear and respect." During the skirmish the father-president was on his knees in the chapel, imploring God to spare his own men as well as "the heathen that they might not die without baptism." [6]

At first the natives were as reluctant to accept baptism as they had been to receive the presents of food offered them. Francisco Palóu tells us that Father Serra won the allegiance of a fifteen-year-old youth, whom he asked to "bring him a little child with the consent of its parents; that he would make it a Christian like ourselves by pouring a bit of water on its head, so that it might become a son of God, and of the Padre, and a brother of the soldiers, whom they call *Cueres*, adding that he would give it clothing so that it might dress like the Spaniards." A small boy was brought forward, but before the venerable padre could complete the sacrament, relatives snatched the child away and fled with him back to their village. According to his biographer, Father Serra, even after hundreds of converts had been baptized at the mission, never recounted this incident in later years without tears in his eyes, attributing his failure to his own sins.[7]

The accounts of the pious Palóu and other early chroniclers of the California missions suggest that the Indians volunteered to become Christians. After undergoing catechetical instruction for several months they were, if still receptive, baptized. Palóu reported that the neophytes of San Juan Capistrano asked "that they might be baptised," rather than "to wait the time necessary for their instruction." [8] In order to accomplish the all-important purpose of saving the souls of the Indians, the missionaries felt justified in offering material rewards to bring them to the missions. Coercion seems to have been employed also. Tribal leaders were bribed or pressured into rounding up a requisite number of candidates for baptism. Once the initial fear of poisoning was overcome, the daily rations of food served to the neophytes proved an inducement which attracted even members of free-roving tribes. "These Indians are usually caught by the mouth," wrote Fra Pedro Font, who visited the San Gabriel Mission four years after its founding.[9]

The purpose of the Franciscans was both to make Christians of the natives and to train them for usefulness in the new colony. The converts joined the mission community, living close by or within the compound and becoming subject to its discipline. Heavy restrictions were imposed on their freedom. They were confined to the mission lands. If they left without permission, they were followed and punished. The unmarried girls were locked at night into *monjerios*; the older boys were also separated from their parents.

In order that they might become vintners, herdsmen, soap-makers, tanners, carpenters, blacksmiths, bakers, and cooks, they were given daily instruction by the artisans who had accompanied the missionaries. It was this neo-phyte population under supervision that built the twenty-one coastal missions and decorated them with colorful fres-coes. They were taught to sing liturgical music and to play stringed instruments. They acquired a speaking knowledge of Spanish, though some of the Franciscans eventually learned to speak, and even to preach, in the native lan-guages.

The missions were successful as training schools. After the first lean years, as the neophytes became expert in growing crops and raising flocks and herds for the profit-able hide and tallow trade, the missions became more than self-sufficient communities. They supplied fresh produce to the *presidios* and *pueblos* and to visiting ships, with the result that the civil administrators of the province began to cast covetous eyes on these prosperous domains of the church.

It is a California tradition that the devoted Franciscans "brought civilization and well-being to the Indians." [10] With great patience and selflessness, they labored to save their souls and clothe their bodies as they taught them useful skills. They were harsh disciplinarians as well as tireless benefactors to their wards. When they were accused by a discharged priest of cruel treatment—heavy floggings and the confinement of wrongdoers in the stocks—the friars explained that "according to the laws they stood *in loco parentis* to the natives, must necessarily restrain them by punishments, and inflicted none but proper penalties, par-doning first offenses, and always inclining to mercy and kindness." [11]

The Franciscans practiced a policy of *reducción*, a sup-pression of the Indians' culture, for which they had little regard. "They [the Indians] led an idle and lazy life, more like that of brutes than of rational beings," wrote Father Jeronimo Boscana, who made a detailed study of the customs and mythology of a tribe living near San Juan Capis-trano.[12] The values of the Indians and the Spaniards were irreconcilable. Hunting, the chief occupation of native males, was for Europeans a recreation, while to live on the bounty of nature seemed unenterprising to a people who had tilled the soil for centuries. The tribal religious practices, even when chronicled by such careful observers as Father Boscana, were regarded as superstitions that must be stamped out to make way for the true faith.[13]

The shamans were suppressed. The chiefs were not allowed to speak to the people, so the previously valued eloquence in the native languages declined. Sweat baths were sometimes permitted, but the burning of the dwelling places and the possessions of the dead was discouraged. The Indians were forced to wear binding clothes and to regulate their lives by the clock. The mission bells, tolling the hours for worship, meals, and work, obliterated the old patterns of diurnal and seasonal change. While the young people were restrained in semimonastic celibacy, the older couples were required to formalize their unions by a marriage ceremony.

The fetters were loosened to the extent that dance celebrations under supervision were permitted occasionally, as well as visits to the wilderness with the obligation to return to the mission. Food-gathering expeditions were allowed when the granaries were low. But the origin of these time-honored tribal practices, which was the Indians' cosmic view of the universe, was discredited by the new teaching. Great distress was caused when the neophytes were discouraged from following traditional taboos.

Father Boscana told the story of a cook at the San Diego Mission who was exhorted by the priest not to diet, as was his custom, after his wife gave birth to a child. When the premature child died, "all the Indians and he himself, attributed it to the eating of meat." A gravely ill youth at La Purisima Concepción forsook the new religion, wrote

Father Boscana, and called on a native healer "who executed with him all his diabolic art," though to no avail, while a neophyte on his deathbed at San Juan Capistrano refused confession with the words, ". . . having lived deceived, I do not want to die deceived." [14]

More than a few neophytes were moved to revolt. Mission Indians, with the help of Gentile groups outside, destroyed the San Diego Mission in 1775, torturing and killing a Franciscan. In 1824 there were simultaneous uprisings at La Purisima Concepción, Santa Inés, and Santa Barbara missions, the rebels holding the soldiers temporarily at bay with captured firearms. But the most common means of resistance was escape. An estimated one out of every twenty-five converts left the missions to find sanctuary in distant *rancherias* or among the free-roaming tribes of the San Joaquin Valley. They were pursued and often recaptured by parties of soldiers from the *presidios,* who also raided the native villages for replacements if they could not track down the escaped *Christianos.*

Indian family life was often a casualty of missionization. Despite the effort of the friars to separate their flocks from contact with the garrisons (the father president, Junípero Serra, moved his headquarters from Monterey to Carmel partly for this reason), they were unable to restrain the soldiers who had come without wives from taking native women. On one occasion the Indian husbands were prevented from interfering by physical restraint—their hands were tied behind their backs. After the soldiers had used them, the women's own people considered them contaminated and they were put through a ritual of sweating and the drinking of herb potions. The children born of such intercourse were secretly strangled and buried.[15] In 1773 the viceroy in Mexico sent a letter to the commander of the garrison in San Diego, granting permission to the soldiers to marry baptized Indian girls at the mission and authorizing the assignment of land to these couples.

It is possible that the attempted destruction of their tribal values and practices made the neophytes more susceptible to the white man's diseases. The Indians succumbed by the thousands to smallpox, cholera, malaria, tuberculosis, syphilis, and measles.[16] Of the total number of converts, estimated at 53,600 during the sixty-five years of the mission era, no more than a third were left at the end of the period.[17] In some cases, entire clans seem to have disappeared.

It had been the intention of the Franciscans that as the neophytes progressed from their apprenticeship to independent status, they would turn over the missions to their former wards and move on to new frontier outposts. But as the years passed, they felt the Indians were not ready for such a step. Civil leaders in California blamed the *padres* and their system for dulling and stupifying formerly vigorous human beings and reducing them to near-slave status, a criticism that, whatever its validity, must be considered in the light of the ambitions of the men who made it. From the very first there had been jealousy and ill feeling between the churchmen and the *commandantes*. Secular discontent increased with the independence movement. When Mexico severed her allegiance to Spain, there was resentment of the power of the Spanish church and its Spanish-born missionaries.

The secularization of the missions was decreed by the Mexican Congress in 1833 and was completed in 1836. As the Franciscans, who had grown elderly in service, were stripped of their temporal power and became simply parish priests, the lay leaders of California permitted their friends and relatives to squander mission property. The governors treated their new holdings as a treasury, paying debts by granting orders for hides, tallow, or grain from the missions as long as the supply lasted, while some of the administrators overseeing the various properties sold utensils, tools, and even tiles from the roofs to "gratify their propensity for gambling." [18] The once beautiful missions with their adobe walls enclosing colorful gardens and fine orchards fell into decay. The buildings at San Juan Capistrano, the "jewel of the missions," were auctioned by the governor in 1845 to two American settlers for $710.

The position of the Indians did not improve under secularization. A scene at San Juan Capistrano, where drunken neophytes staggered around the plaza shouting *"Soy libre!"* was symbolic of what was to be their future.[19] Under the secularization plan, a part of the mission property was to be divided among them, both through the use of the land and by outright ownership, but many of the *Christianos* sold or gambled away their property or neglected to claim it. Though often abused and overworked by the major-domos who controlled the missions, a number of the ex-neophytes stayed on through habit or through the influence of the Franciscans. In 1844 John Charles Frémont met on the trail an Indian from the San Fernando Mission who was honorably returning to the priests who had given him leave to visit his relatives in the mountains. The very embodiment of Father Serra's promise to the Indian boy in 1769, he had "a Spanish costume, jingling spurs and horse equipped after the Spanish manner." [20]

A different sort of Hispanization took place as many former neophytes became servants, laborers, and *vaqueros* on the large *ranchos*. The skills they had learned in the missions made them valuable workers. Though the Mexican *patróns* lived on horseback and took part in the yearly rounding up and branding of their cattle where they could demonstrate their equestrian skills, they depended on Indian labor to perform the menial tasks in the day-to-day running of their estates. In return, they provided food, shelter, protection, and a more tolerant attitude toward tribal traditions than the missionaries had shown. The Indians living a little distance from the main house could build their dwellings and *temescals* undisturbed. The life of Indians on the *ranchos* represented the most harmonious adjustment of the two groups.

But halcyon descriptions of pastoral California in the heyday of the dons ignore the damaging effect of the Indians' dependent status. Though Helen Hunt Jackson's fictional hero Allesandro, an idealized Ibero-Indian, was honored by the Spanish household he served intermittently for his skills as a sheep-shearer and musician, most "domesticated Indians," as they came to be called, were treated more as Captain John Sutter handled his staff of several hundred workers who had not been mission-bred. The affable Swiss had acquired the labor force for running his elaborate ranch community at New Helvetia on the Sacramento River by making treaties with nearby valley tribes. The Indians were fed at large community troughs set down on the ground. They were paid in scrip, with coins stamped with the hours they had worked, for which they could buy goods in Sutter's store. A German-born *ranchero* who maintained a vast estate farther north considered the six or seven thousand Indians on his land as subjects ready to labor for him "whenever I needed them." He paid white workers twenty to fifty dollars a month and Indians one dollar a fortnight plus board and goods.[21]

In general, the California tribes outside the mission sphere met the white man's aggressions with a more belligerent attitude, for the reason, perhaps, that there was less initial attempt at pacification. Beginning in the late years of the eighteenth century, the natives of the Central Valley, the mountains, and the desert occasionally encountered parties of missionaries, explorers, and trappers. Though these meetings were often friendly and marked by the exchange of gifts and promises of mutual forbearance as the whites passed through the Indians' territory, there were occasional clashes. The Yumas along the Colorado River, who had assisted Captain Juan Bautista de Anza as his party moved northwest from Sonora to San Francisco in 1774, seven years later destroyed two missions that had been founded in their domain and attacked a party of colonists, killing all the men and enslaving the women and children.

The Yumas were perhaps the most warlike tribe in California, but when the Spaniards began to raid the villages of the Shoshonean groups in the Central Valley in search of converts or slave labor, the natives, who had learned the use of horses and guns from contact with runaway neophytes, retaliated by descending on the coastal *ranchos* to terrorize the inhabitants and drive off stock. As the white man invaded their hunting grounds, they in turn stole his cattle and horses. The *rancheros* led war parties into the interior to avenge Indian raids or to capture conscript labor, while at the same time protecting a staff of domesticated Indian servants.

The relationship between Hispanized Indians and free Indians was complicated by white intervention. Neophytes were enlisted to accompany the Spanish military parties into the interior. The servants at the *ranchos*, who might receive a warning of an impending attack from the valley, were occasionally punished, even when innocent, for suspected conspiracy. The whites feared that the Indians would unite in a general uprising, forgetting that they were divided by language as well as by geography. Ironically, it was a Spanish-speaking chief of the Jacum Indians in the San Diego area who claimed to have enlisted other, presumably Spanish-speaking, tribes in a plan for recovering California from the white men before the Jacums were suppressed by the commander of the local *presidio*.[22]

Runaway neophytes, who had joined the tribes in the wilderness, often became leaders of the stock-raiding forays on the coast. Their mission training made them effective in guerrilla warfare against the *Californios*. One renowned native leader, who had fled to the San Joaquin area, took advantage of the ill feeling between the civil governors and the Franciscans. After a battle, he found sanctuary in a mission where the father-president concealed him until a pardon was obtained from the governor. Some of the tribes were discovered using horses for plowing and possessing spades, hoes, and other agricultural implements, suggesting the Spanish influence. One chief was described as living in an adobe house, his table spread with plates, knives, and forks. His people raised wheat, corn, pumpkins, melons, peas, and beans.[23] But in general the former neophytes living with free tribes, though carrying the identifying marks of their interlude of servitude with the white race, copied from the alien culture only those techniques that made them effective in combating it.

Americans Subdue the Indians

Whether or not they accepted it and whatever its cost to them, there was a place for the Indians in the Hispanic system. But under the Americans who began to pour into California in the 1840s, and who wrested its control from the Mexican government in 1847, all too often the only policy toward Indians was one of genocide. The previous history of Indian-American relations in other parts of the continent was to be re-enacted on this last frontier. The emigrants who undertook the difficult overland journey across the mountains had acquired their attitudes from hostile encounters with belligerent plains tribes or by absorbing the oft-retold tales of the massacre of other pioneer parties. The hatred of Indians was a part of the code of the mountain men, that group of bold hunters, trappers, and explorers who first crossed the Rockies and the Sierra Nevada. In their expeditions in pursuit of valuable beaver pelts, they took little pains to pacify the natives whose territory they invaded and whose game they appropriated.

As their treatment of Spanish explorers, particularly in the Colorado River area, had been capricious, so the natives sometimes welcomed, and on other occasions attacked, the Yankee intruders. Jedediah Smith, the first white man to reach California by crossing the continent, was set upon by the Mojaves in the desert, by the Umquas in Oregon, and was finally killed by Comanches on the Santa Fe Trail. The survivors of such bloody ambushes broadcast the legend of the treacherous race of red men. Simultaneously, from the time of the Lewis and Clark expedition, Indian guides were relied on by many of the early exploring parties. Truckee, a Paiute scout, was immortalized in the name of a mountain area he passed through after leading one of the first wagon trains across Nevada.

Not far away is Donner Pass, named for the ill-fated party forced to spend the winter of 1846–47 in the snowy Sierra Nevada. During their ordeal two Indian guides were sent out by John Sutter from New Helvetia to help bring them down to the valley. After reaching the stranded homesteaders in their shelters, the Indians accompanied a group on snowshoes who were going to try to break a trail down the mountains to bring help to the others left behind. During the torturous descent through the drifts, the starving band of pioneers set upon these guides and killed them for their flesh, an episode that is generally forgotten, while the Donner Party's cannibalism of white corpses has become legendary.[24] A man from another overland party, who for twenty-one days had nothing to eat but pieces of leather, recalled that when hunting for a buck he saw an Indian and gave chase. "And, sir," said he, "had I caught him, I should have slain and eaten him, as soon as if he had been a deer." [25]

In the Gold Rush era, Indians were murdered with less cause, often the victims of what Bret Harte called "indiscriminate rifle practice." Not all "forty-niners" had as clean a conscience as the California pioneer who boasted that "he never killed an Indian for the sport of it, *for game,* but only in fight, when necessary." [26] The general white attitude was that Indians, like grizzly bears, rattlesnakes, and mountain lions, were a hazard of the trail. Yet pioneer parties that ran out of supplies copied the Indians in converting native plants, such as manzanita berries and acorns, into food.

With the American acquisition of California followed by the discovery of gold, emigrants and fortune hunters poured in by sea and across the continent. The population of whites jumped in one year from 26,000 to possibly 115,000.[27] The former sleepy province, which in the Spanish and Mexican era had consisted of a thin chain of missions, forts, and towns within fifty miles of the Pacific Coast, now expanded its boundaries from San Diego to Eureka on the west, and from the Mojave Desert to Goose Lake near the Oregon-Nevada border on the east. The central region between began to be penetrated and settled everywhere by miners staking gold claims and by pioneers homesteading new land. Groups of Indians who had had no relationship with whites during the Hispanic period were being disturbed. As the wagons with their weary loads of settlers emerged from the desert or took a south cut-off from the Oregon Trail into Lassen, Shasta, and Modoc counties, the local natives came to stare at them. An Indian descendent wrote, " . . . on seeing people of a different color from themselves, they all ran for the hills. They thought that God had sent evil spirits among them to punish them in some way. But they soon learned that the white people were human, so they became friendly toward the emigrants. Every time any of them saw a train of wagons they would meet them. They liked the white man's bread, coffee, and other eatables that the emigrants gave them. It went on thus for several years." [28]

But the two races were soon competing for land. The Indians felt the encroachment of the whites first in the diminishing of their food supply. Those tribes who fled into the mountains to escape the sound of the newcomers' rifles and axes lost their stored hoards of acorns in the foothills. Native fish dams were destroyed by the gold-washing operations of miners. The grass that the Indians cultivated for seed was trampled down by the cattle of the emigrants; their timber was burned. The food-gathering methods of the Indians were dependent on a fairly extensive, undisturbed terrain. An American army officer noted, "They have not any particular boundaries or fixed homes for any great length of time together, but change their locations as taste or their necessities may require. Yet they all have an indistinct and undefined idea of their right to the soil, the trees, and the streams." [29]

The Indians' seminomadic existence, which yet incorporated a sense of belonging to a particular part of the country where their ancestors were buried, came into violent collision with the acquisitive instincts of miners who were staking claims near gold-bearing veins of quartz, polluting streams with hydraulic equipment, and fighting off anyone who threatened their bonanza. Homesteaders were staking claims to new land for which they had endured untold hardships. They had sacrificed much to reach the new country and were not prepared to relinquish lightly any rights they might have had in it.

Miners destroyed the Indian villages "with fire, outrage, and murder, as if they had been so many wasps' nests in our gardens at home," in the words of the Harvard philosopher, Josiah Royce.[30] The settlers were more likely to occupy the land alongside the Indians. A chief near San Bernadino complained of Americans who "are now squatting here, and taking away my land, wood, and water. . . . We have not land enough to plant: my people are poor and hungry; they want something from the government. Some Americans tell us we must go away to the mountains to live; other Americans tell us that we must all live together on some land. We do not understand it; we do not like it." [31] Another chief said, "This is our country; why do the Americans come here? They are good and brave, but they come upon the land of my people. What do they intend to do?" [32]

The first American law in California "for the Government and Protection of Indians," passed in 1850, took the position that the Indians were squatters on settlers' lands. "Persons and proprietors of lands on which Indians are residing, shall permit such Indians peaceably to reside on such lands, unmolested in the pursuit of their usual avocations for the maintainance of themselves and families. . . . The Justice [of the Peace in the township where the Indians reside] shall set off a sufficient amount of land for the necessary wants of such Indians, including the site of their village or residence, if they so prefer it; and in no case shall such selection be made to the prejudice of such Indians, nor shall they be forced to abandon their homes or villages where they have resided for a number of years." [33]

But it proved to be impossible for the two races to live in peaceful proximity. The Indians, hungry and fearing starvation in consequence of "the strangers overruning their country," stole livestock and other possessions of the whites or committed "acts of depradation" to drive them away— shooting arrows into their settlements, stampeding their horses, and attacking hapless wagon trains. A white military party, sweeping into an abandoned Indian camp, found stolen beef, sugar, and tea, and the clothes of a murdered American teamster. When some Indians stole a cow, a hot-headed group, in retribution, killed fifteen "friendly Indians" to the consternation of the commanding general of the United States forces in California, who found himself with "another war on our hands." [34]

In the Indian culture a murderer might win pardon if he made material restitution to the family of his victim. At the opposite extreme, the white miners and settlers, who felt they had an inherent right to the land which the Indians considered their own, treated Indian thievery of white property as a capital offense and were not overly scrupulous about distinguishing the real culprits from convenient scapegoats. A federal Indian agent commented, "If a pack train is attacked or robbed, if a *corral* in one of the valleys is broken into and robbed, the conclusion is instantly reached that the *Indians* are the aggressors, the Oregon rifle or the Pike County revolver is at once called into requisition, and the first red skins, not white, made to pay the penalty." [35]

Both races were indiscriminate in their choice of victims, but with a difference. The Indians practiced *lex talionis,* avenging one death by taking another life, sometimes killing an undefended woman in a cabin or an unarmed prospector. Their attacks on the innocent outraged the whites who, in turn, revenged themselves on entire native villages. "What are the lives of a hundred or a thousand of these savages to the life of a single American citizen . . . ?" ran an editorial in the Shasta *Courier* for April 2, 1852, after an army officer had been killed at Fort Reading. Newly arrived immigrants from Europe found an immediate common bond with the trans-Sierra pioneers in forming volunteer companies to take out after the Indians who lived in proximity to their pioneering communities. Some towns paid a bounty for Indian scalps.[36]

The politicians aligned themselves with the interests of the white settlers. The first governor, Peter Burnett, felt a responsibility to protect exhausted emigrant parties entering the state by the overland trails. After two instances of Indian aggression near the Colorado River and in El Dorado County, he ordered out companies of volunteers to punish the tribes. Over the next decade the legislature appropriated hundreds of thousands of dollars, much of it reimbursed by the federal government, to pay the expenses of volunteer companies made up of settlers defending the frontier.

Regular troops were employed as well. The professional soldiers who were not competing with the Indians for their land were more restrained in their behavior. They took the time to study the Indians' way of life, took a census of tribes in different areas, and in conflicts between Indians and white settlers often took the role of mediators, investigating incidents and sifting evidence to spare the innocent and convict the guilty. After a citizens' group had massacred a large number of Indians, officers protected the Indian women and children at a fort. A general wrote to Governor Burnett:

> That the Indians have been more "sinned against than sinning" since the settling of California by the whites, is the opinion of many old inhabitants, as well as Miners, who have lived in their midst and watched the rise and progress of the many disturbances that have occurred; they are naturally inoffensive, and perhaps less warlike than any other tribes on the continent . . . in fact, all their habits are peaceful, and in their whole character it is not discoverable that *naturally* they possess the first element of a warlike people; but the germ of a hostile spirit has been *created* in them, that without some prompt and decisive action on the part of the General Government, will grow and spread among them a deadly hate towards the whites, which ere long may cause our frontier to be marked with lines of blood.[37]

Governor Burnett made the following assessment before the Legislature six months later:

> We have suddenly spread ourselves over the country in every direction, and appropriated whatever portion of it we pleased to ourselves, without their consent, and without compensation. Although these small and scattered tribes have among them no regular government, they have some idea of existence as a separate and independent people, and some conception of their right to the country, acquired by long, uninterrupted, and exclusive possession. They have not only seen their country taken from them, but they see their ranks rapidly thinning from the effects of our diseases. They instinctively consider themselves a doomed race; and this idea

leads to despair; and despair prevents them from providing the usual and necessary supply of provisions. This produces starvation, which knows but one law, that of gratification; and the natural result is that these people kill the first stray animal they find. This leads to war between them and the whites; and war creates a hatred against the white man that never ceases to exist in the Indian bosom.

After this analysis, he made the prediction that "a war of extinction will continue to be waged between the races, until the Indian race becomes extinct. . . . While we cannot anticipate this result but with painful regret, the inevitable destiny of the race is beyond the power or wisdom of man to avert." [38]

A Federal Plan

The federal government intervened with a plan to negotiate treaties with the Indians by which they would be asked to cede certain lands and agree to live on other lands, in the pattern developed with tribes east of the Sierra Nevada. While state officials continued to call for the removal of all Indians from California, three commissioners appointed by the Department of the Interior arrived in San Francisco and traveled all over the state, attempting to gather together the leaders of different bands of Indians. One of these men, speaking of ". . . the many obstacles [that] have presented themselves in attempting to consummate a treaty" reported that "it would appear that the difficulty of treating with them is in due ratio to the comparative length of time that the whites have been among them." The commissioners discovered that a rumor was circulating among a group in the north that "the object of our party was to collect them, so that the men might be murdered, and the women and children stolen and carried off." In one instance a group that refused "to treat" were punished by a military party.[39]

The commissioners addressed the Indians in the name of "the President . . . the great chief [who] has conquered and owns this country." The policy, as one of them wrote to the Commissioner of Indian Affairs, was "to get [the natives] down from their mountain fastnesses and place them in the reservations in the foothills bordering on the plains; the miners will then be *between* them and the mountains, making a formidable cordon, or barrier. . . . The country set apart for them so far is very poor soil; only a small portion of it is adapted to agricultural purposes, but remarkably well adapted to the raising of stock, and we think it would be good policy to supply them liberally with *brood stock,* in addition to the beef cattle. . . ." [40]

Although only fifty thousand dollars had been appropriated to them by Congress, the three commissioners let contracts for nearly three-quarters of a million dollars for provisions and beef cattle to supply the reservations. They negotiated treaties affecting 139 tribes that would have placed them on eighteen tracts of land comprising 7,488,000 acres, or about 7½ percent of the area of California. [41] Almost immediately a storm of anger arose in the state and was carried to the legislature, where a committee protested that so much land should be given "Indian tribes, wholly incapable, by habit or taste, of appreciating its value." The committee favored allowing mission Indians to resume their roles as servants on the *ranchos* and removing all other tribes outside the boundaries of the state to an unspecified location. The federal government, they said, had "extinguished the Indian title to near one hundred and twenty millions of acres of land" in states east of the Mississippi and removed the Indians. Should not California be treated in the same way? [42] Settlers took advantage of the furor to attack the Indians, and the governor predicted, correctly, that the United States Senate at the instigation of California's senators would reject the treaties. They lay forgotten in the federal archives until after the turn of the century, when a claims suit based on work of the commisisoners in 1851 was filed.

A much more limited reservation scheme was adopted by Congress in 1853. Four sites of from 25,000 to 75,000 acres each were to be developed at Tejon in the Tehachapi foothills; at Hoopa Valley on the Klamath River; at Nome Lackee, near Tehama, in the Sacramento Valley; and at Round Valley on the Mendocino coast. It was originally planned that there would be a military post near each reservation, a scheme perhaps copied from the Spanish mission and *presidio* plan by Edward F. Beale, the first Superintendent of Indian Affairs in California, who also patterned a model grain-growing operation at Tejon after the self-sufficient agricultural enterprises of the missions. Beale devoted energy and enthusiasm into making Tejon a showcase agency where the Indians participated in decision-making.

His successor, Thomas J. Henley, was more of a politician than a social reformer. He neglected Tejon and quarreled with the army over how the Indians were to "come in" to the other reservations. When bands of Indians of diverse origin were arbitrarily assigned to the various preserves, often many miles from their native ground, some refused to move. Henley asked for federal troops "to convey the Indians to the reservation," but the army general, John E. Wool, would not furnish troops to force the tribes to move against their will. Henley said he would not help any Indians who would not agree to move, though one of his agents protested the plight of the Scott's Valley Indians who were adamant against going to the Tehama reservation. "Their neglect, under the severity of winter," he declared, "amounts to cruelty." Henley was reported to have said that "he did not intend doing anything with the Indians till after he saw how the next election went." [43]

Tribal groups continued to be transplanted. The 1850 law that permitted Indians to remain on their ancestral lands was replaced by an 1858 statute that allowed whites to move them to reservations. The former mission Indians maintained that, unlike the "savage tribes" who apparently had no land rights under Mexican or American law, their ownership rights, established by the Mexican government, were guaranteed by the Treaty of Guadalupe Hidalgo by which the United States annexed California. In 1856 a former official of the Mexican government referred to documents in the archives proving that "the parcel of land named San Pasqual was granted to these same Indian families from the mission of San Diego. . . . At the same time were founded, San Dieguito, Las Flores, etc., all by the same order. . . ." [44] A federal committee, however, held that the United States, in acquiring the territory from Mexico, acquired rights in the soil. It was not until many years later that small reservations in San Diego and San Bernadino counties were set aside for the descendents of mission Indians by executive orders in Washington.

The northern reservations were unproductive. The two thousand Indians who were living on them in 1856 could not live by hunting and food-gathering or by agriculture. livered. The sites were in disrepair for lack of federal They were haphazardly supplied by agents who quite frequently collected money for food that was never de- funds to maintain them. Two years later an inspector condemned them as "government alms-houses where an inconsiderable number of Indians are insufficiently fed and scantily clothed, at an expense wholly dispropor- tionate to the benefits conferred. There is nothing in the system, as now practiced, looking to the permanent im- provement of the Indian, or tending in any way toward his moral, intellectual or social elevation. . . ." [45]

Indians on or off the reservation were not free men. One of the first orders concerning them after the American acquisition of California was a ruling that, if not provided with certificates from their employers, they were liable to be arrested and punished as horse thieves. An 1850 statute stated that, "Any Indian able to work and support himself in some honest calling, not having wherewithal to maintain himself, who shall be found loitering and strolling about, or frequenting public places where liquors are sold, begging, or leading an immoral or profligate course of life, shall be liable to be arrested on the complaint of any resident citizen of the county, and brought before any Justice of the Peace . . . who shall examine said accused Indian and . . . if satisfied that he is a vagrant . . . to hire out such vagrant within twenty-four hours to the best bidder. . . . The money received for his hire, shall . . . be, if he be without a family, paid to the County Treasury, to the credit of the Indian fund." This ruling made legal the oft-described Los Angeles "slave mart," a weekly public auction at the prison to which landowners came to buy Indian labor.

The 1850 law forbade a white man to convey an Indian forcibly from his home and compel him to work for him, or to "obtain" Indian children without the consent of their parents or protectors, or to neglect or inhumanly treat Indian wards—prohibitions which speak eloquently about then current practices.[46] The iniquitous indenture labor system which flourished during the first years after the American conquest had its origin during the Spanish and Mexican eras, when extra hands were obtained at harvest time by sending out armed parties to raid the tribes of the interior. Yankee traders also copied the *gente de razón* (people of reason) in carrying on the remunerative business of kidnapping Indian children, and occasionally Indian women, in order to sell them as servants and concubines.

An 1860 amendment to the original law suggested that indentures could be obtained for children as well as adult Indians who were prisoners of war or who "have no settled habitation or means of livelihood, and have not placed

themselves under the protection of any white person."
Male children under age fourteen could be apprenticed
until they were twenty-five, and females till they were
twenty-one years old.[47] Entire families were sometimes
placed under contract. A recent study of 110 persons
indentured in Humboldt County beginning in 1860 indicates
that they ranged in age from two to fifty, with a concentration of children between the ages of seven and twelve,
one of whom was to be held for seventeen years.[48] Fortu-
nately, this indenture law was repealed in 1863.

Indians could not vote though they were sometimes
rounded up and counted to "throw" an election.[49] The
1850 statute that declared that "in no case shall a white
man be convicted of any offense upon the testimony of
an Indian" was amended in 1863 to prohibit from testifying
in an action against a white person those who had one-half
or more Indian blood, Mongolians, and Chinese. It remained
in effect against Indians and Chinese until 1872.

While they were deprived of the rights of citizens and
exploited for their labor, the "domesticated" Indians were
corrupted with alcohol. The neophytes had been conditioned
by the system of the missions, where wine, brandy, and
other treats were offered as occasional rewards for good
behavior. In their own culture they used hallucinatory
agents—jimsonweed, for example—in controlled situa-
tions, in connection with certain rituals, such as the
puberty initiation or the prophecies of religious leaders,
but the intoxicants of the white man were offered to them
as payments or bribes. They had poor resistance to these
blandishments, for which they gambled away their property
and sold their women. There had been no prostitution
among the villagers in their native state.

"[The Indian] can never see why he is sold out to
service for an indefinite period for intemperance," wrote
B. D. Wilson, a Southern California pioneer in 1852, "while
the white man goes unpunished for the same thing, and

the very richest, or best men, to his eye, are such as tempt him to drink and will pay for his labor in no other way." [50] As a response to the gravity of the problem, the punishment for furnishing liquor to Indians was increased from a minimum of twenty-dollars fine and/or five days in jail in 1850, to a maximum of five-hundred-dollars fine and up to three months in jail in 1855.[51] Concurrent statutes prohibited the sale or gift of firearms to Indians. It is a challenging question to decide whether these measures were for the protection of Indians or of whites, and whether they constituted a further infringement upon the civil rights of native Californians. Robert Heizer and Alan Almquist, in their recent study, comment that hunting was both an occupation and a necessity to the Indian and that game "after the white had reduced and scattered it by the use of firearms, was now beyond easy reach of the bow and arrow." [52]

"In the end we shall lose man for man in our encounter with them," Governor Peter Burnett had predicted in 1851.[53] But the whites increased as immigration continued, while the number of Indians drastically declined.

Warfare was not chiefly responsible for the mortality rate among natives. S. F. Cook estimates that three thousand to five thousand Indians fell by the guns of white soldiers or volunteer militiamen and a few hundred more were the victims of individual homicides. But the disruption of food and hunting cycles brought malnutrition and starvation so that the infections introduced by the invaders devastated the natives in their weakened condition.

In the 1830s an epidemic of smallpox depopulated the Central Valley. A Los Angeles pioneer traveling "from the head of the Sacramento to the bend and slough of the San Joaquin . . . did not see more than six or eight live Indians, while large numbers of their skulls and dead bodies were to be seen under almost every shade tree near water where the uninhabited villages have been converted into graveyards." [54] Later a massive vaccination program curbed the inroads of this disease. Scholars have addressed themselves to the question of whether the Indian birthrate fell also. Cook thinks that the natives failed to reproduce themselves, though he finds little factual evidence to substantiate this hypothesis. The Indian population declined perhaps by 50 percent during the decade 1846 to 1856 and 82 percent between 1848 and 1880. [55]

Later Relationships

By 1900 the Indian population of California had declined to 15,500. [56] A meager remnant of a once strong, autonomous race had been pushed by the whites to small reservations, where they were encroached upon by settlers who took the best land; or if they escaped this form of captivity, they were forced to flee to bleak deserts and barren mountaintops, to "places without incentive," or to live as day laborers on the fringes of white communities, banned from white schools and hospitals. Once they were no longer a threat, most Californians forgot about them, unless aroused by some emergency. The year after the close of the Modoc War, the last and most serious conflict in California between the races, citizens of Shasta County petitioned their congressman "for the sake of humanity, and for the protection of your constituents" to provide for the starving Pit River, Fall River, and Hot Creek tribes who were destitute after a season of drought. "In the past season drought and grasshoppers have destroyed roots, currants, and plums, and, as a consequence, the poor creatures have nothing to live upon but fish, which they have dried for their winter store. . . . About one hundred of the buck Indians, through the summer season, were employed by the settlers; but now there is no work for them and all [are] out of employment. . . . The settlers have done all they are able, as they themselves are poor and have their families to support." [57]

As the demands for reimbursing volunteer companies of Indian fighters disappeared from the legislative journals, there began to appear an occasional request to turn a fort into an Indian school or other petitions for relief or welfare programs. The report of a special agent, John G. Ames, and Helen Hunt Jackson's books, *A Century of Dishonor* (1881) and *Ramona* (1884) belatedly aroused Californians to the plight of the natives in the southern part of the state.

In the early years of American rule in California, Indian sympathizers among the white population were unpopular. James Marshall, the carpenter who discovered gold in Sutter's millrace, had to escape from the Sacramento Valley after he had defended some innocent members of a nearby tribe against a mob of angry miners. Bret Harte, two years later, fled Humboldt County after he had condemned in print the massacre and mutilation of sixty Indians on an island near Arcata, where he was a newspaperman. A pioneer woman in Shasta County, during a community extermination of tribal villages, hid an Indian mother and her baby for weeks in her attic, giving the baby paregoric to quiet it every time her husband entered the house. She was repaying the kindness of Indians who had protected her and supplied her with food when she and her blind mother were left alone on the frontier without a man to provide for them.[58]

Another Shasta County woman wrote that when she first saw red men wearing breechclouts and decorated with war paint and feathers traveling to their fishing grounds, she "would pull down all the curtains and put the younger children to bed and give them anything to keep them quiet until the Indians passed the house." But "in later years, I came to know them and they would come to me for advice and medicine when they were sick. I went to many a sick bed in their camps and sang at their funerals." [59] A Modoc County pioneer, who had loaned his hired man a mule to fight "Captain Jack's" warriors in the Modoc War (and never seen either of them again), had an understanding with the Indians in his neighborhood. He was fair in paying a day's wages for a day's work, but he never invited them into his house. When they came to his door hungry, he would fill a pan with biscuits and milk and set it on the ground outside, accepting the venison they brought in return. [60]

Small boys in nearby Surprise Valley were punished for bartering with Indian boys in the native settlement, which was considered dangerous for whites. [61] On the other hand, Indians who were fearsome in their native state became figures of fun on the streets of the towns. The settlers spoke of the "Diggers." The word, which had a derogatory connotation, came from the observation of Indian women grubbing for roots and bulbs with their digging sticks and was often used to describe Indians not dignified with their tribal names, which also were often white designations. (The major Indian linguistic groups in California are called by names in their own languages, except in a few instances where Spanish names are used, but the titles conferred on individual bands seem often to have been chosen by whites and derived from geographical landmarks associated with them; for instance, the Hot Creeks and the Pit Rivers.)

The white regard for Indians can be gauged by the treatment of "squaw men" who married or lived with Indian women. In the egalitarian male world of the gold camps, such unions were commonplace and generally accepted. The peripatetic, improvised frontier society had no vested institutions that came into conflict with these arrangements, though Indian culture and family life were debased by the crude tactics of the forty-niners in appropriating native women. With the arrival of more permanent settlers, accompanied by wives, the Victorian sexual morality of the era was evoked and the "squaw men" often found themselves to be semi-outcasts and their half-breed children despised.

As late as 1901 some of the leading citizens of Lookout, a hamlet in Modoc County, lynched Calvin Hall, a retired U. S. cavalryman, along with his two sons by his Indian wife, his wife's lover, and her fourteen-year-old son by another man. With the exception of Hall, this group, who by birth and association had a pariah status in the community, had formed a gang, tormenting their neighbors with thefts, acts of vandalism, and cruelty to animals. In the absence of effective legal steps to subdue them, the leading citizens executed them in the tradition of vigilante justice. After a widely publicized trial, the accused were acquitted by a grand jury, a verdict that is still defended today by some people in Modoc County.[62]

Eventually representatives of various religious denominations succeeded civil agents in working on the reservations and the California Indians came into contact with various sects, which they might adopt or later reject if new practices conflicted with old customs. Before the turn of the century California Indians copied other native groups in America in performing the "Ghost Dance," one of the purposes of which was to banish the white conquerors. There was a reactivation of shamanism, the native prophets showing the influence of circuit-rider preachers who had visited the villages or reservations. The overlay of Christianity was superficial, perhaps only the emotion was transmitted, for the Indian seers stimulated the people to follow their own ways and reject the ways of the white man. Even with their numbers decimated and their world increasingly proscribed by fences and No Trespassing signs, they kept alive their history and traditions in oral form and passed on to their children the age-old skills.

This cultural continuity in the face of near-extermination

was dramatized by an event that occurred in August 1911, in Oroville. It was there that a man later called Ishi, the last survivor of the Yahi clan, stumbled into the corral of a slaughterhouse in search of food. Barking dogs aroused the local butchers who gathered around him as he stood, gaunt and exhausted, harried to the brink of mere survival. Over the years his people had been cut down in successive campaigns until the settlers were satisfied that all the Yahi, or Mill Creeks, as they called them, were dead. A small remnant had fled the intruders and had penetrated ever more deeply into their hiding places until Ishi alone was left. He stumbled into the corral as a representative of a Stone Age culture who had miraculously escaped the adulteration of white contacts as he had escaped death.

The local sheriff put him in jail to protect him from the curious onlookers who had gathered to see the "wild man." Though he was emaciated from lack of food, he would not eat, drink, or sleep during his first days of captivity. Local Indians and Mexicans tried to talk to him in their tongues, but he did not understand them. Two anthropologists at the University of California, reading about his "capture" in the San Francisco newspapers, were reminded of the lone woman of San Nicolas Island who had escaped when her people were transferred by boat to the Santa Barbara Mission in 1835 and was brought in eighteen years later by seal hunters to the mainland, where she survived only a few months as a curiosity, unable to talk with anyone.

The two professors went to Oroville, secured Ishi's release, won his confidence, and took him to live at the Museum of the University of California, where he demonstrated his native crafts to the public. He was more fortunate than the woman of San Nicolas Island. He was able to converse with interpreters in Yana, a language related to his own. His demonstration of an uncontaminated native culture was of the greatest interest to the anthropologists who befriended him and he was cherished by them as a personal friend until his death, caused by tuberculosis, in 1916.[63]

How extraordinary was Ishi's transformation from a fugitive to a living textbook example of native life, a walking museum specimen! And what a distance there was between the social scientists' new valuation of Indian culture and the life that was being lived by the descendents of the aboriginal people of California on the fringes of white society.

1. A. L. Kroeber, the author of many studies on California Indians, in estimating the number of natives before 1769, accepted the figure suggested by another anthropologist, S. F. Cook, as approximately 142,000. C. Hart Merriam estimated the number to be 260,000. Henry F. Dobyns in "An Appraisal of Techniques with a New Hemisphere Estimate," *Current Anthropology*, vol. 7, no. 4, October 1966, arrived at the number 400,000 by using an estimated percentage of deaths due to disease in comparison with the number of Indians left at the period of highest mortality.

2. For a description of protoagricultural activity in a desert tribe, see Harry W. Lawton and Lowell John Bean, "A Preliminary Reconstruction of Aboriginal Agricultural Technology among the Cahuilla," *The Indian Historian*, vol. 1, no. 5, Winter 1968.

3. Walton E. Bean, *California, An Interpretive History* (New York: McGraw-Hill, 1968), p. 6.

4. John Galvin, ed., *The First Spanish Entry into San Francisco Bay, 1775* (San Francisco: John Howell, 1971), pp. 15-73 *passim*.

5. Don Miguel Constanso, "The Narrative of the Portolá Expedition of 1769-1770," *Publication of the Academy of Pacific Coast History*, vol. 1, no. 4, p. 43.

6. Francisco Palóu, *The Founding of the First California Missions Under the Spiritual Guidance of the Venerable Padre Fray Junipero Serra*, translated and arranged with the aid of Thomas W. Temple II, by Douglas S. Watson (San Francisco: Nueva California Press, 1934), pp. 86-88.

7. *Ibid.*, p. 88.

8. Francisco Palóu, *Life and Apostolic Labors of the Venerable Father Junípero Serra*, trans. C. Scott Williams (Pasadena, Calif.: George Wharton James, 1913 [orig. pub. 1787]), p. 193.

9. Father Fray Pedro Font, *Diary of an Expedition to Monterey by Way of the Colorado River*, 1775-1776, trans. and ed. Herbert Eugene Bolton, in *Anza's California Expeditions*, vol. 4, *Font's Complete Diary* (Berkeley: University of California Press, 1930), p. 181.

10. Marco R. Newmark, *Jottings in Southern California History* (Los Angeles: Ward Ritchie Press, 1955), p. 5.

11. From summary of Fray Fermin Francisco de Lasuen's report to Governor Borica in Hubert Howe Bancroft, *History of California, 1542-1800*, vol. 1 (San Francisco: A. L. Bancroft, 1884), p. 593.

12. Father Jeronimo Boscana, *Chinigchinich*, trans. John P. Harrington, Smithsonian Miscellaneous Collections, vol. 92, Washington, D.C., 1935, pp. 29-30.

13. Interestingly enough, a recent study of a remote rural town in Spain, where local customs tended to supplant the authority of church and state, showed several similarities to California Indian culture. The Andalusians believed in the power of wise women called *sabias*. J. A. Pitt-Rivers, *The People of the Sierra* (London: Weidenfeld and Nicolson Ltd., 1954).

14. Boscana, *Chinigchinich*, pp. 27, 55-56.

15. Hugo Reid's letters of 1852 in Robert F. Heizer, ed., "The Indians of Los Angeles County" (Los Angeles: *Southwest Museum Papers*, no. 21, 1968), pp. 69-70.

16. Scholars are trying to determine whether syphilis originated with the whites or was introduced to Europeans by contact with Indians at the time Columbus discovered America. It seems not to have been endemic among California natives before the arrival of the Spaniards.

17. S. F. Cook estimates a 72 percent reduction in numbers from 53,600 to 14,900. *The Conflict Between the California Indian and White Civilization*, vol. 3, *Ibero-Americana*, no. 23 (Berkeley and Los Angeles: University of California Press, 1943), p. 92.

18. Bancroft, *History of California*, vol. 4, p. 51.

19. Leo J. Friis, *Orange County Through Four Centuries* (Santa Ana, Calif.: Pioneer Press, 1965), p. 19.

20. J. C. Frémont, *The Exploring Expedition to the Rocky Mountains, Oregon and California* (Buffalo, N.Y.: Geo. H. Derby & Co., 1851), p. 366.

21. "The Memoirs of Theodor Cordua," ed. and trans. Erwin G. Gudde, *California Historical Society Quarterly*, vol. 12, no. 4, December 1933.

22. William H. Ellison and Francis Price, eds., *The Life and Adventures in California of Don Augustín Janssens* (San Marino, Calif.: Huntington Library, 1953), pp. 102-103.

23. *Indian Affairs on the Pacific*, Exec. Doc. no. 76, House of Representatives, 34th Congress, 3rd Sess., vol. 9, p. 31. Anthropologists have theorized that agricultural techniques among some desert people were copied from the Colorado River tribes rather than from the missions. *See* Lawton and Bean, *The Indian Historian*.

24. George R. Stewart, *Ordeal by Hunger: The Story of the Donner Party*, new ed. (Boston: Houghton Mifflin, 1960), pp. 123-124.

25. J. W. Revere, "Tour of Duty in California," quoted in Georgia Read and Ruth Gaines, eds., *Gold Rush: The Journals, Drawings, and Other Papers of J. Goldsborough Bruff, April 2, 1849-July 20, 1851*

(New York: Columbia University Press, 1949), p. 682.

26. George Concepcion Yount to Richard Henry Dana, Jr., in *Journal of Richard Henry Dana, Jr.,* vol. 3, ed. Robert F. Lucid (Cambridge, Mass.: Harvard University Press, 1968), p. 904.

27. Andrew F. Rolle, *California: A History* (New York: Thomas Y. Crowell Co., 1963), p. 211.

28. Jeff C. Riddle, *The Indian History of the Modoc War* (1914), p. 15.

29. Letter from H. Day, Capt. 2nd Infantry, June 9, 1850, in *Report of the Secretary of the Interior,* Exec. Doc. no. 4, Senate, 33rd Congress, Spec. Sess., p. 40.

30. Josiah Royce, *California from the Conquest in 1846 to the Second Vigilance Committee in San Francisco* (New York: Alfred A. Knopf, 1948 [orig. pub. 1886]), p. 286.

31. H. S. Burton, Capt., 3rd Artillery, to Capt. D. R. Jones, June 15, 1856, *Indian Affairs on the Pacific,* Exec. Doc. no. 76, p. 126.

32. Adam Johnston to Hon. Luke Lea, *Report of the Secretary of the Interior,* Exec. Doc. no. 4, p. 65.

33. *Laws of the State of California,* 1850, p. 408.

34. Maj. Gen. John E. Wool to Lt. Col. L. Thomas, May 17, 1856, *Indian Affairs on the Pacific,* Exec. Doc. no. 76, p. 118.

35. Redick McKee to Gov. John Bigler, April 12, 1852, *Journal of the Legislature,* Appendix, 1853, p. 719.

36. Report in the *Marysville Weekly Express,* April 16, 1859, quoted in Robert F. Heizer and Alan J. Almquist, *The Other Californians: Prejudice and Discrimination under Spain, Mexico, and the United States to 1920* (Berkeley: University of California Press, 1971), p. 29.

37. Brig. Gen. Thomas B. Eastland to Gov. P. H. Burnett, June 15, 1850, *Journal of the Legislature,* Sess. 2, Appendix, 1851, pp. 770-771.

38. Governor's message, *Journal of the California Legislature,* 2nd Sess., 1851, pp. 14-15.

39. O. M. Wozencraft to Hon. Luke Lea, July 12, 1851, Report of Redick McKee, Sept. 30, 1851, *Report of the Secretary of the Interior,* Exec. Doc. no. 4, pp. 113, 157. Heizer and Almquist, *The Other Californians,* p. 69.

40. O. M. Wozencraft to Hon. Luke Lea, May 14, 1851, *Report of the Secretary of the Interior,* Exec. Doc. no. 4, p. 83.

41. The figure is sometimes given as 8,500,000 acres.

42. "Majority and Minority Reports of the Special Committee to inquire into the treaties made by the United States Indian Commissioners with the Indians in California," *Journal of the Senate,* 3rd Sess., 1852, pp. 598-600.

43. *Indian Affairs on the Pacific,* Exec. Doc. no. 76, pp. 90, 94, 99, 101, 141.

44. *Ibid.*, p. 117.

45. Quoted in Ellison and Price, *Don Agustín Janssens*, p. 49.

46. "An Act for the Government and Protection of Indians," passed April 22, 1850, *Laws of the State of California, 1850*, pp. 408-410.

47. An amendatory act, passed April 18, 1860, *Statutes of California*, 1860, pp. 196-197.

48. Heizer and Almquist, *The Other Californians*, pp. 53-57.

49. Harris Newmark, *Sixty Years in Southern California, 1853-1913* (Boston and New York: Houghton-Mifflin, 1930), pp. 41-42.

50. John Walton Caughey, ed., *The Indians of Southern California in 1852: The B. D. Wilson Report* (San Marino, Calif.: Huntington Library, 1952), p. 27.

51. *Laws of the State of California*, 1850, p. 409; *Laws of the State of California*, 1855, p. 179.

52. Heizer and Almquist, *The Other Californians*, p. 59.

53. Governor's message, *Journal of the California Legislature*, 2nd Sess., 1851, p. 15.

54. George H. Tinkham, *A History of Stockton* (San Francisco: W. M. Hinton & Co., 1880), pp. 23-24.

55. Rolle, *California: A History*, p. 390; Cook, *California Indian and White Civilization*, p. 105. Also, S. F. Cook, "The California Indian and Anglo-American Culture," in Charles Wollenberg, ed., *Ethnic Conflict in California History* (Los Angeles: Tinnon-Brown, 1970), p. 29.

56. This is the figure given by C. Hart Merriam. S. F. Cook believes that the native population reached its low point in 1880 and thereafter began to rise.

57. Letter from the Secretary of the Interior relative to an appropriation to aid the Indians in Shasta County, California, February 25, 1874, House of Representatives, 43rd Congress, 1st Sess., Exec. Doc. no. 158, pp. 2-3.

58. Interview with Thelma Shiplet, Burney, Calif., October 19, 1970.

59. Mrs. M. E. Gregory in "The Covered Wagon," *Shasta County Historical Society Year Book*, 1945, p. 11.

60. Interview with Jefferson Mulkey, Sunnyvale, Calif., October 5, 1970.

61. Interview with Mrs. Kesner Beebe, Susanville, Calif., October 21, 1970.

62. See James O. Souther, *Legend into History: Facts and Fiction of the Lookout Lynching* (New York: Vantage Press, 1968).

63. See Theodora Kroeber, *Ishi in Two Worlds: A Biography of the Last Wild Indian in North America* (Berkeley and Los Angeles: University of California Press, 1961).

2

The Subjugation
of Hispanic California

❧ ★ ❧

THE FATE OF THE INDIANS was echoed in the history of
the Spanish Californians. Like the Indians, the *Californios*
at first welcomed the foreigners who eventually displaced
them as governors of the province and dispossessed them
of their lands. They, too, were unprepared for the disruption
of a peaceful and pastoral way of life. The conflict between
Hispanic and Anglo-Saxon culture, leading to the dominance
of the more aggressive invaders, recalls the relationship
of natives and whites. The parallel cannot be pushed too
far, however, for in the matter of adaptation and survival,
the experience of the *Californios* reflected their closer ties
with the *Norteamericanos.*

California's destiny in becoming an American possession was determined by its position on the periphery of the
far-flung Spanish empire. The rulers of New Spain long
considered it to be a place of nominal importance. The
conquistadores found gold and silver in Central and South
America, but they did not discover the great riches in the
Sierra Nevada. They claimed the Philippine Islands as a
gateway to the Orient, but their westward-bound Manila
galleons, laden with treasure, generally avoided the coast
of California, which had been suggested as a relief station,

and made instead for the more hospitable harbors of Mexico.

The sixteenth-century explorers who braved adverse winds and tides to sail north as far as Monterey named the wilderness they claimed after a fictional island inhabited by Amazons, the invention of a Spanish novelist. (The first navigators thought that the spiny tip of Baja California was an island, rather than a peninsula.) But far from discovering a terrestrial paradise, they found little to attract them to the new country. The extreme hardships of voyages in sailing ships contributed to the isolation of California.

Two hundred years passed before the colonizing expedition of 1769 came to establish a permanent settlement at the order of a Spanish administrator, who conceived an ambitious scheme for consolidating the northern territories against the possible expansionist designs of other European powers. The outposts established by Father Serra and Gaspar de Portolá were the northernmost points in a loose confederation that included Sinaloa, Sonora, Chihuahua, and Baja California. Only the Franciscan missionaries, eager to carry on their work on a new frontier, careless of hardships, desirous of martyrdom, were enthusiastic about this Siberia of New Spain. For the soldiers who guarded the *presidios* an order to serve in San Diego or Monterey was like a sentence of banishment. They were forgotten in their exile, were poorly provisioned, and their pay was sometimes as much as ten years in arrears.

To attract civilian settlers to California, the first governor offered material inducements—20 pesos and rations for the first two years, plus farm animals and equipment.[1] But only the poorest immigrants could be persuaded to come. Occasionally the inmates of jails were shipped north to help populate the newly formed *pueblos* of Branciforte (near Santa Cruz), Los Angeles, and San Jose. The new Californians—both soldiers and settlers—were often of mixed blood, but all segments of the population except the native Indians were dignified with the title of *gente de razón*. *Mestizos* and mulattos enjoyed full citizenship privileges, though their class identification may have contributed to the general prejudice of the mission fathers against them. If there was a hierarchy of color in Spanish California, it was related to the fact, as mentioned earlier, that positions of leadership in the church, state, and military were awarded to men born in Spain. Until Mexico declared its independence, the *criollos*, Spaniards born in the New World, could not aspire to high office, even if their blood was the purest Castilian.

Though California was not attractive to Spanish settlers and was isolated from the rest of the Spanish empire, it began to be visited from the beginning of the nineteenth century by foreigners lured to its coastal regions and even inside its borders by the possibility of rich profits in the fur trade. The English-owned Hudson's Bay Company sent trappers south from Vancouver and Oregon to the Tulare region, while the first American hunters crossed the mountains and the desert from the east. At the same time sea otters and fur seals brought American and Russian ships to California waters. The animals were hunted along the coast from South America to the Pacific Northwest by Indian and Kodiak boatmen employed by American firms or the Alaska-based Russian American Fur Company. As many as eighteen thousand were obtained in one year and were carried aboard New England-owned ships to China, where they sold in the Canton market for three hundred dollars apiece. Yankee trading vessels supplied the hard-pressed Russian colonists at Sitka, but soon the Russians were sending their own ships to "New Albion," following the name earlier bestowed on California by Sir Francis Drake, in the hope of bargaining for supplies with Spanish officials.

The Spaniards, who had a ban against trading with foreign ships, were somewhat wary of these foreigners, suspicious that their fur-hunting, petitions for supplies, and their use of off-shore islands to careen and repair their vessels masked more sinister motives. There was some foundation for these fears. The weakness of the *presidios,* where a garrison might consist of two or three men and a few unreliable cannon, was observed by the sea captains of other flags, among them the Englishman, George Vancouver, who visited California in 1792–1793 in the course of implementing the Nootka Sound Treaty in which Spain gave up exclusive rights on the northern Pacific Coast.

Some crewmen from an American ship, trading along the coast in 1803 in violation of Spanish law, were seized when they landed to bargain for furs. After they were rescued there was an exchange of cannon fire with a shore battery, but no casualties resulted on either side. "Our second broadside seemed to have caused the complete abandonment of their guns, as none were fired afterwards," wrote an officer, "nor could we see any person in the fort, except a soldier who stood upon the ramparts, waving his hat, as if to desire us to desist firing." The captain concluded that "at great expense and considerable industry, the Spaniards have removed every obstacle out of the way of an invading enemy. . . . The conquest of this country would be absolutely nothing; it would fall without an effort to the most inconsiderable force." [2]

Nikolai Rezánov, Tsar Alexander I's chamberlain, who came to San Francisco from Sitka in the spring of 1806 on board the *June,* wrote: ". . . in the course of ten years we should become strong enough to make use of any favorable turns in European politics to include the coast of California in the Russian possessions. . . . The Spaniards are very weak in these countries. . . ." [3] At this time he was betrothed to the daughter of the *commandante;* however, before the marriage could take place, Rezánov died accidentally while traveling in Siberia.

The Russians waited only six years before establishing

a colony and a fort near Bodega Bay, north of San Francisco. They secured title to the land from Indian tribes for three blankets, three pickaxes, three pairs of trousers, two axes, and some glass beads, according to tradition,[4] but ignored the protests of the Spanish government and continued to hunt sea otters in the forbidden waters of San Francisco Bay harbor. The two northernmost missions at San Rafael and Sonoma were founded partly for the purpose of counteracting Russian influence, but the Californians were at the same time attracted by the possibility of trade with the new colony. Relations between the two groups of Europeans remained generally amicable, though the Russians evaded California duty regulations in trading with foreign ships at Bodega Bay and in other ways maintained their independence. Prompted by the failure of their ambitions to expand their colony and the near-extermination of sea otters, the Russians abandoned Fort Ross in 1841 and sold its assets, largely on credit, for thirty thousand dollars to the Swiss colonist, John Sutter.

The Mexican Era

After the wars of independence brought Mexican rule to California in 1821, trading was carried on more freely with foreign vessels. The California-born *criollos* were growing up in a province that was increasingly open to international influences as the ties with Spain were cut, as the Spanish-born clergy lost their power. The natives were imbued with regional pride, which made them increasingly resentful of the officials sent up from Mexico City to govern them. When the mission lands were divided into *ranchos,* some of these *Californios* or their fathers and uncles were awarded title to vast acreages, and inherited the position of the Franciscans in managing princely estates and governing and protecting a large retinue of family, servants, and dependents. They acted as arbiters in regional affairs, led military expeditions against Indians in the interior, and assumed much the same role in their country seats as did the *alcades* in the towns, who combined the function of judge, mayor, and sheriff in one office. Only simple institutions were required in this pastoral and patriarchal society.

After the first hardships of pioneering, the Californians of property settled into a pleasant outdoor life with many intervals of dancing, horseracing, cockfighting, and bull-baiting. Since attendance at mass and community fiestas generally took the place of formal schooling, the literacy rate was very low. The *peons,* mainly Indians, performed the manual labor while the upper classes enjoyed a life of relative ease and prosperity. Land was cheap and plentiful, the cattle that roamed the "thousand hills" were the source of wealth. The *patrón,* who presided over the candlelit dining table while entertaining chance travelers with wines, brandies, *frijoles,* and *tortillas,* spent his days on horseback. In some communities, horses ran free at the disposal of anyone who wished to catch them, while beef was so plentiful that the carcasses were sometimes left for carrion after the more valuable hides had been skinned. The Californians, spendthrift with their natural resources, welcomed the initiative and diversified interests of foreign traders who brought needed supplements to their barely self-sufficient economy and supported the provincial treasury through the customs duties which were levied on foreign cargoes.

When the sea otters had been nearly killed off, a new trade in hides and tallow developed as an adjunct to cattle-raising on the missions and *ranchos.* Ships from England, France, Germany, Italy, Hawaii, and Mexico came to trade, but the majority were American. An agent for the Boston firm of Bryant and Sturgis won the market from a British company by bidding up the price of hides to two dollars apiece, with the result that the United States came to be

known in California as "Boston," and hides—the main
form of currency—were called "California banknotes."

The foreign visitors brought the prejudices of different
cultures to their experience on the Hispanic frontier. Even
in earlier encounters Americans had evoked Puritan standards in their judgment of the charming Californians.
Harrison G. Rogers, a clerk of a fur-trapping expedition, in
gratitude for the openhearted hospitality of Father Sanchez
at the San Gabriel Mission, had been moved to deliver him
a sermon in the Calvinist style. When the Harvard-educated
Richard Henry Dana visited the West Coast ports in 1834–
1835 as a sailor on a Boston merchantman, he was seduced
by the color and the freedom of life on shore but condemned his hosts as "an idle, thriftless people," who "can
make nothing for themselves." [5] He observed them with a
sharp eye as they came aboard the *Pilgrim* to look over the
stock of spirits, condiments, boots and shoes, hardware,
furniture, and notions. He found their dress flamboyant.
He judged the young men from the better families to be
"dissolute and extravagant when the means are at hand;
ambitious at heart, and impotent in act; often pinched for
bread; keeping up an appearance of style, when their poverty is known to each half-naked Indian boy in the
street. . . ." He noted "the fineness of the voices and beauty
of the intonations of both sexes. . . . A common bullock-
driver, on horseback, delivering a message, seemed to
speak like an ambassador at an audience. In fact, they
sometimes appeared to me to be a people on whom a curse
had fallen, and stripped them of everything but their pride,
their manners, and their voices." [6]

Dana's was a typical Anglo-Saxon view. Sir George
Simpson, governor-in-chief of the Hudson's Bay Company,
wrote after a visit in 1841–42 that "the population . . . has
been drawn from the most indolent variety of an indolent
species, being composed of super-annuated trappers and retired office-holders and their descendents. . . . In all but

the place of their birth, the colonists of Spain have continued to be genuine Spaniards. . . . Foreigners and natives cordially mingle together as one and the same harmonious family. In a word, the Californians are a happy people, possessing the means of physical pleasure to the full, and knowing no higher kind of enjoyment." [7]

Many of the foreign visitors were of the opinion that the amiable *gente de razón* were too indolent to develop the commercial possibilities of their province. The next step was to conclude that they should make way for a more energetic race of pioneers. "In the hands of an enterprising people, what a country this might be!" Dana wrote.[8]

A transition was already underway, for some of the visitors were becoming permanent residents. Americans, Englishmen, Frenchmen, Germans, and men of a few other nationalities, former ship's officers or chance voyagers saw the commercial possibilities of this outpost of Mexico and responded to the charm of its inhabitants. These strangers, in turn, often held a greater attraction for the California ladies than did the local *cavalieros*. (The sickly Governor Echeandia lost the San Diego beauty he loved to an American sea captain, Henry Delano Fitch.) As the young men with their strange accents and their faces bronzed from months at sea recovered their land legs on the streets of the little California towns, the local belles decked themselves out in their best finery and persuaded their fathers to give balls and parties. A current piece of doggerel ran:

> Already the senoritas
>   Speak English with finesse,
> "Kiss me!" say the Yankees,
>   The girls all answer "Yes!" [9]

Dana's own uncle had arrived in Santa Barbara in 1826 and claimed as his bride the sixteen-year-old Josefa Carrillo, who bore him twenty-one children. Large families were the fashion and were no encumbrance in the sparsely

populated province. William E. P. Hartnell, an Englishman who, as Don Guillermo, became one of California's
most prominent citizens, married a daughter of another
prominent Santa Barbara family, Maria Teresa de la
Guerra, who gave birth to twenty-five sons and daughters.

The "Mexicanized gringos" adopted the manners of the
country, Hispanized their given names, and brought up their
children as "Spaniards, in every respect," at least in Dana's
chauvinistic view. They were allowed to settle permanently
and become the beneficiaries of land grants on condition
that they become citizens of Mexico and converts to Catholicism, a step they rationalized by saying that "a man must
leave his conscience at Cape Horn." [10]

Thomas Oliver Larkin, a native of Charlestown, Massa-
chusetts, who became the United States consul in 1843
after ten years of residence, enjoyed a cordial relationship
with the government in Monterey without changing his
citizenship or his religion. In other respects he was typical
of the foreigners who, Dana noted, were "fast filling up the
principal towns, and getting the trade into their hands."
They opened stores stocked with goods from the incoming
vessels and acted as middlemen in arranging transactions
between the owners of cargo ships and the *rancheros*,
with occasionally a little remunerative smuggling on the
side. Their experience as world travelers was wider than
that of most Californians. Familiarity with the markets of
the Northwest and East, and an awareness of the possibilities of trade with the Orient, gave them a strategic advantage, in view of the more provincial orientation of their
hosts.

However, the *nativos*, who bestowed their largesse in
the form of land grants on these emigré merchants, found
themselves in some difficulties with another group of
foreigners who had come without permission and were to
be found as the proprietors or habitués of grog shops on the
back streets of the little coastal towns. To the upper-class

Californians these uninvited guests were as objectionable in their appearance as the native *cholos* (lower classes), nor were they well behaved. Deserters who had "jumped ship" mingled with former backwoodsmen and trappers who held to the honorable tradition of despising "greasers" as they hated Indians. They were the generic descendents of the pioneer trailblazers Jedediah Smith and James Ohio Pattie, who had shown their scorn for the "mighty dons" when they appeared along the coast in the 1820s. Dana tells how a few years later forty Kentucky hunters and trappers invoked frontier justice in Los Angeles to avenge the murder of a Mexicanized gringo while "a general, with titles enough for an hidalgo . . . issued a proclamation as long as the fore-top-bowline," threatening their destruction, "but never stirred from his fort; for forty Kentucky hunters, with their rifles," Dana boasted, "were a match for a whole regiment of hungry, drawling, lazy half-breeds." [11]

Perhaps one of this group was Isaac Graham, a former trapper who later set up a whisky distillery near Santa Cruz.[12] He brought in a group of his cronies to help Juan Bautista Alvarado depose the current Mexican governor and proclaim California "a free and sovereign State" in 1836. But when Alvarado reneged on his alleged promise to give Graham a land grant, the young governor was soon complaining of the "insulting familiarity" of the American's "drunken followers." [13] Alvarado and his cousin José Castro credited rumors that a troublesome group of drifters and brawlers, led by Graham, were plotting to overthrow the new regime.

Accordingly, on April 5, 1840, a plan was formulated by the ruling *junta* to arrest all foreigners who had entered the country unlawfully, except those who had married local women and established themselves as citizens. About forty "undesirables," mostly Americans, were taken prisoner and shipped to Mexico. Through the intercession of the United States and British governments, they were released and compensated for their losses. When Isaac Graham on his return to California was asked his opinion of Spaniards, he replied, "A corral is not big enough to hold me and one of them." [14]

In 1844 Graham revenged himself by bringing in a hundred riflemen to aid the last Mexican governor, Manuel Micheltorena, in his losing fight against the Californians under Alvarado and Castro. His ally was John Sutter, the Swiss emigrant, to whom Alvarado had awarded a small kingdom on the inland frontier, a tract of eleven leagues (nearly forty-five hundred acres to the league) which he had been allowed to select himself. Further, he was given authority to act as *represente del gobierno en las fronteras del Rio del Sacramento,* to administer justice, repress "savage Indians," check illegal trapping and fishing, and prevent robberies by "adventurers from the United States." [15] Ever mindful of his own interests, Sutter, only two years after becoming heir to his fiefdom, promised cynically, "If they will give me satisfaction and pay the expenses . . . I will be a faithful Mexican." [16] He had arrived in Monterey after brief sojourns in St. Louis, Santa Fe, Oregon, Honolulu, and Sitka, visiting all the places where interest in California was awakening. He was aware that the opening of the Southwest trails and the Columbia River route to adjacent territories was bringing settlers who were antipathetic to Latin culture and religion. Buttressed by his assured position and his strategic location—away from the eyes of the Monterey officials, but on the route of the Hudson's Bay trappers and trans-Sierra explorers—Sutter was fired by the stirrings of change and was ambitious to play a leading role if the weak Mexican ruler should give way to the intrusion of a stronger power. In the meantime he would win what concessions he could. Governor Micheltorena gave him the right to award land grants to new settlers (reinforcing his independence of the *nativo* leaders) on condition that he join Graham's vendetta against them.

The prudent Larkin maintained his neutrality in this new crisis as he had during the deportation of the "undesirables," promising to "assist a new Gov. the same as I did the old one. I am very sorry a single Foreigner took up arms in the late affair," he wrote.[17] As consul, however, he was playing an active role in representing the interests of the United States in acquiring California or at least preventing a foreign power from doing so. Provincial affairs were colored by the increasingly strained relations between Mexico and the United States, which had suffered when American settlers north of the Rio Grande established a Texas Republic in the same year that Andrew Jackson offered to buy California, New Mexico, and Texas. The suit for California and New Mexico was renewed under the Tyler administration amid rumors that Great Britain and France were pursuing their own negotiations with Mexican officials.

Tyler's successor, James Knox Polk, took office as the proponents of Manifest Destiny were urging that the Stars and Stripes should fly over land from the Atlantic to the Pacific, while American settlers were rushing into Oregon territory and while Larkin was reporting on the alleged intrigues of the British consul in Monterey. It was rumored that France, which was sending a consul to Monterey, also entertained an ambition to acquire "the pear" that was "near ripe for falling." In October 1845 Larkin was appointed a "secret agent," in addition to his regular consular duties. The document which reached him via a courier from Washington, after a six months' delay, contained the following instructions on American policies in California from the then secretary of state, James Buchanan:

> The future destiny of that Country is a subject of anxious solicitude for the Government and people of the United States. The interests of our Commerce and our Whale fisheries on the Pacific Ocean demand that you should exert the greatest vigilance in discovering and defeating any attempts which may be made by Foreign Governments to acquire a

control over that Country. In the contest between Mexico and
California we can take no part, unless the former should
commence hostilities against the United States; but should
California assert and maintain her independence, we shall
render her all the kind offices in our power as a Sister
Republic. This government has no ambitious aspirations to
gratify and no desire to extend our Federal system over more
Territory than we already possess, unless by the free and
spontaneous wish of the Independent people of the adjoining
Territories. The exercise of compulsion or improper influence
to accomplish such a result would be repugnant both to the
policy and principles of this Government.[18]

Larkin's new assignment, which he took to be one of
encouraging a peaceful transition to American rule, was
but an extension of his previous policy of watching developments and fostering a favorable attitude toward the
United States among the Californians. He was aware of
the futility of the quarrels among the *nativos*—the rivalry
between the new governor, Pio Pico, in the south and the
leaders in Monterey—and believed that some of them
would prefer to be under the American flag than to continue their factionalism or their periodic struggles with
Mexican officials. "The fate of this Country . . . must, in my
opinion, change by some means," he wrote to his friend
Abel Stearns, whom he had appointed to be assistant "con-
fidential agent" in Los Angeles, adding a personal foot-
note, "I myself as a trader prefer everything as it is. The
times and the country are well enough for me."[19]

He made an assessment of the most notable individuals in the province, shrewdly evaluating their abilities and
sentiments toward the United States and other possible
foreign conquerors. On his list of almost eighty men were a
large number of respected emigré traders and *rancheros;*
among the *nativos* were listed the important leaders Pio
Pico and Juan Bandini from Los Angeles, the young north-
erners Alvarado and Castro, and their uncle General Mari-

ano Vallejo, whose Sonoma ranch was as much a port of call for foreign visitors as was Sutter's New Helvetia. Another of Vallejo's nephews, the patrician Pablo de la Guerra from Santa Barbara who would play a prominent part in gringo politics a few years hence, was further removed from the influences of American settlements which were stirring in the Sacramento and Napa valleys. In 1840 he had "congratulated" his amiable uncle on the large number of foreign settlers in the country "who are hard drinkers, but will perhaps, like wine, improve with time." [20] Larkin wrote that Don Pablo "like many others imbibes prejudice against Americans from observing the first Emigrants who came to California from the Mountains." [21]

Larkin was busy promoting the arrival of still more settlers. One of his Mexicanized gringo friends was urging him to bring in an "American population . . . sufficiently large to play the Texas game." [22] Larkin asked "Doctor" John Marsh, a Yankee *ranchero* from the Mt. Diablo region, to bestir himself. "I should like to have you shake off your apathy and idleness, come forth into the field, and write for the Country [where] you intend to live. You are a good writer, know well the country, its people and recources [*sic*], whether it will grow hemp, Cotten [*sic*], wheat or corn, what fruit wild or cultivated, know the soil, climate, rivers and Bays." [23]

Marsh had been doing just this sort of publicity for a number of years. The Western Emigrant Society had been formed in Missouri, partly in response to his enthusiastic letters on California which appeared in the St. Louis *Republican* in 1840, though cold water was thrown on the doctor's efforts by the Mexican minister in Washington, who was startled that a colonist of foreign birth, a guest of the country, should be encouraging his former compatriots to join him en masse.

Mexican officials also took note of the topographical expeditions of naval officers under Charles Wilkes in 1841 and John Charles Frémont with an army party two years later, which combined a scientific study of the flora and fauna of the region with an assessment of the politics and defenses of the *Californios*. Frémont's report of this trip, *An Exploring Expedition to the Rocky Mountains, Oregon and California,* excited great interest among restless men east of the Rockies, as did Lansford W. Hastings' propagandistic *Emigrants' Guide to Oregon and California,* which was also published in 1845.

Both books were used as trail guides by prospective settlers. (Hastings was a better publicist than a pathfinder; it was in following his "cutoff," which he had never taken himself at the time he wrote the book, that the Donner Party fatally lengthened their journey.) Though he first visited his land of promise in a year of severe drought, Hastings was unstinting in his praise for it. "In my opinion," he wrote, "there is no country, in the known world, possessing a soil so fertile and productive, with such varied and inexhaustible resources and a climate of such mildness, uniformity and salubrity. . . ."

He was less enthusiastic about the inhabitants. He found them to be "scarcely a visible grade, in the scale of intelligence, above the barbarous tribes by whom they are surrounded. . . . The higher order of Mexicans are perhaps about equal to the lower order of our citizens throughout our western states . . . these semi-barbarians, intend to hold this delightful region, as against the civilized world." [24] As these remarks circulated among the Californians, one of them offered a retort which gave Manifest Destiny a new definition. "The idea of those gentleman," he wrote, "is that God made the world and them also; therefore, what there is in the world belongs to them as sons of God!" [25]

In the spring of 1846, Hastings was at Sutter's New Helvetia, rejoicing at the number of people who had responded to his appeals. About 250 had come the previous

year and more than twice as many were to follow in 1846
—not in the flood-tide surge envisioned by the promoters,
but in sufficient numbers to make their presence felt. Hastings wrote to John Marsh, "I hope, Sir, the false impression
that our people design to wrest this country forcibly from
the Californians will not be promulgated . . . for it is not
true. *But they cannot be expelled from the country, nor
must their expulsion be attempted!* What consummate folly
it is for the natives of the Californias to attempt to check
the emigration to this country. They might just as well attempt to arrest the thundering wheels of time, to restrain
the mighty water's flow, or to extinguish the blazing light
of civil and religious liberty!" [26] For their part the *Californios* were beginning to regret their open-handed hospitality
to those who, as an official warned, "advance more and
more in their design to destroy our political system and de-
prive us of our native country." [27]

The strangers were entering the country by the back
door, applying for admittance to Sutter at his chosen location along the Sacramento River, rather than to officials
along the coast. New Helvetia became a hospitable way
station for exhausted trans-Sierra travelers as Sutter's wel-
come and the sun of the valley beckoned the weary pioneers down from the mountains. More generous than his
"neighbor," John Marsh, who encouraged emigrants and
then charged for his hospitality, Sutter opened his stores to
replenish the colonists' dwindling supplies and his blacksmith shop to repair their broken equipment. Moreover, his
establishment was large enough to offer living accommodations and temporary employment to those who needed a
base from which to investigate the opportunities in the new
country while they recovered from the rigors of their trav-
els. Eventually most of them struck out on their own,
armed with passports and land grants supplied by Sutter.
Some stayed close by to have the protection of his fort,
while the hardier adventurers went north to the Feather

River, the Bear River, Butte Creek, and even to Deer Creek in what was to be Lassen County, bestowing English names on these hitherto unexplored parts of California. By 1846 it was possible for a traveler bound for Oregon along the interior to find overnight accommodations in a scattering of *ranchos* north of New Helvetia and very far from the bases of the *Californios.*

Officials in Monterey deplored Sutter's assumption of authority and were uneasy about the presence of an undetermined number of foreigners who had entered the country illegally, yet nothing was done to enforce any restrictions against them. Until he was reminded that the impending war between Mexico and the United States made closer surveillance necessary, *Commandante* Castro pledged that his "friendly feeling" and "all the protection within the scope of my authority" would be extended to "foreigners residing on the frontier." [28] A more militant order issued on April 17, 1846, reminded government officials that foreigners who were not naturalized could not hold lands and were liable to expulsion whenever the government ordered it. The settlers were tense. They felt that they were occupying their homesteads as squatters because, since they despised Romanists and Latins, they would not become citizens of Mexico. Nor did they have any assurance of support from the United States. They felt they could not claim the protection of any government and were alone responsible for their conduct.[29]

American Conquest

Into their midst at this moment came the ardent and impetuous John Charles Frémont with sixty armed men, including seasoned scouts like Kit Carson and backwoodsmen from Tennessee. Though the settlers established an immediate rapport with these newcomers they must have reminded Castro of Isaac Graham's followers, who had involved him in such difficulties six years before. The *commandante* seems to have sensed the equivocal intentions of the young explorer who claimed that he had come to survey a practicable route to the Pacific.

Frémont, like Larkin, was privy to his government's ambitions in California and was imbued with the teachings of his father-in-law Senator Thomas Hart Benton, one of the leading exponents of Manifest Destiny. Furthermore, he had been warned of the probability of the outbreak of war with Mexico. As an official American representative (he had received a duplicate copy of Buchanan's letter to Larkin), he decided not to watch and wait, but to act. In defending his provocative behavior, which was debated during his lifetime and is still a subject of intense controversy, he wrote later, "My private instructions were, if needed, to foil England by carrying the war now imminent with Mexico into California." [30]

His calculated action was to return to "the department" after Castro ordered him to leave. His re-entry from Oregon, passing through the Sacramento and Napa valleys, acted as a spark to tinder in touching off an uprising of agitated settlers. So began the Bear Flag revolt, so named because the participants raised aloft over the captured fort at Sonoma a homemade standard decorated with the emblem of a grizzly bear and the words "California Republic." This one-month, one-town republic was a local affair, but the somewhat capricious actions of the participants, including Frémont, left a lasting legacy of bitterness. The rhetoric of the Bear Flaggers was borrowed from the patriots at Concord and Lexington, and drew its heat from the memory of the defenders of the Alamo. A proclamation issued on June 15, 1846, denounced a regime "which has shamefully oppressed and ruined the producing inhabitants of California," and called on "patriotic citizens" to help "establish a liberal, a just and honorable Government. . . ." [31]

Their justification for their actions was that they were

liable to expulsion by the local authorities, but without any
real opposition some of the heterogeneous "army" that
rallied under the Bear Flag felt themselves to be on dubious ground. As a group stood outside the house of Mariano
Vallejo while others who had surprised the general inside
drew up articles of capitulation, a Yankee officer asked,
"What are the orders of Captain Frémont in relation to
these men?" Getting no answer, he declared, *"Gentlemen,
I have been deceived; I cannot go with you. I resign and
back out of the scrape.* I can take my family to the mountains as cheap as any of you." [32] The leader who reunited
the group told them that if they were not conquerors they
ran the risk of being simply robbers.

When Larkin in Monterey received the news that Vallejo, the Americans' best friend, and three people in his
household had been taken prisoner, he was incredulous.
"I can hardly believe it and do not understand the affair." [33]
Sutter, deposed of his authority at New Helvetia by Frémont, had to play host to the Vallejo party as well as to the
garrison that was guarding them, those who Don Mariano's
brother called "Pike County blackguards" because they
dared to refer to men "of the purest blood of Europe" as
"greasers." [34] Sutter and Larkin, who had set the stage for
rebellion by urging American emigrants to cross the mountains, were now swept aside by the rush of events. Larkin
philosophized, "If they have started the big Ball to roll forever and thro' and thro' C[alifornia], I can not stop it." [35]

Warfare in California had always been conducted in a
ritual and relatively bloodless manner, with a fine show of
bravado and the fatalities limited to a mule or two. When
three Californians were summarily executed by Frémont's
soldiers as they landed in a boat near Suisan Bay, Castro
declared he no longer doubted whether his men were strug-
gling against "savage hordes . . . or against civilized soldiers." [36] The Californians were considerably relieved when
the *osos* ("bears") were replaced by a legitimate conqueror.

Commodore John D. Sloat and the Pacific Squadron arrived in Monterey early in July to announce the outbreak of the Mexican War and to claim California for the United States. Pio Pico, Alvarado, and Castro fled to Mexico, and Frémont, promoted to the rank of major by Sloat's successor, Commodore Robert Stockton, led a force which included some of the Bear Flag guerrillas to subdue the South.

The contrast in Hispanic and Yankee battle style continued in this second phase of the war. When Frémont's lieutenant, Gillespie, showed himself too arbitrary in the military occupation of the south, the Angelenos rose up in protest and carried the field in several skirmishes. Their tactics involved maneuver and surprise as well as superb horsemanship. The defeat of General Stephen Kearny's forces at San Pascual was a brilliant episode in comparison with the bumbling performance of the captors of Sonoma. Lighthearted gallantry rather than brutal assault characterized the California War. There were few casualties as the *Californios* upheld their honor by seizing the initiative; and the Americans, in regaining control, proved that if they could not erase the memory of the depradations of the first weeks, they could be generous conquerors.

The Mexicanized gringos tended to play a neutral role, protecting *nativo* in-laws, and exerting their influence to shield the innocent and to prevent excesses on both sides. A few resident foreigners were taken prisoner. Larkin was held in Los Angeles a few weeks "closely confined . . . but had never less than 4 or 5 meals sent to me a day. . . . The Mexicans and C[alifornians] appeared desires [*sic*] to out do each other in obtaining my good will." [37]

As the contest came to a close, the Americans began quarreling with each other. Frémont presided at the capitulation of Cahuenga on January 13, 1847, in the same month that Kearny complained to the secretary of war that Frémont and Stockton had resisted his authority in forming a government in California. "The pathfinder" was courtmartialed on a complaint by Kearny the following year, 1848, in which the conquest of California was confirmed by the Treaty of Guadalupe Hidalgo, which officially ended the Mexican War. In this treaty the United States agreed to pay fifteen million dollars in exchange for 918,000 square miles of former Mexican territory, which included California, the present states of Utah, Nevada, New Mexico, and a part of Arizona. The resident population was offered the choice of crossing the border to Mexico or remaining, either as Mexicans or, if they made no declaration to the contrary, automatically becoming American citizens in a year. In either case they would retain all rights to their land, freedom to practice their religion, and protection "in the free enjoyment of their liberty and property." [38]

The postwar era started with general goodwill and amnesty. Larkin resumed his affairs in Monterey. Mariano Vallejo, showing no rancor for the damage inflicted on his property by Yankee insurgents, shaved his whiskers according to the latest American fashion to march in the victory parade.[39] Jessie Benton Frémont, who followed her husband to California, experienced no hostility, despite the fact that her name "represented only invasion and defeat." She shared a house in Monterey with the wife of the *commandante* who had ordered Frémont to leave "the department" such a short time before. "Madame Castro, true to the nature of Spanish women, sent daily a cup of milk for my little girl, for she had saved a cow for her children. This was another turn of the wheel. I had the name which to her represented total loss, for her husband had not returned from Mexico after we took her country, and yet her motherly feelings were stronger than the natural resentment for lost position and fortune." [40]

Castro, Alvarado, and Pio Pico returned from exile to find California in the throes of social upheaval following the discovery of gold. The northern leaders, still in their thirties, retired into obscurity as *rancheros*. Alvarado had to give up a ten-square-league property in the Mother Lode country for three thousand dollars to cancel a debt to Larkin and another Yankee moneylender, who sold the land to Frémont. When gold was discovered within the boundaries of Las Mariposas in 1849, it came to be known as the "ten-million-dollar tract." Alvarado, who had been California's most youthful governor, complained that his only reminder of his past honors was when his landlord addressed him as "Your Excellency" when asking for the rent. Castro eventually returned to public life but in Baja, not Alta, California, while Pio Pico remained a colorful local figure in Los Angeles and left gringo politics to his brother, Andrés.[41]

The transition into the new era was eased by the attitude of the American military leaders of the first government of occupation. They persuaded *Californios* to serve with Yankees in various official capacities during the first two years after the capitulation of Cahuenga. Leonard Pitt, the able biographer of the *Californios,* notes the "cosmopolitan" character of the provisional government: of the 157 men installed in office from 1847 to 1849, seventy-four were born in the United States or Britain, five in continental Europe, and forty-eight in California and Mexico.[42]

Harmony prevailed in the old capital of Monterey where the Reverend Walter Colton, a Congregational chaplain who had arrived with the American fleet, served as *alcalde.* He was a little shocked by a system that vested so much power in one office, but he exercised his authority with discretion. Under Mexican rule, there had been no confinement of wrongdoers. The *gente de razón* paid a fine while Indians were whipped. Colton introduced compulsory labor, requiring prisoners to make fifty adobe bricks a day. Some of the local customs troubled Colton's Sabbatarian principles, but he did not interfere. Monterey continued to be serenely Hispanic in character, though Jessie Benton Frémont found that the ladies wanted new dresses "as they wore them in the States" for a Fourth of July ball.

Yankee *alcaldes* had more difficulties in San Jose, a town rent by civil unrest, where members of the Pacheco family, still smarting from the war, asserted their independence of gringo rule. Mexicans, Chileans, and Indians predominated, and Spanish was the principal language of business and the street. It was spoken even in the Napa Valley, the stronghold of the Bear Flag rebels, when some survivors of the Donner Party arrived there in May of 1847. In a letter to a friend, young Virginia Reed, clearly entranced with her novel surroundings, showed off her newly acquired vocabulary, which contained the usual American corruptions of the language of the country. *Vaquero* came out as "bocarro," *lassos* as "lasses," and *riata* as "reatter." "Tell Henriet," she wrote, "if she wants to get Married to come to California she can get a spanyard any time." [43]

The Constitutional Convention of 1849

Two years later, the province, which had been settling down to some of its prewar tranquility, was transformed by the arrival of hundreds of fortune hunters from all over the globe. The changes in store for the *Californios* were forecast at the constitutional convention of 1849, which was called twenty months after the fateful discovery of gold flakes in Sutter's millrace. Suddenly, 100,000 new arrivals overwhelmed the small nucleus of about 13,000 Spanish-speaking Californians. This ratio was reflected in the roster of delegates to the convention. There were eight with Spanish surnames; a small number of foreign residents from the Mexican era including Sutter, Larkin, and Abel Stearns; the strident publicist for American interests, Lansford W. Hastings; and the rest were relative newcomers. Twelve had lived in California one year or less. William M. Gwin, a Southern politician who had arrived four months earlier, drew a sharp rebuke from José Antonio Carrillo when he referred to that fiery Angeleno as a "foreigner." Under the "length of residence" on the roster, Carrillo could boast *"Toda la vida* ("All my life")." At fifty-three, he was the oldest delegate. The average age was thirty-six.

The convention opened with a show of amnesty between old and new Californians. Vallejo and John Sutter escorted to the rostrum the former Bear Flag officer, Robert Semple, who was installed as chairman; the two *rancheros,* who had emerged from the vicissitudes of war, flanking the huge Kentucky frontiersman, who had come to California in a buckskin dress and a foxskin cap. Appreciative laughter greeted Vallejo's proposal that the state seal should show a *vaquero* lassooing a bear. The design that was accepted was an amalgam of the past and the present: a bear quietly standing and eating grapes at the feet of the Roman goddess Minerva, who surveyed a miner plying his pickaxe and ships on the Sacramento against a panoply of mountains.

The convention was more influenced by recent events in California and the nation than by the concerns of the old residents, a divergence that was translated into a north-south split on fundamental issues. The interests of the clamorous multitudes mining in the Sierra foothills, transforming the little port town of Yerba Buena into the bustling first city of San Francisco, tended to prevail over the opposing views of the predominantly agricultural southern districts, since the delegate strength of the north was almost six times that of the south, The dispute over the size of the new state was compromised by setting the boundaries at the forty-second parallel on the north, and on the east, a line from Lake Tahoe to the Colorado River.

The "cow county" members petitioned in vain to create a separate territory in the south; they felt they would be taxed unfairly since land rather than mineral wealth was to be the basis for assessment. (In Mexican California land was not taxed; the revenues had come from duties levied on foreign cargoes.) They further lost a motion that seats in the legislature should not be apportioned on the basis of population alone but in recognition of greater financial contribution. They were outvoted on a motion to place the new state capital in Santa Barbara.

Since all but two of the native delegates were from the south, the *Californios*, in particular the eloquent Pablo de la Guerra, led the fight for the interests of this region and succeeded in snatching two concessions from the northern (and overwhelmingly gringo) majority. Tax assessors were to be locally elected and the legislature must print all laws in Spanish. Also, the Mexican law that women retained rights to their own property after marriage was put into the new constitution.

Knowing that California would more easily win admission to the union as a "free soil" state, the delegates—after much disagreement—voted unanimously to bar slaves. Then they hotly debated the question of excluding free blacks, an issue that united delegates who were born south of the Mason-Dixon line with those concerned with individual entrepreneurship in the mining districts. Ultimately the prohibition on the entry of free Negroes was dropped, but in another strongly contested racial issue, one in which the *Californios* took an active part, Indians, Africans, and their descendents were deprived of the franchise.

The *nativos* and others protested that limiting the privilege of voting to white male citizens was a violation of the Treaty of Guadalupe Hidalgo, which guaranteed the full rights of citizenship to all former citizens of Mexico. Property ownership or recognition of membership in the *gente de razón* had been the criteria for citizenship in Mexican California (the aboriginals were excluded by this means). Pablo de la Guerra reminded the convention that "many citizens of California have received from nature a very dark skin; nevertheless, there are among them men who have hitherto been allowed to vote, and not only that, but to fill the highest public offices." [44] Manuel Dominguez, clearly a *mestizo,* was sitting in their midst as a delegate from Los Angeles, yet the majority voted in favor of the "white males only" limitation, with the following rider attached: "Provided that nothing herein contained shall be construed to prevent the Legislature, by a two-thirds concurrent vote, from admitting to the right of suffrage, Indians or the descendents of Indians, in such special cases as such a proportion of the Legislative body may deem just and proper." [45] This gesture to the *Californios* was meaningless in the context of majority public opinion at the time. The legislature was more inclined further to restrict than to enlarge the privilege of the franchise. In 1857 Dominguez was barred from testifying in a San Francisco courtroom.

Hispanic Southern California

The constitution was ratified and California was admitted to the Union on September 9, 1850. The *nativo* delegates may have left the convention with the feeling that their way of life was being eclipsed by a new era, but those who returned south were soon reassured by the unchanged character of the landscape. For almost a generation to come, those speaking Spanish would be in the majority in San Luis Obispo, Santa Barbara, San Diego, and Los Angeles. Today's largest city in California, Los Angeles had a population of about five thousand in the mid-1850's. The old families, those of Mexican origin and the Mexicanized gringos with whom they had intermarried, dominated the social and cultural life of the little *pueblo.* A few fugitives from the gold mines, including Chinese and Sonorans, drifted into town, as well as a trickle from the vast army of immigrants arriving to the north.

A young German-Jewish merchant, Harris Newmark, gives a clear picture of the Hispanic quality of early Los

Angeles.[46] When he arrived as a youth in 1853, he found he had to learn Spanish rather than English. Mexican measurements were used, court proceedings were translated, and the newspaper was bilingual. Houses were of the traditional adobe construction; the city water was carried through *zanjas,* or irrigation ditches, from the river; and people traveled in either heavy, squeaking, two-wheeled carts called *carretas,* which were pulled by oxen, or by foot or on horseback. Since there were no hitching posts, horsemen tied a long *riata* onto their saddlehorns, keeping hold of the other end as they entered a house or store. Shopkeepers were expected to throw in a *pilon,* or trifle, when a customer made a purchase. The traditional sports, especially horse racing and cockfighting, occupied the men, while both sexes celebrated even such an American holiday as the Fourth of July with a parade of colorfully garbed horsemen and barbecues that lasted for several days.

The "cow counties" profited from the Gold Rush. Longhorns were for a brief period valued at seventy dollars a head, though the price soon dropped to sixteen dollars. The high beef prices enabled the *Californios* to continue their traditional, comfortable way of life with a few embellishments. Those *paisanos* who went to dig for gold, however, were suddenly and rudely exposed to the nativist sentiment against all *Latinos* in the mining districts. In 1848, before the worldwide migration converged on California, the approximately thirteen hundred local Spanish descendents who traveled to the Sierra Nevada realized some good fortune and brought home their gold dust without undergoing any disturbance. But by the following year they were confused with the newly arrived Sonorans, Peruvians, and Chileans, and told that "foreigners" had "no right" to be there.[47]

They reacted either by retiring from the scene (dignified retreat was the pattern of the upper-class *hacendados*) or by joining the stigmatized Mexicans from across the border. If Sonorans and *Californios* were one and the same in the eyes of the Yankee argonauts, they could meet the blanket discrimination by combining forces to harass the common enemy. Mexican badmen had come north to waylay travelers laden with gold. Following their example, some of the young *nativos* defied the persecution of the gringos by fulfilling their expectations of the behavior of an outlaw group—by stealing cattle and robbing stage coaches in classic *bandido* style. The contest, however, was not always along ethnic lines; sometimes it was between new ruffians and old residents, or between *ricos* and *peons*. Mexicans might run with Yankee robbers, while upper-class Californians joined the Anglo-Saxon vigilance committees that punished the outlaws. Perhaps the most famous *Californio* outlaw was Monterey-born Tiburcio Vasquez, whose crimes, which led him to the gallows, were motivated by a desire for revenge against the Yankees.

The Land Controversy

The landed gentry among the Californians felt the hostility of the new citizens of the state most strongly when the fortune hunters came down from the mountains. Many of the forty-niners were frustrated and penniless, in need of some stability after months of wandering, and anxious to recoup their losses by farming. They wanted land. They knew that homesteaders had always been given encouragement on the American frontier. In nearby Oregon, by order of Congress, settlers received an allotment of 640 acres apiece. California settlers petitioned the government for only 160 acres. "Give us the means and inducements of having a fixed and settled population and California is destined to sit as the Queen of the Pacific." [48]

In 1852 Congress opened 500,000 acres of "Public Lands" to settlers who were to be given land warrants for 160 acres apiece at two dollars an acre; but this was a paltry offering in comparison with what was denied them. They were blocked from acquiring the land where mining operations were in progress and from between thirteen and fourteen million acres of property suitable for agriculture which was held by a few hundred *Californio* families, who had acquired it in the prewar era when it was of negligible value. Among the approximately 800 Mexican land grants were a few that ran in size from 133,000 to 1,775,000 acres!

The contrast between the old Hispanic and the new American era was nowhere more dramatically evidenced than in this land controversy. The settlers protested the inherent inequity of the situation: that the descendents of a defunct regime should monopolize a vast empire which had appreciated in value through the change of flags. The clamorous newcomers were ready to replace the cattle-raising of the Spaniards with the techniques of intensive land cultivation that they had learned in their home communities across the seas or over the mountains. California now belonged to the United States, they argued. If it was to fulfill its promise to its pioneers, the great Mexican *ranchos* must be subdivided.

Some solution to the problem that would have partially satisfied the land-hungry emigrants and the cash-poor *Californios* might have been reached had there been more time and a smaller population. But there were too many impatient settlers. Most of them had no knowledge of the guarantees of the Treaty of Guadalupe Hidalgo, which promised former citizens of Mexico all rights to their land. Coming from the laissez-faire atmosphere of the gold-mining camps, the would-be farmers did not stand on ceremony. They acted as they did in their collisions with the Indians. When they saw vacant land, they appropriated it and put up fences and homesteads; "improvements" were a warranty of possession. If they suspected that the property belonged to an absentee owner, they rationalized their appropriation of it by recalling that the Stars and Stripes and not the banner with the eagle and the snake flew over California. The city of Oakland was created when Americans settled on the San Antonio *rancho* belonging to the Peralta family and refused to move.

These squatters (or settlers, depending on the viewpoint) had the ear of the new state legislature, and William Gwin, who had become one of Californa's first senators, pleaded their cause in Congress. Gwin's Land Act of 1851 challenged the validity of the old California land grants. Under its provisions, the owners would be forced to provide documentary evidence of the authenticity of Mexican titles. California's second senator, Frémont, opposed Gwin's bill (his *Rancho Mariposas* would be under scrutiny) but left the argument to his father-in-law, Thomas Hart Benton, who favored a bill that would uphold the legality of the land titles and force the homesteaders to furnish the burden of proof against them. His eloquence was unavailing; Gwin's bill passed easily. It should be noted that it was supported by some who had confidence in their documentary proof of title as a method to oppose the squatters. To others who were competing with rival claimants for their titles, it seemed logical to require a complete review of all holdings.

A three-man commission sat in San Francisco from January 1852 to March 1856 to hear evidence. It took, on an average, seventeen years for a decision to be rendered in each of the over-eight-hundred cases, starting with the presentation before the commissioners which would be challenged up through the courts. Spanish texts, and measurements in *varas* and leagues, caused delays. The grants were frequently overlapping and vaguely defined, with no fences between neighboring properties since the branded cattle roamed at will. The boundaries of one not untypical *rancho*, San Antonio, were drawn from a bullock's skull to a fork in a cow path, then to a brush hut, past a sycamore tree, and ended at a hatchet-blazed stump.[49] For a title to be approved, the grant had to have been surveyed, recorded, and occupied; not over eleven leagues in size; and awarded before 1847. A few eleventh-hour grants by Governor Pio Pico were challenged, but the commissioners approved at least one spurious title. Another set of examiners exposed this fraud in which a French adventurer, in order to gain control of over a half-million acres of choice San Francisco land, forged an 1843 title with the signature of a former Mexican governor obtained in 1852.

Ultimately, 604 grants covering nearly nine million acres were confirmed, while 209 claims involving four million acres were rejected. The commissioners, though unfamiliar with Mexican procedures, were considered to be fair. In fact, the settlers who challenged their decisions in the higher courts accused them of favoring the grantees. But the *Californios* had to put out money, always a scarce commodity, to travel to San Francisco or even to Washington, and more money to pay lawyers to take their cases up through the district tribunals or to the Supreme Court. There was still more outlay to get court injunctions against squatters who were not waiting for a legal decision before settling on the disputed lands. In order to obtain cash, the *Californios* had to mortgage their estates at usurious rates, since they could not obtain reasonable loans without clear title. Benton had predicted, quite accurately, that Gwin's bill would force them into such prolonged and costly litigation that they would lose their property even if their titles were confirmed. Beset as well with the problems of bad management and a poor cattle market, very few of the *rancheros* emerged from the ordeal with their estates intact.

Nor did the years of uncertainty benefit the settlers, though in some cases they were selling the cattle, cutting the orchards, and fencing off the access roads of the true owners. The settlers continued to be favored by the government. In 1852 Senator Gwin introduced a bill in Congress which, had it passed, would have allowed the settlers to take over eighty-acre tracts of unoccupied land in Mexican grants, and if the grants were confirmed, the owner would be compensated with an equal amount of public land. Another law, which was passed and later declared unconstitutional by the state supreme court, would have required grant holders to pay squatters for their improvements or to sell them the land at its appraised value. On the other hand, settlers protested that "in some cases, the grantees have been allowed to extend their claims over land upon which settlers have made valuable improvements, and which was always supposed to be part of the public domain. . . . It is hard, indeed, that the land-holders should now be allowed, after settlers have made the land valuable, to extend their boundaries so as to cover that which was never before claimed." [50]

Though the literacy rate was not high among the Spanish-Americans, their side in the land controversy got some coverage in the vernacular press. The activities of a young Los Angeles journalist, Francisco P. Ramirez, who took up the cudgels for his *compadres* in his *El Clamor Publico* in the late 1850s, have been described in detail by Leonard Pitt in his excellent biography of the *Californios*.[51] The *rancheros'* plight was movingly recounted in Spanish in the gringo-dominated legislature by Pablo de la Guerra in 1856. He pleaded for those who

> . . . lay prostrate before the conqueror and ask for the protection of the few possessions which remain to them in the bad luck into which they had fallen . . . those who had been sold like sheep—those who were abandoned and sold by Mexico. They are unfamiliar with the prevalent language now spoken in their own country. They have no voice in this Senate, except such as I am now weakly speaking on their behalf. . . . I have seen old men of sixty and seventy years of age weeping because they have been cast out of their ancestral home. They have been humiliated and insulted.

They have been refused the privilege of cutting their own firewood. And all those who have committed these outrages have come here looking for protection . . . the Senate sympathized with them, though it does not hear the complaints of *la clase Espanole* . . . after suffering all these injustices and enduring all kinds of injuries, now we find that the legislature is hungry to get from us our last penny, simply because the squatters are more numerous than we.[52]

Don Pablo was much discouraged by his minority status in the legislature. He struggled to speak English, which he called "the idiom of birds," whereas Spanish was "the language of God." His uncle, Mariano Vallejo, urged him not to lose heart, "It may be the last time that we will be represented in the Legislature of California and it is necessary for you not to abandon the position. . . ."[53]

Richard Henry Dana returned as something of a celebrity to California in 1859 to find that Pablo de la Guerra and Andrés Pico were "the only men of Sp[anish] descent in a Senate of 40 members, in a country wh[ich] was Mexican 13 years ago! In the Assembly, of 80, there is but one Mexican."[54]

The northern politicians who dominated the legislature and declared themselves "teetotally and universally against anything Spanish" passed a number of laws in the mid-fifties which the *Californios* took to be aimed at repressing their way of life: an edict preventing cattle from roaming at will, Sunday "blue laws," a temperance referendum, and an antivagrancy act called the "Greaser Law." Section 2 of this 1855 edict named as liable to "be disarmed by any lawful officer, and punished. . . . All persons who are commonly known as 'Greasers' or the issue of Spanish and Indian blood . . . who go armed and are not known to be peaceable and quiet persons, and who can give no account of themselves. . . ."[55]

The legislation on temperance and vagrancy, though reflecting the prevailing disdain for Spanish-Americans, was an attempt to counteract the social anarchy which was a legacy of the Gold Rush. The society was in a period of transition from the lawlessness of the frontier to the creation of more stable communities. The offensive word "greaser" was dropped the following year. Perhaps the most direct attack on the *Californios* was the refusal of the 1855 legislature to translate the laws into Spanish.[56]

The *Californios* continued to hold a few seats in the legislature. In 1875 Romualdo Pacheco filled out the incumbent governor's term of office for almost a year, but his chief importance was as a symbol of a bygone era. It was only in their own communities in local politics that Spanish Californians played a significant role. In the mid-1850s they were able to defeat on their home ground (but not for statewide office) the "Know-Nothings," members of the American party who campaigned against Catholics and "foreign influence." The "Ignorantes," though they succeeded in electing a governor, were thoroughly trounced in the "cow counties" by *Californio* Democrats. Some of the *Californio* Democrats switched to the Republican party and supported its presidential candidate, John C. Frémont, in 1856. Mariano Vallejo did not endorse his former captor (whom he had, however, supported in his senate race), but a group of leading *nativos* reevaluated "the pathfinder's" role in the conquest of California and pronounced his conduct "humane and gentlemanly." [57]

It was shortly afterward that Andrés Pico pressed once again for the separation of California into two parts, with the section that included San Luis Obispo, Santa Barbara, Los Angeles, San Diego, and San Bernardino to "be segregated from the remaining portion of the state." [58] This was to be called the "Territory of Colorado." The division became tied to the slavery issue (the Southern California gringos were sympathetic to the South) and out of fear that the new territory would not be "free soil" like the north, the legislature overrode a popular referendum approving separation.

Californios, in general, pledged loyalty to the Union

side in the Civil War. Salvador Vallejo was persuaded to give up his prejudice against gringos to lead a "native cavalry" unit, which patroled the Colorado River. His brother went east to tour the war camps and to renew acquaintance with the Union generals Sherman, Halleck, Hooker, Sheridan, and Grant, who had visited him at Sonoma during their tours of duty in California after the conquest. Don Mariano had an audience with Abraham Lincoln in which he praised the conquerors of California: "The Yankees are a wonderful people—wonderful! Wherever they go, they make improvements. If they were to emigrate in large numbers to hell itself they would irrigate it, plant trees and flower gardens, build reservoirs and fountains and make everything beautiful and pleasant, so that by the time we get there, we can sit at a marble-top table and eat ice cream." [59]

This was a typically gracious remark by a man who had lost heavily through Yankee aggressiveness. When Dana visited Sonoma in 1859, he commented on the eclipse of the Vallejo family fortunes. The poignant spectacle of the *Californios* in decline seemed to touch the New Englander on his return.[60]

When he had first come to California in 1834–35, Dana had met the young Juan Bandini of Los Angeles who, he wrote, had returned from his education in Mexico "accomplished, poor, and proud, and without any office or occupation." He found Bandini to be "the best representation of a decayed gentleman I had ever seen." [61] Bandini, who forgave this indictment, became a leader in Southern California, but in his later life typified the *Californios* who lost their wealth through being unable to come to terms with the economics of the new era.

The *Californios'* credo called for them to protect and support relatives, even when family labor was inefficient. They were used to employing many hands in exchange for room and board. The idea of each man working for himself with the aid of mechanized equipment was one they instinctively rejected. The egalitarian free-enterprise system was foreign to them. When one old *ranchero* first saw a mowing machine, he exclaimed, "The Yankee is but one finger shy of the devil!" [62] *Vaqueros* did not readily convert to farming or sheep-raising, even when years of drought and the division of the large *ranchos* ruined the cattle business. The *Californios* were incurably extravagant; if any windfall came their way, they celebrated by calling in all their friends and giving elaborate fiestas. Juan Bandini, like many of the other old *hacendados*, had gringo sons-in-law who connived behind his back to protect his interests. But the humiliation embittered him, for shortly before his death in 1859, he protested in a quotation from the Scriptures, "Our inheritance is turned to strangers/ our houses to aliens./We have drunken our water for money/ our wood is sold unto us./Our necks are under persecution/we labor and have no rest." [63]

Another personage from the old era failed to make a successful transition. John Sutter, like Bandini, extravagant and with no business acumen, was ironically the victim of his own liberality toward emigrants. When the news was broadcast that gold was discovered at Coloma, his lands were trampled over and his employees deserted in the mad stampede to the foothills, leaving his multiple enterprises to languish. He sold part of his land to settlers, but the Supreme Court found a part of his grant invalid and he went bankrupt while trying to reimburse those to whom he had awarded subtitles. A "squatters riot" took place in the new city of Sacramento in 1850 on land which he had sold. He was swept aside by the mass migration of new settlers to California, whom he had encouraged to come, not without self-interest, for he had hoped to play a leading role among them. In the total transformation of the social order, he became an antediluvian figure, traveling every year to Washington to petition Congress (in vain) for some recompense for his services to the young state.

Charles M. Weber, another European from the pre-American era, succeeded where Sutter failed. He organized a profitable company for trade and mining, and on his Mexican land grant of 48,747 acres laid out the city of Stockton, which he named for the commodore whom he had met during the war with Mexico. Though squatters contested his ownership, he was awarded a clear title to his land in 1855, and this was later confirmed by a United States patent signed by Lincoln six years later. (The president is said to have hesitated on the grounds that it was "such a big farm.") Weber, who began life in California as a trader, miller, salt-producer, and shoemaker, was a wealthy and respected man at the time of his death in 1881.

Thomas Larkin also moved with the times. He transferred his business to San Francisco as that new city eclipsed the old Mexican capital in Monterey as a center of trade, and he became one of California's first millionaires. But shortly before he died of typhoid fever in 1858, he wrote wistfully of the "halcyon days" of the Mexican era.

Southern California retained a Spanish flavor until the railroad brought in hundreds of thousands of newcomers. First the Southern Pacific linked the "cow counties" with the northern part of the state in 1876, transforming the size and complexion of the quiet southern *pueblos* to the degree that in 1880 only a quarter of the people in the vicinity of Los Angeles were Spanish-speaking. In 1887 the Santa Fe inaugurated cross-country rail service, bringing 120,000 tourists, health-seekers, and would-be settlers to the city. As real estate business boomed and new areas were opened up to receive the influx of people from the East and Middle West, the Hispanic traditions necessarily declined, and were visually evident mainly through tortilla vendors and fiestas on the "Cinco de Mayo." Leonard Pitt describes one "symbolically confusing" celebration that commemorated both Mexican Independence Day and the completion of a section of the railroad. Reginaldo del Valle, "a Californian born in the American period, paid tribute to Mexican liberty by speaking in English to a gringo crowd about Yankee progress." [64]

This was typical of the cross-blending of cultures achieved by some members of the old families whom Pitt characterized as "gringoized Mexicans"; for example, the Los Angeles legislator and judge, Ygnácio Sepúlveda, who represented the Wells Fargo Company in Mexico City and later served there as an American chargé d'affaires. Aristocratic Hispanic antecedents were an asset in public life, and in family connections as well. Intermarriage continued in the second generation, with *Californios* cementing their link with the majority group by marrying Yankee women, and Americans turning their backs on the hustling mercantile society by forming an alliance with Spanish-surname families, a link with the fragrant past.

Another and undoubtedly larger group of *Californios* merged with the new immigrants from Mexico and became indistinguishable from them in the Sonoratowns of the Anglo communities. In the second generation some *nativos* bearing distinguished names took to crime and continued the tradition of the California *bandidos*. Their exploits, like so much else in the Hispanic past, were alternately romanticized and vilified by American commentators. California writers often portrayed the Spanish descendents in terms that suggested genteel decay or spurious pretensions to grandeur.[65] In the 1870s the San Francisco bookseller, Hubert Howe Bancroft, who was undertaking a multivolume history of California, performed an invaluable service by contacting the chief surviving figures of the Mexican era just as they were in danger of being forgotten or were dying off, and collecting their memoirs. Bancroft's version of the controversial years before and during the American conquest served as an antidote to the more chauvinistic treatment generally favored in earlier histories.

His revision set the stage for an upsurge of interest in

California's Hispanic heritage. As "the 'Spaniards' went
into apotheosis, 'Spanish California' became a cult," Leonard Pitt has written.[66] Herbert Bolton and a group of His-
panophile followers at the University of California pursued
the investigation on a scholarly level. The writings of Helen
Hunt Jackson and Nellie Van de Grift Sánchez awakened
a romantic fervor that made effective the public-relations
campaign of Charles Fletcher Lummis and others in such
projects as restoring the missions, which had fallen into a
state of decay. It is significant that the rediscovery of California's Spanish traditions was undertaken by Anglo-
Saxons, even by some not mentioned above, who had a
mercenary motive in evoking romance for the sake of at-
tracting tourists.

The Arcadian version of California's past isolated an
era and a people out of context in the interest of nostalgia.
The more recent correction is to place the *Californios*, as
the historians Moses Rischin and Leonard Pitt have suggested, in the history of the total migration of Spanish-
speaking people to California, and it is in this light that we
will next take up their story.[67]

    1. *Reglamento para el gobierno de la provincia de Californias,
aprobado por S. M. en real orden de 24 de Octubre de 1781*, Reim-
preso en la Imprenta del Colegio de Santa Clara, 1874, pp. 53-55.
    2. Quoted in Robert Glass Cleland, *A History of California:
The American Period* (New York: Macmillan Co., 1939), p. 96.
    3. *Ibid.*, p. 61.
    4. Heizer and Almquist, *The Other Californians*, p. 66.
    5. Richard Henry Dana, Jr., *Two Years Before the Mast* (Phila-
delphia: David McKay, 1916 [orig. pub. 1840]), p. 83.
    6. *Ibid.*, pp. 83, 84, 86, 257.
    7. Sir George Simpson, *Narrative of a Journey Round the World
during the Years 1841 and 1842*, vol. 1 (London: Henry Colburn,
1847), pp. 296, 385, 386.
    8. Dana, *Two Years Before the Mast*, p. 187.
    9. Quoted in Leonard Pitt, *The Decline of the Californios: A
Social History of the Spanish-Speaking Californians, 1846-1890*
(Berkeley and Los Angeles: University of California Press, 1966;
paperback ed., 1970), p. 23.

10. Dana, *Two Years Before the Mast*, p. 88.

11. *Ibid.*, pp. 185-186.

12. Bancroft writes that Isaac Graham, a native of Kentucky, came to California, probably from New Mexico, in 1833, '34, or '35. Herbert Hugh Bancroft, *History of California*, vol. 3 (San Francisco: A. L. Bancroft, 1885), pp. 762-763.

13. *Ibid.*, vol. 4, p. 3, fn. 1.

14. *Ibid.*, p. 7, fn. 6.

15. *Ibid.*, p. 137.

16. *Ibid.*, pp. 239-240, fn. 29.

17. Larkin to Abel Sterns, March 4, 1845. A selection of letters edited by John A. Hawgood, *First and Last Consul: Thomas Oliver Larkin and the Americanization of California* (San Marino, Calif.: Huntington Library, 1962), p. 20.

18. Secretary of State James Buchanan to Larkin, October 17, 1845, in George Hammond, ed., *The Larkin Papers*, vol. 4, Doc. 337 (Berkeley: University of California Press, 1953), p. 44.

19. April 27, 1846, Hawgood, *First and Last Consul*, p. 59.

20. Bancroft, *History of California*, vol. 4, p. 110, fn. 2.

21. Hammond, *Larkin Papers*, vol. 4, pp. 325-326.

22. Alfred Robinson to Larkin, quoted in Bean, *California: An Interpretive History*, p. 87.

23. July 8, 1845, Hawgood, *First and Last Consul*, p. 25.

24. Lansford W. Hastings, *The Emigrants' Guide to Oregon and California* (Princeton, N.J.: Princeton University Press, 1932 [orig. pub. 1845]), pp. 133, 113, 122.

25. Bancroft, *History of California*, vol. 5, p. 56.

26. March 26, 1846, Hawgood, *First and Last Consul*, pp. 52-53.

27. Francisco Arce to Vallejo, February 15, 1846, quoted in Bancroft, *History of California*, vol. 5, p. 56, fn. 3.

28. Castro to Weber, April 12, 1845, *ibid.*, vol. 4, p. 605, fn. 35.

29. Simeon Ide, *A Biographical Sketch of the Life of William B. Ide* (Glorietta, N.M.: Rio Grande Press, 1967 [orig. pub. 1880]), pp. 51-52.

30. *Century Magazine*, vol. 19, new series, p. 919.

31. William Brown Ide, *Who Conquered California? History of the Conquest of California, in June, 1846, by the "Bear Flag Party"* (Glorietta, N.M.: Rio Grande Press, 1967 [orig. pub. 1880]), p. 56.

32. *Ibid.*, pp. 43-44.

33. June 18, 1846, Hawgood, *First and Last Consul*, p. 73.

34. Pitt, *Decline of the Californios*, p. 27.

35. June 18, 1846, Hawgood, *First and Last Consul*, p. 75.

36. Pitt, *Decline of the Californios*, p. 30.

37. February 11, 1847, Hawgood, *First and Last Consul*, p. 88.

38. Article IX, Treaty of Guadalupe Hidalgo.

39. Pitt, *Decline of the Californios*, p. 37.

40. Jessie Benton Frémont, *A Year of American Travel* (New York: Harper & Bros., 1878), p. 107; Jessie Benton Frémont and Lt. Francis Preston Frémont, "Great Events during the Life of Major General John C. Frémont and of Jessie Benton Frémont, 1891 (University of California, Bancroft Library, Berkeley), p. 120.

41. Pitt, *Decline of the Californios*, pp. 138-139, 35.

42. *Ibid.*, p. 39.

43. Quoted in Stewart, *Ordeal by Hunger*, p. 361.

44. J. Ross Browne, *Report of the Debates in the Convention of California, on the Formation of the State Constitution in September and October, 1849*, Washington, D.C., 1850, p. 63.

45. Article II, Sec. 1, California Constitution of 1849.

46. Harris Newmark, *Sixty Years in Southern California, 1853-1913*, 3d ed. (Boston and New York: Houghton Mifflin, 1930 [orig. pub. 1916]), pp. 33-34, 77-78, 84-85, 113-116, 157-162.

47. Pitt, *Decline of the Californios*, pp. 50, 51, 56.

48. Memorial to the Senate and House of Representatives of the United States in Congress Assembled, *Journal of the State Senate*, 3rd Sess., 1852, p. 582.

49. Pitt, *Decline of the Californios*, p. 90.

50. Gov. John B. Weller to the Senate of California, April 17, 1858, *Journal of the Senate*, 9th Sess., 1858, p. 599.

51. Pitt, *Decline of the Californios*, pp. 181-194.

52. *Ibid.*, p. 117.

53. *Ibid.*, pp. 145, 146.

54. *Journal of Richard Henry Dana, Jr.*, vol. 3, p. 919. In fact, de la Guerra served in 1857 and Pico in 1858.

55. Statutes of 1855, *Laws of the State of California*, p. 217.

56. Pitt, *Decline of the Californios*, p. 198.

57. *Ibid.*, p. 200.

58. Approved April 15, 1859, *Statutes of California, 1859*, p. 310.

59. Pitt, *Decline of the Californios*, pp. 240-241.

60. *Journal of Richard Henry Dana, Jr.*, vol. 3, pp. 903, 910.

61. Dana, *Two Years Before the Mast*, p. 257.

62. Pitt, *Decline of the Californios*, p. 254.

63. *Ibid.*, p. 116.

64. *Ibid.*, p. 274.

65. Mary Austin, *California* (paintings by Horace Sutton) (New York: Macmillan Co., 1914), pp. 87-93 *passim;* Frank Norris, *The Octopus* (New York: Sagamore Press, 1957 [orig. pub. 1901]), p. 15; January 23, 1917 entry in *The Diary of Cora Baggerly Older* (Los Altos, Calif.: Local History Studies, Foothill Community College District, California History Center, Winter, 1971), p. 6.

66. Pitt, *Decline of the Californios*, p. 284.

67. Moses Rischin, "Continuities and Discontinuities in Spanish-Speaking California," in Wollenberg, *Ethnic Conflict in California History*, pp. 45-60; Pitt, *Decline of the Californios*, pp. 291-296.

3

The Gold Rush Population

⚔ ★ ⚔

THE GOLD RUSH brought rapid and revolutionary changes to California, setting in motion a pattern that continues to the present day whereby new men and new enterprises are continually supplanting the old or the recently established. Even before California became officially a state, its citizens were forced to improvise hasty solutions to the problems created by instantaneous growth. The arrival of people from all over the world, first in response to the discovery of gold and later in pursuit of other less dramatic forms of wealth and opportunity, has kept the society in a perpetual state of ferment into the third quarter of the twentieth century.

The values, institutions, and respected men of the pre-American era were swept aside by the bonanza-seekers of 1849, who quadrupled the population in a single year as they swarmed over the region the Spaniards had called *tierra incognita*. But by no means were all the newcomers suited for the adventure. Like other great migrations of history, the Gold Rush that peopled California encompassed great human tragedies. Family ties were ruptured; the weak and the unfortunate were felled by the rigors of the new life; and in the competition for wealth and power, the dominant group, with a cruelty as pitiless as the elements of nature on the transcontinental trek, banished those who were considered inimical to the evolution of a stable society. The transformation of an inchoate mass of humanity on a lawless frontier into a more ordered community was inevitably a costly process as far as individuals were concerned.

The social revolution set in motion by the Gold Rush began even before the multitudes arrived from distant places of the earth. It began, in fact, in May of 1848, soon after Samuel Brannan, a former Mormon leader who had arrived two years earlier with a band of fellow "saints," walked through the streets of San Francisco waving a bottle of dust and shouting, "Gold! Gold! Gold! From the American River." After James Marshall had found the first flakes in the millrace he was building for Sutter early in January, he and the captain of New Helvetia and their associates tried to keep the discovery a secret as long as possible. When the news leaked out, the discoverers could not resist confounding the skeptics by showing them nuggets, with the result that by April rumors began to circulate in San Francisco and men gathered on street corners to discuss reports from the Rio Americano. Some of the more gullible left for the Sacramento Valley, usually in secret, for fear of ridicule. "A few fools have hurried to the place, but you may be sure there is nothing in it," was the report that the military governor, Richard B. Mason, received in May.[1]

Brannan, who had a general store at Sutter's Fort, was convinced by the amount of gold brought in by his customers that the potential treasure was extensive. He prudently laid in supplies enough to meet the needs of an army of gold-seekers before publicizing his news.

When he did make the announcement, the response was instantaneous and wholesale, both in San Francisco and the other coastal settlements. Laborers dropped their tools, and sailors and soldiers quit their duty posts, to rush to the interior. The newspaper *Alta California* reported the cataclysmic effect many months later: "Like fire, the news spread throughout the land. The conservative industry of the country was dead; the plow was left to rust in the furrow, the crops to decay and waste where they grew, and the cattle to stray and wander where they chose." [2] Storekeepers left their shops (occasionally with the doors open so that customers might help themselves to perishables). Doctors and lawyers abandoned their clients. Municipal officials closed their offices. The jailor in San Jose took his prisoners, ten Indians, to dig with him. "Burn the barn if you cannot dispose of it otherwise," was the message sent to a stable-keeper by two of his brothers already at the diggings. [3]

By mid-June three-quarters of the male population of San Francisco had gone to the Sacramento area. Goods rotted in the holds of ships or sat on the wharves with no one to remove them, for the gold mania had revolutionized the labor market. The yeoman who had been content with a dollar a day "proudly refused ten," and the mechanic who was accustomed to earning two dollars "now rejected twenty for his day's services." A contemporary observer noted, "It was certainly a great country . . . . Every subject was as lofty, independent and seemingly rich as a king." [4]

Soon, the *alcalde* of Monterey, the Reverend Walter Colton, complained, "The gold fever has reached every servant in Monterey; none are to be trusted in their engagement beyond a week, and as for compulsion, it is like attempting to drive fish into a net with an ocean before them. . . . The gold mines have upset all social and domestic arrangements in Monterey; the master has become his own servant, and the servant his own lord. The millionaire is obliged to groom his own horse, and roll his own wheelbarrow. . . ." [5]

The maelstrom struck those old settlers who stood directly in the path of the incoming tide of humanity. Sutter,

as we have seen earlier, was unable to turn the extraordinary events on his land to his own profit. After losing his
retinue of workers, he was overrun first by prospectors and
then by settlers and squatters who built the city of Sacramento on a part of his *rancho*. Eventually his fort was converted into a hospital, after he had retired to a more humble abode.[6]

Theodor Cordua, who had come via Hawaii from
Germany, had a prosperous *rancho* where Marysville now
stands. There he had organized a community in micro-
cosm, producing candles and soap, curing hides and furs,
raising wheat, corn, potatoes, and onions. With the discovery of gold, his staff deserted, and though land and cattle increased in value, the shortage of labor brought his
multiple enterprises to a standstill. He wrote, "These were
the beautiful golden times in which almost all the old and
well-to-do Californians became poor." [7] In 1848–49 he sold
his land and cattle for thirty thousand dollars and opened
a store in the mines which did not prosper. He was still in
the Sacramento Valley in 1854, but broken in health as
well as property, he is said to have returned to the Hawaiian
Islands where he died.[8]

Peter Lassen, a Danish blacksmith who had come to
California in 1840 and acquired a Mexican land grant on
Deer Creek in Tehama County, was as much in the mainstream of the overland emigrant traffic as Sutter had been
earlier. Associated with the settlers' side in the Bear Flag
revolt (he had entertained Frémont and his men), soon
after the American acquisition, he set in motion a scheme
to divert trans-Sierra travelers south by the so-called Lassen cutoff, with the idea of reaping some profit by selling
them supplies. He went out with the prospecting parties
hunting for gold, contributing his knowledge of the foothill
country and its native inhabitants. "Old Pete," described
as "honest," "ignorant," "kind," and "stubborn," was generous to those who broke down on the trail, but he was im-

prudent in his business affairs. He sold a half-interest in his prosperous *rancho,* well-stocked with cattle, horses, sheep, and hogs, and invested the money in an abortive steamboat speculation that ruined him financially.[9]

The California pioneers discovered that the transformed economy which seemed to offer so many glittering prizes was, like the Sacramento River, full of treacherous shoals. However, there were two veteran Yankee landowners in the valley, John Bidwell and Pearson B. Reading, who successfully made the transition into a new era of mining, and subsequently amassed fortunes by returning to agriculture.

By the summer of 1848 the gold-seekers had reached previously remote locations, for they did not remain long at Coloma but soon spread out over a wide area from the Tuolumne River in the San Joaquin Valley to the Trinity River in the north. Miraculously, gold, until now invisible, was discovered everywhere. The first diggers came to the scene with spoons, then pickaxes appeared, and soon the amateurs were copying the techniques of the more experienced miners in using pans and rockers in the streams to separate the valuable ore from the worthless silt. Eventually, mule-drawn crushers, sluices, and heavy hydraulic equipment for moving masses of earth would be brought into use, but 1848 was the year of placer mining, in which a relatively small number of men—from six to nine thousand—working largely with hand tools, extracted ten million dollars worth of gold from sandbars, stream beds, and river bottoms.

There was little conflict or crime during this first season of 1848, and very few rules. Many stories were told of men carelessly leaving their valuables, even their pokes full of dust, in the public thoroughfare, so to speak, and coming back to find their treasure intact. The home folks were in the field and they had plenty of room to operate without getting into each other's way. They moved around a great deal, always hopeful that a bigger strike awaited them around the next bend of the river. There was no law governing mining on public lands in a territory that was no longer a part of Mexico but not yet officially a state in the American union. In August of 1848, Governor Richard Mason wrote after visiting the goldfields: "It was a matter of serious reflection to me how I could secure to the government certain rents or fees for the privilege of obtaining this gold; but upon considering the large extent of the country, the character of the people engaged, and the small scattered force at my command, I resolved not to interfere but to permit all to work freely, unless broils and crimes should call for interference." [10]

The miners themselves formulated impromptu rules about the use of the land. In general, a man's claim was recognized as long as he worked it. If he left to try his luck in another area, he forfeited his right to his first diggings. The year 1848 was a profitable as well as a peaceful one. Some of the miners made a hundred dollars a day; a few occasionally realized five hundred. Bancroft estimates that the average take was about a thousand dollars per man for the season.[11] The Hispano and Yankee Californians continued a practice of the old era in employing groups of native laborers to do the heavy work. The latter accepted food and baubles in exchange for the gold they unearthed. Significantly, it was a party of Oregonians, smarting from trouble with Indians in their own territory, who objected to this system and drove a California settler and his aboriginal work corps from their claim on the Trinity River.[12]

Outsiders Arrive

In the autumn over a thousand prospectors came down from Oregon, while several thousand Mexicans crossed the border from Sonora. Shortly afterwards, boatloads of men from Hawaii began to arrive in San Francisco, soon to be followed by Chileans and Peruvians. As most of the Californians were hurrying back to the coast at the onset of the rainy season in October, they met these neighbors coming in.

The news of gold in California took longer to make an impact on the eastern United States and Europe, though excited rumors were circulating even before President Polk, after receiving confirmation by Mason of the extent and value of the discovery in the Mother Lode country, reported this information in his message to Congress on December 5, 1848. Soon the sort of wholesale restlessness that had emptied the California coastal settlements seized young and old on the eastern seaboard. "The name of California was in every mouth"; Bancroft wrote, "it was the current theme for conversation and song; for plays and sermons. Every scrap of information concerning the country was eagerly devoured." [13]

A hastily concocted *Emigrant's Guide to the Gold Fields* (thirty pages for twenty-five cents) was selling in New York, and soon suppliers and outfitters were offering "California goods"—pistols, bowie knives, maps, money belts, hatchets, and axes. A New York newspaper on December 11 reported, "The gold mania rages with intense vigor, and is carrying off its victims hourly and daily. . . . Vessels are about to sail from all Atlantic ports, and our young men—including mechanics, doctors, lawyers, and we may add, clergymen—are taking leave of old associations, and embarking for the land of wealth, where the only capital required for making a fortune is a spade, a sieve, or tin colander, and a small stock of patience and industry." [14]

A French envoy in Washington took a less sanguine view as he cautioned, "There is without doubt some gold on the shores of the Sacramento, but it requires a good deal of silver to come at it." [15] Noting that probably two hundred ships from Bangor to New Orleans as well as vessels from Europe and the islands of the Pacific were being outfitted and would reach California within the year, the *Alta California* warned, "This extraordinary excitement and emigration fills us with an undeniable dread—not that we doubt the inexhaustibility of the mines, but that we fear the suffering and disappointment which so many of this vast crowd must undergo. . . . Thousands of those who come here will do well, but we cannot but believe that there will be hundreds who will have abandoned comfortable homes to seek for gold in a land where privations only will be their reward." [16]

The sober voices, however, were drowned out by the chorus of excited promoters who, like Horace Greeley, proclaimed, "We are on the brink of the Age of Gold!" [17] All available ships were hastily converted to carry an optimum number of passengers, many of whom had formed companies or associations by pledging money themselves for the trip to the goldfields or accepting the backing of wealthier men who could not go but who were willing to finance proxies to bring back a fortune. In fact the loans were seldom repaid and most of the companies disbanded after reaching California. [18]

Similar arrangements were being made in European cities where the fabulous prospects of El Dorado excited the same frenzy. Early in January, five different California trading and mining companies were registered in London with an aggregate capital of £1,275,000. [19] Joint stock companies were being formed in France and the government held a giant lottery, *L'ingot d'or*. The prize was a gold nugget from California and the proceeds were to be used to finance the passage of five thousand immigrants. Posters proclaiming "Gold! Gold! in California!" appeared in Australian cities in February, touching off a ferment and launching a fleet of vessels filled with prospective miners. [20]

It was not the lure of treasure alone that drew adventurers halfway around the world. With the end of the Mexican War, restless young Americans thirsted for new enterprises, new chances for risk and daring. In Europe political and economic conditions increased the impetus for immigration. A Frenchman wrote, "La misère de 1848 [les] avaient lancés comme une marée montante vers le pays d'or. . . ." [21] Europeans left home with or without the encouragement of their governments. They were seeking freedom from political oppression, mandatory conscription, limited opportunities, pinching poverty, and even starvation, such as the thousands fleeing from Ireland in the wake of the potato famine of 1846–1847. The British Isles (Ireland in particular), Germany, and France contributed the largest number of European immigrants to California at this period. Only a few came from Scandinavia, which was relatively prosperous at this time. The influx from Norway, Sweden, Denmark, Southern Europe, Italy, Portugal, Armenia, and Greece, as well as Eastern Europe, came a decade or two later, at which time the British Isles, France, and Germany also markedly increased the number of immigrants to California.[22]

The Argonauts who came from the Pacific were less motivated by a desire to become permanent citizens, though many of the Europeans also fell into the category of transient fortune hunters. A goodly number of the men from all over the world intended to return home with their wealth, but some were unable to do so, notably the Chinese, who began to arrive after 1850 and who were trapped in the bonds of peonage by the labor contractors who paid their passage. Though almost every generalization about the character of the population that came to California can be refuted, there was some correlation between the immigrants' intentions (whether to leave after a short time or to remain) and the distance they traveled to reach the land of promise. Compare, for example, the Germans and the Irish, who came thousands of miles to get away from difficulties in the Old World, with the near neighbors from just across the borders, who regularly commuted back and forth to the goldfields. Those who brought families, as did many members of the trans-Sierra wagon parties, were much more likely to be permanent residents.*

Much was written in the annals of the legislature in favor of those who intended to become permanent citizens and against those who would tap the wealth of the state and subsequently carry it away, but the discrimination between groups was not always strictly along these lines. For example, the Oregonians who carried off a considerable fortune were treated as no different from local settlers who rightly belonged in the field, while the Sonorans were regarded as foreign interlopers. The resentment of foreigners of distinctive appearance—Hawaiians, Mexicans, and Latin Americans—began almost as soon as they arrived. Anglo-Saxons and Germanic peoples who tended to assimilate quickly were treated differently, as we shall see.

It has been said that the forty-niners in general, by a process of natural selection, were young and physically robust, and in economic circumstances fell between the category of extreme poverty and great wealth. The pioneer-historian, Theodore H. Hittell, found that they were by and large a literate group of men by the standards of the day. But it is certain, as the *Alta California* predicted, that not all of them were suited, either temperamentally or physically, to the trials they had to undergo.

Only for the neighbors across the borders was California easy to reach. Ships occasionally took 163 days to get from London to San Francisco. For the immigrant passage a mutual deception was often practiced, with the ship-owners hastily fitting out vessels that were barely equipped for the long run, while the too eager passengers hurried the

* The Bancroft history attributes the greater number of real settlers in the wagon parties to the fact they were often people from the small towns and farms of the Middle West who were fitted for pioneering. A more convincing explanation may be that more of them brought their families along than did the Argonauts who arrived by sea.

ill and infirm through a cursory health inspection only to have them die in mid-Atlantic when supplies ran short and overcrowding produced epidemics of sickness. Six years after the first gold-seekers sailed from European ports, William Powell, a Welshman, immigrated to California with his wife and five children, paying £30 for their passage from Liverpool to New York. He had the benefit of the advice of those who had gone before, such as the "Hints for emigrants to the goldfields of California," which appeared in *The London Times* of March 11, 1853:

> . . . take strong soled shoes for your early morning salt water bath on ship; take dark clothes as the ship is dirty; take strong tin cooking utensils that fit inside each other; small bags for flour and rice; parties with messes from 3 to 9 form on board.

Though the Powells laid in some last-minute supplies of "pincer nails, screws, shoes, gun and pistol, bed, bowl, cord, nets, brandy and oranges" before boarding, the head of the family was soon making his own list of extra provisions needed beyond the "ship allowance" that was distributed to each passenger and cautioning, "See that you get all the articles of sea stores you paid for." He records in his diary:

> May 7—An awful storm last night. Nearly lost a sailor from top mast. I am on the second watch, 1 a.m., for fear our boxes should be robbed.
>
> May 9—Strong wind. The hook of the top yard broke by the shieve and the smash of the rope with the rattle of the sheet sail in the wind made a pounding like thunder or a cannon shot. The crew ran from all parts of the ship. The shieves, like balls, tumbled to the sea. The ship was then turned on one side.
>
> May 10—Flocks of large fishes follow us, as well as small birds like sparrows. Ship stores have given out. Very cold. We wear big overcoats every day. . . .
>
> May 12—The doctor sprinkled Chlorride of Zinc and sea

water about the floor of the cabin to purify the foul air under decks.

May 14—Many parties now in want of flour and sugar; no butter, cheese or bacon. We have plenty yet and can spare some bacon, cheese and sugar.

During the rigors of the voyage when there was "nothing but water and roaring waves," he comforted himself by remembering that "Noah and his family were safe in the Ark above 12 months."

The Powells reached New York just a little over thirty days after leaving England and were soon encountering "land sharks" and "humbug hawkers," who tried to palm off inflated-priced tickets to California. The canny new arrivals avoided falling into their clutches and paid the standard fare (seventy-five dollars for adults) to travel from the East Coast to the West Coast by the Nicaraguan route, much improved since it had opened four years earlier, but still tedious.[23]

There were three main sea routes to California from the Atlantic. The passage around Cape Horn was most popular in 1849—15,597 persons reaching San Francisco by this long voyage as opposed to 6,489 who risked the hazards of the new crossing on the Isthmus of Panama.[24] On the Central American trek, the passengers were landed at Chagres, carried upriver in dugout canoes, transferred to mules or wagons at Cruces, and at Panama on the West Coast were picked up by another steamer to continue the journey. This would have been tolerable except for long delays en route. Tickets were sold to more passengers than the steamers could accommodate, with the result that men were paying up to $150 to sleep on a coil of rope on deck or in the rigging, rather than postpone their arrival at the goldfields. Delays crossing the Isthmus exposed the travelers to yellow fever and cholera and some few, in order to escape contagion or to avoid spending all their money, attempted the

the desperate and usually futile expedient of starting up the coast in log canoes.

By 1850 some of the difficulties had been straightened out, and the following year the alternate route through Nicaragua, which had been pioneered by Cornelius Vanderbilt, was offering some competition to the Panama crossing. Young Harris Newmark was enchanted with the scenery of this passage, even though "men, women, and children, we were parched and packed like so many herring. . . . The heat was indeed intense; the mosquitoes seemed omnivorous . . . the native officers in charge of our expedition pestered us with their mercenary proceedings." After the river trip, the party debarked to continue the journey on muleback. "Imagine, if you please, nine hundred men, women, and children from northern climes, long accustomed to the ways of civilization, suddenly precipitated, under an intensely hot, tropical sun, into a small Central American landing [advertised in a London newspaper as offering 'all the comforts of life'] consisting of a few huts and some cheap, improvised tents (used for saloons and restaurants), every one in search of a mule or a horse, the only modes of transportation. . . . Each one of the nine hundred travelers feared that there would not be enough animals for all, and the anxiety to secure a beast caused a stampede." [25]

By the time the Powell family took the Nicaraguan route, the accommodations had improved to the point where passengers were no longer sleeping on the decks, and the women and the luggage were conveyed by carriage rather than by mule to the Pacific port, the motto being "from ocean to ocean in 21½ hours." Several passengers died of "cholera morbus," which was attributed to their having eaten too freely of the native fruits. Newmark had been led to believe that brandy in his drinking water would render him immune to any contagions. With the primitive notions then in vogue respecting the causes and cure of diseases, it is not surprising that many passengers from the Central American crossings arrived in California in the last stages of illness.

The Panama route became more popular than any other passage, particularly after a railroad was built across the Isthmus in 1855, though the clipper ships continued to bring freight around Cape Horn. Up until 1851, however, more people came to the West Coast by the transcontinental route. The wagon parties started from St. Joseph or Independence, Missouri, traveled to South Pass in the Rocky Mountains, and then cut south from the Oregon Trail. A southern route followed the Santa Fe Trail and then crossed the desert into Southern California. A few unfortunate groups entered Death Valley, a "seventy-five mile strip of perdition"; one man later recalled "the protracted rage of thirst," and on a different route another forty-niner remembered "the fearful long drive 83 miles no grass nor water." Little guessing what hardships lay ahead of them, an estimated twenty thousand people, ready to start the journey West, gathered east of the Platte River in May 1849, and soon the landscape showed an unbroken stream of animals and wagons. Families started off in high spirits, with well-stocked rigs, the men wearing backwoods garb, and, Bancroft has noted, the mild-mannered and timid carried a bristling arsenal of pistols, knives, and rifles. They were, however, less troubled by Indians than by an outbreak of cholera that struck even before they reached the mountains, leaving some victims dead and frightening some still healthy members into turning around and going home. Some recouped their strength by breaking the journey to spend the winter with the Mormons at Great Salt Lake.

Latecomers on the trails that season had a difficult time because the first wagon parties had depleted the forage along the route in picketing their animals at camp stops. Later parties were also alarmed to find mute evidence of the hardships of those who had gone ahead of them: discarded possessions, trunks disgorging once-cherished objects that had been packed so hopefully and later thrown out to lighten the load when the oxen gave out. These souvenirs of home were left to the ravages of the elements just as the graves of those who had died en route were exposed to depredation by wolves. A fork in the road might be marked with notes to friends in the rear, instructing them as to the best route ahead, or it might mark the grave of combatants who had died in an altercation, for tempers grew short as the difficulties increased.

Under conditions of extreme adversity, human nature was revealed at its best and at its worst. One man left his wagon for the use of those who followed, inviting them to help themselves to its contents, while another destroyed tools he could not carry rather than let others benefit from them. Some stayed behind to care for the sick, while others left them to die on the trail. As conditions worsened, the instinct of many was to hurry forward and save themselves. J. Goldsborough Bruff, who started out with a company organized in Washington, D. C., described the effects that a few weeks on the trail had on the people he met: "It is a queer sight now, to observe the straggling emigrants coming up and going in. Wagons of every kind, oxen, horses, mules, bulls, cows, and people—men, women, children, all packed. A few weeks travel has wrought a great change in their circumstances—many of them I recognized as old acquaintances as far back as Pittsburgh, and all along our western waters, and over the long travel. Large companies, fine animals, a great amount of provisions & stores, and smiling faces were now a [sic] scattered, broken, selfish stragglers, dusty in faces and dress, and many of them, thin with hunger, as well as anxiety." [26]

Bruff, like many others, was separated from his company. As captain, he had been tireless in fulfilling his responsibility toward the other sixty-five members in the party, only to be abandoned by them when he was struck down by illness in the mountains. Two companions remained faithful, but one never returned from a hunting trip and the other went ahead to the settlements to bring out help. Fearing he would die if he remained alone any longer in the wilderness, a year after he had started in high hopes, Bruff, with his dog, began dragging his way to Lassen's *rancho*, a step at a time; he was too weak to shoot game, so he was subsisting mainly on carrion meat. During this painful trek, he gave equal space in his diary to record his latest dinner (of coffee grounds and a broth made of deer hooves, an inch of candle, and an ounce of tallow) and the fact that he had found on the trail a currently popular book, James' *History of Chivalry*, which in spite of his weakness he had picked up and dried.[27]

The transcontinental crossing was so telling on the strength of both men and animals that government relief parties with provisions were sent out from the establishments to help the pilgrims over the last part of the journey. Opportunists, those who would in the words of a trail leader, "take a biscuit out of a woman's mouth," interfered with the just distribution of supplies and some reaped a profit by selling their own foodstuffs at exorbitant prices; others, however, showed mercy to their neighbors in distress, provisioning them, nursing their sick, burying their dead, and comforting widows and orphans.

Chaotic Conditions

As the exhausted people stumbled out of the mountains, they found some places of rest with old settlers in the sparsely populated valleys and foothills. Much stamina and some little trail sense were required for those who set out immediately to pan for gold. Venturing into the towns called for a different sort of hardihood, for the changes were so sweeping—and of such constant occurrence—that longtime residents were as much at a disadvantage as the latest greenhorn. Though the old Spanish *pueblos* to the south remained relatively untouched by the ebb and flow of the gold hunters, fire, flood, and plague added to the chaotic dislocation of the new towns. Perhaps 15 percent of the population of Sacramento was carried off by an epidemic of cholera in 1850, eight months after the river overflowed its banks and inundated the town. But there were always those who profited from disaster. During the flood, while boatmen were charging an ounce of gold worth sixteen dollars to ferry stranded citizens to safety, a saloonkeeper, sitting on his counter a foot above water, announced he was ready to serve any customers that came along.[28] Similarly, after one of the frequent fires that leveled the tents and flimsy packing-case dwellings of San Francisco, a woman was discovered serving drinks from some boards pulled from the embers.

San Francisco, the phoenix rising not once, but five or six times from its ashes, was undergoing the most drastic changes, doubling its population every ten days. The little port town, described by an earlier visitor as a place of fog, fleas, winds, and sterility,[29] had a population of eight hundred in 1848. By 1850 it had grown to twenty-five thousand, though figures were unreliable since people were so continually coming and going. There were not enough dwellings to house the multitudes that came down from the diggings or poured off the ships that arrived daily. Tents and improvised sheds were rented at exorbitant prices. The *Alta California* described the dislocation:

> When a stranger arrives in the harbor of San Francisco
> . . . the city looks to him like a great camp scattered over the
> hills without any apparent order or regularity. Mingled with
> the houses which he sees rising in all directions, he observes
> numberless tents which give him the impression that all this
> is but temporary and will soon vanish away when the specu-
> lative schemes of these adventurers have either been realized
> or defeated . . . he hears of prices paid for a few feet of ground,

greater than any realized at home, in cities which have been occupied for centuries. . . . He learns that rents are ten times greater than at home, and if it appeared strange to him that the fee of property should be so enormously high, it seems like the wildest infatuation in all these people to pay a rent which in twelve or eighteen months will equal the whole value of the property. . . .[30]

Food prices at restaurants were exorbitant (though a few places served dinner for a dollar), interest rates were prohibitive, city lots which had been worth sixteen dollars rose in value to several thousand, while a brisk speculation in real estate took place, though the titles were not clear. Since there were no services, a few people sent their laundry to Canton or Hawaii or bought new linen to replace soiled clothes. Since housing was so short, some of the approximately five hundred ships in the harbor served as dormitories. Though boardinghouses and restaurants sprang up everywhere, there was no time for permanent improvements, such as street lights and sewers. When hills were leveled, the excavated sand was thrown into the bay. There were no sidewalks and in the rainy season mud was so deep that men and animals had trouble negotiating a passage. A sign was posted at Clay and Kearny streets: "This street is impassable, not even jackassable!" [31] To construct crossings, surplus cargoes too expensive to store were used, "such as tobacco, iron, sheet-lead, cement, beans, salt beef! . . . Thus entire lines of sidewalk were constructed of expensive merchandise in bales and boxes. . . . A sidewalk was made from Montgomery St to the mail steamer office 'of boxes of 1st class Virginia tobacco, containing 100 lbs. each, that would be worth 75 cts a pound!' . . . Tobacco was found to be the cheapest material for small building foundations. Foundations subsequently were sometimes worth more than the house. Some Chile beans sunk for a crossing on Broadway would have made a fortune for the owner a few weeks later." [32]

The overturning of traditional values and practices seems to have produced a kind of frenzy in some who were on the scene. A British sea captain who arrived in November 1849 wrote that the city was "a very uncomfortable place. The gambling is truly awful to witness. . . . Dollars and gold bars are piled around the gaming tables but there is no robbery; wages are too high."[33] Another English correspondent wrote, "Much of San Francisco is built on piles in water. Loose sand blows constantly. . . . The merchants thrive on others' property [left behind]. . . . Houses rent for $500 to $8,000 per month. I never saw such go-ahead people. They rebuild before the embers are cool. This city is hell upon earth. The worst characters are here. There is plenty of law but no justice. You may with truth write against people coming here from Old England. . . ." [34]

The mayor agreed that San Francisco was not ready for the invasion. John W. Geary, who had become the *alcalde* in 1847, protested:

> We are without a dollar in the public treasury. . . . You have neither an office for your magistrate, nor any other public edifice. You are without a single police officer or watchman and have not the means of confining a prisoner for an hour; neither have you a place to shelter, while living, sick and unfortunate strangers who may be cast upon our shores, or to bury them when dead. Public improvements are unknown in San Francisco. In short, you are without a single requisite necessary for the promotion of prosperity, for the protection of property, or for the maintainance of order.[35]

Chaotic as it was, San Francisco was a truly cosmopolitan city. It had never been so distinctively Spanish as Monterey or San Jose, since its early leaders were emigré merchants. Now it became a gathering place for men from all over the world, some camouflaged in frontier garb or miner's costume ("red flannel shirt, belt with knife and pistols, mining boots pulled over trousers, straw hat with wide brim"); others, flaunting their native dress. A veritable babble of languages was to be heard on the streets. It was said that those who could speak English, French, and Spanish had the advantage.

The *Alta California* frequently described this *"omnium gatherum* of Humanity," [36] declaring that "the community of San Francisco is a prefect *olla podrida,* although its principal ingredient and general character is American. The Americans are the onions and flavor, and season the whole dish." Then follows the sort of thumbnail characterization of each nationality so popular with writers of the period, who never failed to apply the adjective "volatile" to the Frenchman and "stolid" to the German, while reserving their most fanciful language for the Chinese. [37]

The finer distinctions were ignored in such a catalogue, but they did not escape the eyes of the immigrants themselves, thrown together on this frontier, where, for better or for worse, former social status counted for nought. A young Frenchman, observing his compatriots, reported that gentlemen were carrying trunks for persons who a year before they would not have had as servants. Former doctors, lawyers, and merchants were blacking boots and washing dishes in a restaurant. An ex-cavalry officer was selling wood, while an admiral's son was taking people in a boat to tour the bay. To the observer's disgust, a marquis, who "had all the earmarks of a strayed sheep of the aristocracy," was charming the Californians who were "not too particular," and yet another unsavory acquaintance from home "posed as a prosperous, honest and reputable citizen." The young emigré asked, as have so many other travelers meeting their compatriots abroad, "Where have these rustic field mice come from, with their coarse manners, and red noses, their cheap language. . . ?" [38]

Another fortune hunter who had exhausted his physical and material resources at the diggings returned to San Francisco to find two formerly affluent friends from the East disguised in new roles, one driving an ox team for three hundred dollars a month, the other carrying bricks for some masons.[39] Before the Chinese assumed the duties of servants, a few Irishmen, Frenchmen, and Italians worked as houseboys. With the leveling of rank, some of the forty-niners found it convenient to drop their old names and past histories and assume a new identity. "French Pete," "Kanaka Joe," "Boston," and "Kentuck" of Bret Harte's *The Luck of Roaring Camp* were part of the same tradition that produced the period song:

> Oh, what was your name in the States?
> Was it Thompson, or Johnson, or Bates?
> Did you murder your wife
> And fly for your life?
> Say, what was your name in the States? [40]

The fire-eating "chivalry" man from the South and the "hot-headed abolitionist" mixed and mingled with the young bloods of Europe and the Pacific. Most of them were under thirty, unrestrained by family or hometown taboos or by the presence of women. (An 1850 census noted that females constituted only 8 percent of the total population of California and only 2 percent in the mining districts.[41]) The freedom to kick over the traces, cut a wide swath, adopt new modes of behavior in a place that had no rules was irresistible to many. Some traditional customs fell into disrepair on the long trip to California. William Powell, the Welsh immigrant, had scant success in stopping the card-playing on board a steamer bound north from Nicaragua, as he moved among his fellow passengers "with a short sermon, saying, 'Today is the Sabbath of the Lord thy God. Keep it holy.'" [42] In Sacramento, the seventh day was commemorated by a sharpster who made the Bible a device for a betting game. Sundays at the diggings were spent by the prospectors in housework and visiting. Revelry rather than piety marked the day of rest; most of the fights occurred then. Actually, Sabbatarian sobriety was not a part of life in Hispanic California and came only with the evolution of a more stable American- and Protestant-dominated society, along with the arrival of wives and mothers.

Stories are told of the homesickness of the men separated from their loved ones, those who rushed to meet the mail steamers to get letters from home. (The Pacific Mail Steamship Company inaugurated service to San Francisco in the fall of 1848.) Even more poignant are the stories of miners, starved for the sight of a woman, dancing around a bonnet or walking miles to catch a glimpse of a settler's wife. To men far from home the warmth of the saloon and the gambling parlor, however crude, was more attractive than their Spartan living accommodations, and even more alluring were "the ladies of the demi-monde." Along with gamblers and confidence men, ex-convicts from Australia, and bandits from Mexico, came the prostitutes, some of whom, like the monte players, profited handsomely, though the shortage of women of any sort led to quarrels of passion and jealous rage. The French critic spoke disparagingly of a "poor, strolling actress" who had come with her compatriots to San Francisco, one who "has chosen her path in life: the theatre, the street, and the alcove. This she may be able to follow for many years to come, for the stores carry chiffons, wigs and curls; the dentists, teeth; and the perfumers, rouge to replace what is missing. . . ." [43] Was she perhaps a member of the French vaudeville company, under the direction of Mesdemoiselles Eleanora, Adalbert, and Placine, who entertained at the Adelphi Theatre in January of 1851?

There had always been a shortage of Caucasian women in California. The story is told that the father of Mariano Vallejo, having assisted at the birth of a girl child—the daughter of a friend—immediately requested that she should be given to him in marriage when she became fourteen years old. During the Gold Rush years the native women, the settled Mexican California women, the new camp followers, and the few settlers' wives lived their separate lives with very little mutual contact. The mother of Josiah Royce, whose reminiscences of those days were appropriately entitled *A Frontier Lady*, noted that when a businessman brought his mistress to a gathering, the other women present refused to be introduced to her. Mrs. Royce felt that many of the forty-niners were in danger of moral shipwreck in being cast off from the customary restraints of established society.[44]

If the freedom of the mining camps allowed for a fine spontaneity in social relations, the hardships and risks were very great, as a correspondent for *The London Times* noted: "I really don't know what puts it into people's heads to leave good homes and civilized society to come here to snatch up gold dust, exposing themselves to all sorts of dangers." [45] Another writer complained that the wrong people were arriving, too many clerks unsuited to manual labor.[46] Many would-be prospectors were unprepared for the physical rigors, plying a pickaxe in an icy stream in temperatures that occasionally went over one hundred degrees, blistering their hands, spraining their arms and backs. Others were harassed by the nomadic, unregulated life.

Physical disease claimed many victims. Some invalids were carried off the ships in San Francisco and at once became public charges. By the early 1850s hospital facilities had been set up. The 1852 annual report of the State Marine Hospital in San Francisco provides information on the contagions that afflicted the population—cholera, typhoid fever, pneumonia, and tuberculosis being the most lethal (though the latter two infections occurred relatively infrequently). Yellow fever, called Panama fever, was, as has been mentioned, contracted by people who crossed the Isthmus. Rheumatism, dysentery, scurvy, diarrhea, and malaria were common ailments among the overland wagon parties and among the miners in the camps, who also suffered occasional outbreaks of smallpox and erysipelas. Of the 2,283 patients admitted to the hospital in the year 1852, about one-seventh died. The roster gives some insight into the composition of the population at that time. Only 63 women and 17 children were patients, and only 51 of the whole group paid for their treatment.* More foreigners than Americans were admitted, in keeping with the larger foreign population of San Francisco, though the 1852 census for all of California indicated a ratio of slightly under 40 percent foreign-born people to 60 percent American citizens.[47]

The Stockton Hospital had more Americans than foreign-born patients. Its trustees noted, "A large number of those admitted had just arrived in the country, after a tedious and protracted journey across the plains, or from Mexico, debilitated, exhausted and diseased, without employment and without means, proper objects of our interest and compassion. The majority of those received from San Francisco were brought into the country by the Pacific steamers, and were generally ill with dysentery, diarrhoe [*sic*], and Panama or typhoid fever." The Stockton Hospital also cared for the insane and among these patients for the year 1852, it was reported that there was almost an equal number of Americans and foreigners.[48] The resident physician at Stockton wrote, "It is fearful to contemplate the amount of mental excitement, the violent passions, the ungoverned tempers and continual turmoil prevailing throughout the entire population of the State." The delusions of some of the madmen took the form of fantasies about wealth and the ownership of great tracts of land. One patient claimed all of California and Hawaii, "held a lien on Russia for several millions, and strictly prohibited the erec-

---

* An 1851 law, aimed chiefly at curbing the arrival of Chinese, required the masters of a foreign vessel to post a bond for each passenger against the cost of medical treatment or relief or support.

tion of a hospital or a Methodist church in all his possessions." [49]

In the journals and diaries of forty-niners were recorded a number of suicides of those who had become despondent over bad luck or who had been unable to bear the anarchic confusion of the times. Gradually new forms of the regulation of men's relations began to be created in the mining camps and the new cities. Partnerships, which offered practical as well as psychological security, were common in the first placer-mining days.[50] As surface gold became scarcer, more sophisticated techniques for moving large quantities of earth had to be devised, which required cooperative action between groups of men. Companies, in which each miner gave up some of his independence for the mutual benefit of a number of people, were an outgrowth of the change in mining methods.

During the period of most intense competition—for example, in 1852, when 100,000 miners were elbowing each other from Mariposa to the Klamath River—the friction was constant. Gone were the days when a man could leave his valuables hanging from the nearest tree. Larceny was the most common crime in California and was often treated as a capital offense. The earliest mining-courts had been impromptu affairs, called into session when a case of serious injustice required the deliberation of all members of a camp. Charles Shinn, who wrote one of the earliest studies of frontier government in California before statehood, found the folkmoot courts at the diggings to be a reflection of Anglo-Saxon Germanic tradition, for which he had an exaggerated reverence. Later scholars acknowledge the miners' indebtedness to Mexican mining laws as well as to mining techniques.

The Californians of that period favored direct action rather than calm deliberation, with the result that the innocent often paid the penalty when an angry mob of vigilantes in the cities or lynchers in the diggings would not wait for a careful sifting of the evidence. Ear-cropping and flogging were administered when the offense was not too grave; some "undesirables" were simply banished. A number of "suspicious" characters were ordered to leave the town of Shasta in 1851 after a hay yard had been burned down —an episode that may have been the basis for Bret Harte's story, *The Outcasts of Poker Flat.* At the diggings the stigma often fell on prostitutes, gamblers, and thieves, and in San Francisco was applied to the petty criminal element, among them the Botany Bay convicts known as "Sydney Ducks." But more and more frequently foreign miners were indiscriminately attacked or driven from their claims by the dominant Americans, not on the basis of their criminal proclivities—though this was offered as a rationalization— but because the nativist sentiment remaining from the recent war with Mexico made the persecution of foreigners of Latin extraction almost an act of patriotism.

Anti-Foreign Sentiment

The onus fell particularly on the Sonorans, who were profiting from the Gold Rush by stripping the store shelves in their border towns, sending up their prostitutes and monte gamblers; furthermore, they were clever and experienced miners. (Consider the Spanish names used in the diggings: *placer, bonanza, arastras,* the latter, an ore-crushing mechanism drawn by a mule.) Like the "Cousin Jacks" from Cornwall, the Mexicans knew how to look for gold. They sometimes obtained their pay dirt by "coyoting" —that is, "sinking a square hole to the bed-rock, and then burrowing from the bottom along the ledge," or winnowing the dust in the wind to sift down the heavier gold.[51]

The other neighbors, the Oregonians, were soon complaining about "the Mexican dandies" with their extravagantly ornamented costumes, who pranced along "as if the ground was not good enough for them to walk upon." [52]

Another observer reported, "The Mexicans are disliked and almost hated by the other miners because of their frequent quarrels as well as their customary disturbing, dizzy life. They are shunned or crowded out if their presence cannot be otherwise avoided." [53]

It was not only the Sonorans who were singled out for disapproval. As noted in an earlier chapter, the American citizenship of the *Californios* was challenged and the other Latins were scorned. The victims of the first lynching at a place called Hangtown were a Chilean and a Frenchman. The only woman to be lynched in the mining camps was a Mexican woman, who was hanged with her Latin-American lover by a maddened crowd at Downieville on July 5, 1851 because she had stabbed an American intruder. When the Chileans fled to San Francisco, they were attacked by a gang of rowdies, mainly mustered-out soldiers, who called themselves "Hounds," or "Regulators." These bullies, who had been extorting "money, goods and effects from different persons," tore down the tents in the Chilean settlement, destroyed or stole the contents, and beat and threatened the inhabitants, including women and children, for the Chileans had brought their families. After a public indignation meeting was called by the *alcalde*, the leaders of the Hounds were shut up in a ship in the bay (the state prison at San Quentin had not yet been built). The *Alta California* commented: "The events and conduct relative to foreigners, which has recently transpired in the mines, has, no doubt, tended to give assurance to these reckless men. . . ." [54]

Anti-foreign agitation emanated from high places. General Persifor F. Smith, the commanding general of the army in Monterey, arrived in 1849 in time to send out relief wagons to help bring in overland emigrant parties but, aroused by the number of foreign adventurers he met en route to California through the Isthmus, he said he would "consider everyone who is not a citizen of the United States, who en-ters upon public land and digs for gold as a trespasser." [55] His successor, Brigadier General Riley, repudiated the doctrine of trespass but Yankee veterans, frustrated in the diggings, persuaded themselves that the Mexicans they met were plotting to retake California.[56]

Part of the resentment was caused by the fact that the Sonorans and *Californios* sometimes brought Indian laborers to dig for them. It was demeaning to the Yankee to work alongside a gang of *peons*. They had an equal detestation for those few black men who were brought in by their masters from the southern states. It was claimed that some ex-slaves were not told that the California constitution had outlawed involuntary servitude (on a motion introduced by a miner of Irish ancestry) and they were made to work for their freedom. When some Texans brought slaves to dig at Rose's Bar on the Yuba River, they were served notice to take them out of the district.

It was one of these slaveholders, Colonel Thomas Jefferson Green, who, as a member of the legislature, introduced a bill to impose a tax of twenty dollars a month on foreign miners. He warned that the discovery of gold had in other nations "excited the wildest cupidity, which threatens California with an emigration overwhelming in number and dangerous in character. Tens of thousands have already arrived in our country, and they are the commencement of a vast multitude, *en route* and preparing to come hither, of the worst population of the Mexican and South American states, New South Wales, and the Southern Islands, to say nothing of the vast numbers from Europe. Among others, the convicts of Mexico, Chili [*sic*], and Botany Bay, are daily turned upon our shores, who seek and possess themselves of the best places for gold digging, whether upon their own or on account of foreign employers, and carry from our country immense treasure." He made the point that the tax would bring revenue to Calif-fornia while putting American gold miners on an equal footing with "the foreign proprietor." [57]

The bill was passed and tax collectors were sent to the Mother Lode country. At Sonora in the southern mines the foreigners reacted angrily, posting notices in several languages calling upon Mexicans, Peruvians, Chileans, and Frenchmen to unite for the purpose of "putting an end to the vexations of the Americans in California. If you intend to allow yourselves to be fleeced by a band of miserable fellows who are repudiated by their country, then unite and go to the camp of Sonora. . . ." [58] The French collected their "grisettes," called up Alsatians and Basques to join them, and contributed to the crowd of about four thousand aliens who gathered in Sonora on May 16, 1850 to defy the collectors until they were routed by a company of Mexican War veterans.

The tax collectors continued to have difficulty getting the foreigners to pay as well as protecting the rights of those who *had* paid and who were nevertheless being driven from their diggings by Americans, "common justice demanding," said one collector, "that they should be protected in their labor or the money returned." [59] Moreover, swindlers passing themselves off as tax collectors tried to extort the twenty-dollar fee from the strangers in the camps. It is generally agreed that English-speaking foreigners—Britishers, Irishmen, and Australians—were ignored, while the miners of Latin origin were ordered to pay the tax. The *Alta California* noted, "While the human devils that hail from the penal colonies are allowed all the rights of our own citizens because they speak the English language, a quiet and laborious people have been driven from among us because they did not speak that language." [60] The merchants of Stockton, who had earlier protested the Mexicans' undercutting of prices and flooding the market with pack mules, wrung their hands over the decline in profits now that they were departing.

The Foreign Miners' Tax, which brought in a revenue of $26,574.89 between July 1 and December 15, 1850,[61] was denounced by the *Alta California* as "decidedly unconstitutional, unjust, impolitic, opposed to every principle of our free institutions, behind the age, illiberal and foolish." [62] It was revoked the following year by the legislature. But since it sanctioned existing prejudices, particularly in its selective application, the nativist sentiment was infused with new vigor. A candidate for office in Sacramento warmed up the crowd by referring to Mexicans as "the enemy." In different camps, the American miners passed exclusionary resolutions, one of which proposed that a committee of three United States citizens at each locale decide which foreigners were "respectable," allow them to remain if they gave up their arms, except in special cases, while banishing the rest altogether.[63] In the first state census, taken in 1852, Mariposa County in the southern mining district reported that its estimated 1,571 foreign population (as compared with 2,788 Americans) were "unsettled and migratory." [64] In the same year a group of Frenchmen and South Americans were driven from their Mariposa claims just as they were preparing to reap the profits of their labor in turning the course of a river, exposing ore-rich gravel.

Only two mining counties, Calaveras and Tuolumne, had more foreigners than Americans in the population in 1852.[65] In general the prejudice was less intense in the northern districts, though an American doctor's wife, who accompanied her husband to two camps on the Feather River in 1851–52, reported that after a Fourth of July fracas, the people of Spanish ancestry, many of whom are "highly educated gentlemen . . . think that it is the grand characteristic of Columbia's children to be prejudiced, opinionated, selfish, avaricious, and unjust." [66] The French miners had concluded that "la justice favorise généralement les Américains aux depens des étrangers." [67]

The French fled to San Francisco where they became

merchants, ran restaurants and hotels, or earned their living, at least temporarily, as hairdressers and bootblacks. The French colony was located near Clay, Kearny, Commercial, and Sacramento streets. French money circulated in town, the language was spoken widely, and Gallic culture took root in San Francisco so that by the time Richard Henry Dana returned to California in 1859 it was contributing a very distinct and charming flavor to the life of the city. The more restless among the French Argonauts returned home or went to Sonora as colonists or to other parts of Latin America on filibustering expeditions in an effort to keep adventure alive on soil congenial to Latins.

Filibustering was a by-product of the Mexican War and the Gold Rush. A number of Americans also followed the Latin Americans back across the border, for by 1854 the Chileans and Peruvians were going home and the Sonoran migration to California, having reached its peak in 1850, was moving in the opposite direction.[68] Yankee veterans of the Mexican War and other restless individuals plotted expeditions to wrest more territory from the republics south of the border, though with scant success. These forays into foreign soil were undertaken by the more erratic elements of the population and had no widespread support from the majority of sober-minded prospectors who were preparing to settle down as citizens.

However, the warfare between Yankees and Latin Americans was continued on an individual basis in California as a number of the disaffected Mexicans who remained revenged themselves for their unfair treatment at the hands of gringos by robbing and murdering them. There were more Mexicans in the state prison in 1855 than men of any other foreign nationality, but for every *bandido* captured, others, whose exploits were as legendary as their elusiveness, were contributing to a sheriff-versus-badman saga, which was the ultimate and tragic result of the Yankee-Hispano confrontation in the goldfields. Predictably, American veterans of the Mexican War were commissioned by the governor to capture the most fearsome badman of all, the legendary Joaquin Murieta. Though considerable doubt remains as to whether the right man was caught, Joaquin's head and the hand of his chief cohort, three-fingered Jack Garcia, were pickled in whiskey and displayed throughout the state for profit and shock value.

The foreigners of Latin background were particularly ready to join the attack on the Chinese, who were the next group to be singled out for prejudicial treatment. While a Frenchman in San Francisco was writing about *le peril jaune* ("the Yellow Peril") Mexican *bandidos* in the mining areas took special pains to rob and terrorize the gangs of coolie laborers who were filtering into the picked-over diggings that the others were deserting. In 1849 there were reported to be 54 Chinese in California; by January 1850, 791 were recorded; and by the end of the year 4,000 had arrived. The Tai-Ping rebellion of 1850 in southeastern China, followed by an economic depression, induced immigrants, mainly young men of peasant stock, to leave their families at home and try their fortunes in the country of the "golden moutains." At first, the "Celestials," as they were called, were praised as quiet, patient, and industrious. A reporter for the *Alta California* predicted that "The China Boys will yet vote at the same polls, study at the same schools and bow at the same Altar as our own countrymen." [69]

Appreciation of their virtues declined when, in 1852, 20,026 more arrived, most of whom had had their passage paid by rich entrepreneurs among their own countrymen, who required them to work at the mines as indentured laborers. This system was as unpopular with American miners as had been the competition of Indian and black labor. A legislative committee inveighed against "hired serfs" and "untaxed slaves," and categorized as undesirable "the inhabitants of the Pacific Islands" and "many others dissimilar from ourseves in customs, language and education." These could not be welcomed as were "the inhabitants of European countries . . . who come as freemen to seek a home, to find religious and political liberty, and to become citizens of a Government they have learned to know, to honor, and to love. . . ." [70]

Laws Affecting Racial Minorities

The Foreign Miners' Tax was revived in 1852 at three dollars a month, later increased to four dollars a month, and was invoked chiefly against the Chinese. It was called "An Act to Provide for the Protection of Foreigners, and to Define their Liabilities and Privileges." A foreigner was defined as a "person, not being a citizen of the United States, or who shall not have declared his intention to become such (California Indians excepted)." Though most Chinese did not want to become citizens, a federal law of 1790, which stipulated that only "free white persons" could be naturalized, was belatedly invoked against them to deny them rights that were accorded to citizens. In a characteristically accommodating manner they willingly paid the Foreign Miners' Tax, which for years provided a quarter of the revenue of the state. After it ceased to have any practical value, the state supreme court declared it unconstitutional in 1870.

In an 1854 amendment to the 1850 law, Chinese, like Indians and black men, were prohibited from testifying in court either "in favor of or against a white man." The question had come up in *The People* v. *Hall,* a case concerning a white man convicted of murder on the testimony of Chinese witnesses. The twenty-nine-year-old chief justice of the state, Hugh C. Murray, maintained that "the words Indian, Negro, Black and White, are generic terms, designating race. That, therefore, Chinese and all other people

[who] are not white, are included in the prohibition from being witnesses against whites." He argued that since the Indians had Asian ancestors, the Chinese and Indians should be categorized together. He characterized the Chinese as "a race of people whom nature has marked as inferior, and who are incapable of progress or intellectual development beyond a certain point, as their history has shown; differing in language, opinions, color, and physical conformation; between whom and ourselves nature has placed an impassable difference. . . . The same rule which would admit them to testify, would admit them to all equal rights of citizenship, and we might soon see them at the polls, in the jury box, upon the bench, and in our legislative halls." [71]

Other blanket laws awarded the privileges of citizenship to whites only—for instance, the act defining the organization of the state militia in 1855, which stipulated as subject to military duty "All free, able-bodied white citizens, between the ages of eighteen and forty-five years, residing in this State. . . ." [72]

The state enactments concerning Negroes reflected the national struggle between the abolitionists and the pro-slavery faction in Congress. As isolated as was the West Coast from the storm center in Washington, free-soil-versus-slave-territory agitation played a part in California's Constitutional Convention and in the deliberations of the legislature, since the state's new leaders brought with them the passions of their sectional differences.

California's first governor, Peter Burnett, originally from Tennessee, had succeeded in introducing a measure to outlaw free blacks in Oregon (later incorporated into the constitution) before he came to the Gold Rush. In his inaugural message before the first session of the legislature in San Jose in December 1849, he proposed to revive the ban that had been argued and dismissed at the Constitutional Convention in Monterey two months earlier. Burnett suggested that there were "but one of two consistent courses to take in reference to this class of population—either to admit them to the full and free enjoyment of all the privileges guaranteed by the Constitution to others, or exclude them from the state. . . . We have certainly the right to prevent any class of population from settling in our State, that we may deem injurious to our society. Had they been born here, and had acquired rights in consequence, I should not recommend any measures to expel them. They are not now here—except a few in comparision with the numbers that would be here—and the object is to keep them out." [73]

The legislature did not follow his suggestion and continued the less controversial, if inconsistent, policy of admitting black people and curtailing their rights. Most of the Negroes in California had been brought by white men as slaves or servants; the small number in the state reflected the constitutional ban on slavery.* Their anomolous position was reinforced by a stringent fugitive slave law which was invoked when owners leaving California to return to the southern states attempted to reclaim the slaves they had brought with them. Since the black person claimed as a slave could not testify against the white claimant, he or she had no recourse in a state court. The first fugitive slave law, passed in 1852 and extended by the legislative sessions of 1853 and 1854, covered the period from before California was admitted to the Union until one year after the enactment of the law.

Three years after the law's expiration, a Mississippi schoolteacher in Sacramento reclaimed his former slave, Archy Lee, in order to take him back home with him. The action was contested by early civil-rights advocates, including blacks who raised money on Lee's behalf. But Peter Burnett, then on the bench of the superior court, ruled in favor of the white man on the grounds that he was travel-

* The 1852 census recorded 2,070 Negroes and 572 mulattos.

ing, not sojourning, in California. As Archy Lee was being carried away from the coast in a steamer, he was rescued through a writ of habeas corpus, and his former owner was charged with abducting him. The United States commissioner who then ordered him freed was a Southern proslavery man who transcended his own prejudice in the interest of justice, deciding that Lee's former owner was not simply passing through "with his property" but had been a resident of California for a year.[74]

The frontier with its opportunities for wealth and its fluid social patterns enabled some black people to realize a prosperity and acceptance they had not known in the communities of the East. (Peter Biggs, who came to California with the army in 1846, set up as a barber in Hispanic Los Angeles, married a local woman, and became an ornament at all the local balls and festivities.) Black leaders emerged to challenge the limitations on full citieznship for blacks, organizing a Franchise League in 1852 and disseminating their views in a San Francisco publication called the *Mirror of the Times*. With the expiration of the fugitive slave law in 1855, a black convention was held to petition for the repeal of the law which prohibited Negroes from testifying in the courts. This was not accomplished until 1863 and the law remained in effect against Chinese and Indians until 1872.

Another minority group which came during the Gold Rush, the Jews, inspired minor legislative response in the form of a law requiring peddlers to buy expensive licenses, and an 1855 bill, introduced but not passed, which sought to impose a prohibitive tax on merchants who observed the Sabbath on Saturday and opened their stores on Sunday. The several thousand Jews who came to California beginning in 1849, many of them refugees from political strife in Europe, made an invaluable contribution in starting stores and banks in remote mining areas as well as in Stockton, Sacramento, and San Francisco. A good deal of prejudice, standard for the era, is recorded in miners' diaries; some Jews are reported to have traded under assumed names.[75]

Most Jews arrived on the West Coast with goods to sell or money to buy supplies or, at least, with a connection with an established firm that stood ready to finance a new venture in the placer region. A common practice, according to one observer, was for a representative of a firm in the city to spy out the prospects of trade at new diggings, and if the situation augered well, to send back word to a partner to come ahead. The prosperity of a mining town could be gauged "by the number of Jewish shop-keepers it maintained and the size of its Chinatown," in the opinion of another man from the gold country.[76]

Evolution of a More Stable Society

Chinese and Jews (but not blacks) were included in the category of approximately sixty thousand foreigners listed in the 1852 census who were concentrated in the mining districts and the new northern cities. San Francisco had more foreign-born residents than Americans and by 1856—less than a decade after the beginning of the Gold Rush—had thirteen daily papers and as many weeklies printed in English, French, German, Spanish, Italian, and Chinese. In a ten-year period the portal to California was transformed from a tent city on the sandlots to the nucleus of an imposing metropolis. Wharves, factories, foundries, and refineries attested to its commercial prosperity, while schools, churches, and orphan asylums proclaimed the beginning of family settlement. New ordinances closed the bars and the gambling halls (but not the theatres) on Sundays, and outlawed bullfighting, bear-baiting, cockfighting, and horse racing on weekdays as well.

Bancroft drew an analogy between the frequent fires that removed the flimsy structures of the town, making way for permanent construction in stone and brick, and the activities of the Vigilance Committees of 1851 and 1856 that helped rid the community of some of the worst criminal elements. The 1851 Committee subdued members of underworld gangs, including the Sydney Ducks, who were plaguing more sober citizens; the 1856 group, which had wide civic support, reflected the merchants' frustration with the corruption of city politicians and the ordinary channels of law enforcement. Hanging, banishment, deportation, and turning victims over to "the authorities" were the punishments inflicted by the self-constituted bodies that attempted to impose their own order on a city where ballot boxes were stuffed, voters were intimidated, and one thousand unpunished homicides occurred between 1849 and 1856.[77]

Crime was such a serious problem in California after the Gold Rush that the legislature apportioned far more money for prisons than for public education. Though criminals were perhaps almost as numerous as children in the predominantly bachelor society of the day, the expenditure worked out to two thousand dollars spent for each convict as compared with nine dollars for each child.[78]

The regular government was weakened by the transient character of the population, accompanied by widespread indifference to civic responsibility. Less than one-fifth of the people in the state turned out on a rainy day in November 1849 to ratify the constitution and to elect the first state officials.

This was the situation—a peripatetic population rent by anarchic impulses—that gave birth to vigilantism, a phenomenon defended by nineteenth-century commentators and historians but more recently deplored. Richard Henry Dana in his observations of 1859 noted that the miners took the law into their own hands. "Without this, they could not have lived." [79] He praised the operation in San Francisco of "that peculiar invention of Anglo-Saxon

Republican America, the solemn, awe-inspiring Vigilance Committee of the most grave and responsible citizens, the last resort of the thinking and the good, taken to only when vice, fraud, and ruffianism have intrenched themselves behind the forms of law, suffrage, and ballot, and there is no hope but in organized force, whose action must be instant and thorough, or its state will be worse than before." [80]

The Harvard philosopher Josiah Royce, who applied a moral judgment to his scrutiny of his native state, heartily condemned the intolerant spirit in the mining camps that led to the persecution of outcasts and foreigners. However, he condoned the vigilance committees in San Francisco as a necessary antidote to irresponsibility. The wages of sin— carelessness—must be paid in violence. [81] Later historians have condemned the vigilante movements, challenging the motivation of the leaders, criticizing the practice of inflicting punishment without due process, and arguing against treating larceny as a capital offense and hanging as a substitute for imprisonment. [82]

If the assumption of authority by a group of citizens had a purgative effect on San Francisco, the state legislature demonstrated a selective policy toward the various elements of the general population, which had a somewhat similar result. American miners were not taxed. American settlers were awarded 160-acre parcels of land at two dollars an acre and were favored, as noted earlier, in their contest with the *Californios* over Mexican land grants. The first session authorized borrowing huge sums to defray the cost of warfare with the Indians and later a considerable amount was appropriated to assist overland immigrants.

During the first years of fiscal imbalance, while the mines were yielding millions, the state treasury was empty. In addition to bonds, the state revenue came from the Foreign Miners' Tax and from property taxes that were levied most heavily on Southern California *rancheros*. Gambling operations, saloons, itinerant vendors, caravans, and traveling shows were taxed. A three-dollar poll tax levied on all male citizens was frequently evaded. In 1852 John McDougal, the second American governor, admitted that the six "grazing counties," with a population of 6,000, paid almost twice as much in property and poll taxes as the northern counties, which had a population of 120,000.[83]

The first state census was taken in the peak year of the Gold Rush, 1852, in which eighty million dollars was extracted from the Mother Lode country (after which the yield gradually decreased till it reached a plateau of seventeen million annually from 1865 to 1900).[84] Yet, in 1852, more capital was invested in livestock than in mining. California, "without a competitor" in mining, surpassed twenty-two states out of the Union in livestock production, and though agriculture was in its infancy, the extraordinary yield realized in raising grain in the small amount of acreage that was under cultivation forecast a future source of wealth in the state.

More capital was being invested in quartz mining than in placer mining.[85] As the surface gold was taken off, groups of miners organized to buy and operate the more expensive crushers and hydraulic equipment needed to extract deeply embedded veins of ore. An 1852 law stipulated that capitalists could acquire rights to mineral veins, deposits, and quicksilver mines. Since mercury was used in the refining of gold, the quicksilver mines at New Almaden near San Jose, where Mexican and Cornish miners labored under Amercan managers, became valuable enterprises. Fewer men were needed in the new type of mining. The individual entrepreneurship of the early days was abandoned as joint-stock companies or large corporations, run by a few capitalists and employing largely Mexican and Chinese labor, were started.

One of these new mine operators hailed J. Goldsborough Bruff on the eastward-bound steamer for Panama in June 1851. Having secured interest in a valuable mine, he was returning home to bring out his family. Bruff had last seen him "the mere skeleton of a man—worn down by disease and want, whom I lifted out of a wagon, at my camp in the fall of 1849. . . . He is now a hale, robust person, who can as easily throw me upon his shoulder as I before lifted his emaciated frame out of the wagon. . . ." [86]

This success story was unusual. Not many of those who had "seen the elephant" had such good fortune. More were in the position of Bruff, who, far from becoming a rich man, had barely escaped with his life and was returning gratefully to hearth and family, his only wealth being in anecdotes to astonish the incredulous and in his journals and drawings to prove the truth of his stories.

The extravagant events of 1849 and after inspired many pens, with the result that the Gold Rush as a legend renewed world-wide interest in California. The German-born artist, Charles Christian Nahl, who had arrived in 1850, produced sketches of life in the gold camps that were later the basis for ambitious oil paintings. Mark Twain, though arriving very late on the scene in 1861, caught in his tall tales told in dry understatement the atmosphere that lingered about the frontier settlements, a combination of romantic extravaganza and sardonic humor. The flamboyant Cincinnatus H. ("Joaquin") Miller capitalized on the public's fascination with the *bandido* Joaquin Murieta as he fulfilled the stereotype of the homespun man of the West. "The poet of the Sierras" appeared in England in red shirt, high boots, and sombrero—to great effect, though his popularity abroad was not as lasting as that of Bret Harte, whose tales of the unlucky and the unwanted touched a tender chord in his readers.

Some California real estate promoters wanted to sup-press Bret Harte's stories on the ground that his portrayals discouraged the kind of immigrants they wished to attract to the state. The stories were as influential in their way, if not as electrifying, as the contemporary press reports from the goldfields. A visiting dignitary from England, the Duke of Manchester, startled the formally attired guests at a gathering on a country estate near San Francisco by appearing among them in high boots and a red flannel shirt, wishing to put them at their ease by wearing what he understood from reading Mr. Harte was the regulation Western costume.[87]

England continued to be hospitable to Bret Harte and his frontier romances after America had tired of them. "I grind out the old tunes on the old organ and gather up the coppers," he said in his exile. The pioneer scenes of his youth continued to provide him with "copy" many years after he had expressed his aversion to the wanton cruelty he witnessed in the Golden State—the killing of Indians, the persecution of foreigners and outcasts—by proposing to Noah Brooks that they found a "Society of Escaped Californians." [88]

They were not alone. Though the figures are far from accurate, in all likelihood between a quarter and one half of the Argonauts sailed for home or traveled on to further adventure in Latin America and Australia, many of them, as we have seen, having been encouraged to move on.[89]

Among those who stayed and were ready to take up a more settled life were "self-selected, venturesome, strong young fellows" who were looking for wives. Lincoln Steffens tells how his mother and her sister, English-born gentlewomen, ventured from "the crowded east" where girls without a fortune were at a disadvantage in finding husbands. Equipped to support themselves, they came to California, "the easiest man-market in the world at that time," and promptly married two young men chums whom they met at their first boardinghouse.[90] They apparently were no more deterred than had been the gold-seekers by the thousands of miles they had to travel to reach their goal.

For several years after becoming a focus of interest all over the world, California was accessible only after a long sea voyage or tortuous wagon crossing. But in the late fifties Congress allocated appropriations for mail and passenger service across the barrier of mountains and deserts, and enterprising companies bid on them. Technological developments brought rapid changes. The colorful Pony Express was in operation only about a year and a half before being displaced by transcontinental telegraph lines. The Butterfield stages that ran between St. Louis, San Francisco, and Los Angeles were succeeded by the first railroad across the Rockies and the Sierra Nevada. Completed in 1869, the railroad passed not far from the place where members of the Donner Party had perished in their harrowing crossing twenty years earlier.

In the headlong rush of progress, past eras survived in strange juxtaposition with the new developments, "telephones, and telegraphs, and newspapers, and advertisements running far ahead among the Indians and the grizzly bears." Robert Louis Stevenson noted these incongruities in the Napa Valley in 1880 where, in the dawn of the machine age, "bucks, and bears, and rattlesnakes, and former mining operations [were] the staple of men's talk." [91]

People settled in different areas of the state on the basis of their occupations, which were tied to their regional origins. Those from the south central states seemed to gravitate to the agricultural valleys, following in the footsteps of the first backwoodsmen, hunters, and trappers, who had avoided the coastal settlements frequented by seafaring New Englanders. The farmers who fought the representatives of the railroad at Mussel Slough in 1880, an incident immortalized by Frank Norris in *The Octopus,* were chiefly Missourians. Former Texans were to be found in El Monte in Southern California and in Tulare County, while transplanted Easterners from Vermont and Maine built houses along the Mendocino coast similar to the ones they knew from birth. Moving west, men sought a reminder of home, but they were soon caught up in the demanding problems of the new state, the controversies over the use of the land and water involved in hydraulic mining, cattle-raising, farming, and railroad-building.

Climate was an important factor in the pattern of settlement. Regional economy was dependent on a rainfall which varied from over one hundred inches annually in the far north to less than twenty inches a year in the south, until techniques were devised to alter what nature provided. The first major commercial crops, wheat and barley, were grown by the "dry farming" method, the seed planted during the rainy season. Later, rivers were channeled into irrigation canals. Underground water was pumped to the surface. These innovations, combined with the demise of the cattle business and the breaking-up of the huge *ranchos*, changed the pattern of land use. As mining and stock-raising declined, agriculture became an important source of wealth.

The location of the terminus of the first transcontinental railroad in Sacramento further encouraged the settlement of the central part of the state, which had come into prominence in the Gold Rush, the southern "cow counties" remaining rural and Hispanic for another decade. But a startling metamorphosis took place when the railroads reached these areas in the late seventies, about the time that grazing land was being converted to agricultural use. Citrus growers, tourists, and health-seekers transformed the country of the *vaqueros* into "the Italy of America."

A rate war between the Southern Pacific and the Santa Fe railroads, which drastically reduced fares from the Midwest, was accompanied by a strenuous publicity campaign. Soon the Southern California cult excited in restless Easterners a frenzy reminiscent of the gold fever that had brought people to San Francisco thirty years earlier. The new treasure-seekers who came West were generally older and less robust physically than the forty-niners. The average health-seeker was depicted as "middle-class, middle-aged and middle-western," [92] a description that could also be applied to visitors who came for the scenery or the sun.

Appropriately, instead of mining the land with pick and shovel, the newcomers tapped its wealth by speculation. The boom of "the freakish eighties," as a Los Angeles pioneer dubbed the era, gained momentum when the victims of real-estate promoters became promoters themselves in short order, ready to believe and persuade others that some barren sandy waste bristling with builder's stakes would soon be a verdant oasis linked by streetcar lines with the rest of the southland. In the furious speculation, lots which had been valued at a few dollars were suddenly selling for thousands.[93] The boom thrived on illusion—the desert would be made to bloom and poor men would become millionaires. When it collapsed, the remains of what had been hopefully platted towns were put onto wagon beds and moved out ahead of the angry creditors.[94] But the developing agricultural enterprises, particularly the citrus industry which provided a real basis for potential wealth, cushioned the shock.[95] And of the thousands of visitors who had come to Southern California for curiosity or speculation, many remained, giving the region a decidedly Anglo-Saxon American character. Whether they were New Englanders in Santa Barbara, Iowans in Long Beach, or Hoosiers in Pasadena, the new Californians settled down to lead lives not too different from those they had led in Boston or the Middle West. Yet they may have felt a little freer, a little more audacious, for they had arrived in quest of a promised land like the San Franciscans of the same era, whom the novelist Kathleen Norris described as "people who had come on a great adventure." [96] This was also true of the settlers who came from overseas.

1. Bancroft, *History of California*, vol. 6, pp. 53-54.
2. *Alta California*, February 1, 1849.
3. Bancroft, *History of California*, vol. 6, p. 62, fn. 20.
4. Frank Soule, John H. Gihon, M. D., and James Nisbet, *The Annals of San Francisco, together with the Continuation, through 1855, compiled by Dorothy H. Huggins* (Palo Alto, Calif.: Lewis Osborne, 1966 [orig. pub. 1855]), p. 214.
5. Rev. Walter Colton, USN, *The Land of Gold, or Three Years in California* (New York: D. W. Evans, 1860), pp. 247, 253.
6. Bancroft, *History of California*, vol. 6, pp. 99-107 *passim*.
7. "The Memoirs of Theodor Cordua," ed. and trans. Erwin G. Gudde, *Quarterly of the California Historical Society*, vol. 12, no. 4, December 1933.
8. Bancroft, *History of California*, vol. 2, p. 767.
9. Georgia Willis Read and Ruth Garnes, eds., *Gold Rush: The Journals, Drawings, and Other Papers of J. Goldsborough Bruff. April 2, 1849–July 20, 1851* (New York: Columbia University Press, 1949), *passim*.
10. Bancroft, *History of California*, vol. 6, p. 89, fn. 10.
11. *Ibid.*
12. *Ibid.*, pp. 72-73.
13. *Ibid.*, p. 117.
14. *New York Herald*, quoted in Read and Gaines, *Gold Rush*, p. xxxii.
15. *Ibid.*, p. xvii, quote of Maj. William Tell Poussin from the *Washington Daily Globe*, March 3, 1849.
16. *Alta California*, April 19, 1849.
17. Bancroft, *History of California*, vol. 6, p. 119, fn. 13.
18. *Ibid.*, pp. 120-121; also fn. 16.
19. *Ibid.*, p. 124.
20. Doris Marion Wright, "The Making of Cosmopolitan California: An Analysis of Immigration, 1848-1870," *California Historical Society Quarterly*, vol. 19, 1940. Part I, p. 328; Part II, p. 71.
21. *Notre Centenaire: le guide france californien du centenaire*, edité par Jehanne Bietry-Salinger (San Francisco: Pisani Printing and Publishing Co., 1949), p. 2.
22. Wright, *Cosmopolitan California*, Part I, p. 340.
23. *The Diary of William Powell*, ed. by his great-granddaughter, Mary Powell Flanders.
24. Wright, *Cosmopolitan California*, Part I, p. 342.
25. Newmark, *Sixty Years in Southern California*, pp. 15, 16.

26. Read and Gaines, *Gold Rush*, p. 212.

27. *Ibid.*, March 31, 1850, p. 328.

28. *Ibid.*, p. 402.

29. Capt. Cyrille Pierre Théodore Laplace, quoted in Bancroft, *History of California*, vol. 4, p. 153.

30. *Alta California*, February 18, 1850.

31. Bancroft, *History of California*, vol. 6, p. 198, fn. 44.

32. *Ibid.*, p. 198, fn. 45.

33. *The London Times*, February 6, 1850.

34. *Ibid.*, September 9, 1850.

35. Quoted in Oscar Lewis, *San Francisco: Mission to Metropolis* (Berkeley, Calif.: Howell-North Books, 1966), p. 58.

36. *Alta California*, February 7, 1851.

37. *Ibid.*, March 8, 1850.

38. "A Frenchman in the Gold Rush," translated from the Journal of Ernest de Massey by Marguerite Eyer Wilbur, *California Historical Society Quarterly*, vol. 5, March 1926, pp. 15, 20, 21.

39. *The London Times*, January 2, 1850.

40. *California Songster*, quoted in Carey McWilliams, *California: The Great Exception* (New York: Current Books, Inc., 1949), p. 72.

41. Bancroft, *History of California*, vol. 6, p. 221.

42. *Diary of William Powell*, entry of June 24, 1855.

43. "A Frenchman in the Gold Rush," p. 26.

44. Sarah Royce, *A Frontier Lady* (New Haven, Conn.: Yale University Press, 1932), pp. 113-114.

45. Dispatch from San Francisco, July 31, 1850 in *The London Times*, September 9, 1850.

46. *Ibid.*, October 22, 1850.

47. Annual Report of the Trustees of the State Marine Hospital in San Francisco for 1852, Doc. no. 21, *Journal of the Assembly*, 4th Sess., 1853; *Journal of the California Senate*, 4th Sess., Doc. 14, 1853.

48. *Journal of the Assembly*, 4th Sess. 1853, Appendix B, pp. 39-40.

49. Report of resident physician to the Board of Trustees of the Asylum for the Insane of the State of California, *Journal of the Senate*, 5th Sess., 1854, Doc. no. 1, pp. 23, 26.

50. Charles H. Shinn, *Mining Camps: A Study in American Frontier Government* (New York: Alfred A. Knopf, 1948 [orig. pub. 1884]), p. 105.

51. Bancroft, *History of California*, vol. 6, p. 88, fn. 8.

52. Wright, *Cosmopolitan California*, Part I, p. 325.

53. *Ibid.*, pp. 325-326.

54. *Alta California*, August 2, 1848, steamer ed., p. 1.

55. Pitt, *Decline of the Californios*, pp. 55-56.

56. *Ibid.*

57. Report of Mr. Green on Mines and Foreign Miners, *Journal of the Legislature,* 1st Sess. 1850, pp. 493, 496.

58. *Alta California,* May 25, 1850.

59. Statement of L. A. Besancon, *Appendix to the Journal of the California Legislature,* 2nd Sess., 1851, p. 662.

60. *Alta California,* March 7, 1851.

61. *Appendix to the Journal of the California Legislature,* 1851, p. 547.

62. *Alta California,* March 7, 1851.

63. Royce, *California,* p. 285.

64. *Journal of the California Senate,* 4th Sess., Doc. 14, 1853, p. 23.

65. *Ibid.,* pp. 15, 52.

66. Mrs. Louisa Amelia Knapp Smith Clapp, *The Shirley Letters from the California Mines, 1851-1852,* edited by Carl I. Wheat (New York: Alfred A. Knopf, 1949), pp. 158-159.

67. E. Auger, *Voyage en Californie* (Paris, 1857), quoted in Royce, *California,* p. 288, fn. 56.

68. Wright, *Cosmopolitan California,* Part I, p. 325.

69. *Alta California,* May 12, 1851.

70. Report of the Committee on Mines and Mining Interests, April 16, 1852, Appendix, *Journal of the Legislature,* 1852, pp. 830-831.

71. Chief Justice Murray in *The People* v. *Hall,* October 1, 1854, 4 California, 399.

72. *Laws of the State of California, Statutes of 1855,* p. 136.

73. Gov. Burnett's message, December 21, 1849, *Journal of the Legislature,* 1st Sess., 1850, pp. 604, 605.

74. Bancroft, *History of California,* vol. 6, p. 715, fn. 52.

75. *Ibid.,* p. 222, fn. 3.

76. *The Autobiography of Charles Peters* (Sacramento: La Grave Co., 1915), p. 139, quoted in Robert E. Levison, "The Jews in the California Gold Rush" (Ph.D. thesis, University of Oregon, Eugene, 1968), p. 12.

77. Rolle, *California: A History,* p. 247.

78. Bean, *California: An Interpretive History,* p. 194.

79. *Journal of Richard Henry Dana, Jr.,* vol. 3, p. 916.

80. Richard Henry Dana, Jr., *Two Years Before the Mast and Twenty-Four Years After,* The Harvard Classics, vol. 23 (New York: P. F. Collier & Son, 1909), p. 414.

81. Royce, *California,* p. 219.

82. Bean, *California: An Interpretive History,* pp. 136-150; John Walton Caughey, *California* (New York: Prentice-Hall, 1940), pp. 351-352.

83. Gov. McDougal's Message, January 7, 1852, *Journal of the Assembly,* 3rd Sess., 1852, p. 12.

84. Bean, *California: An Interpretive History*, p. 199.

85. *Journal of the California Senate*, 4th Sess., Doc. 14, 1853, pp. 9-11.

86. Read and Gaines, *Gold Rush*, p. 495.

87. Gertrude Atherton, *Adventures of a Novelist* (New York: Liveright, Inc., 1932), p. 65.

88. Margaret Duckett, *Mark Twain and Bret Harte* (Norman: University of Oklahoma Press, 1964), p. 83.

89. It is estimated that 268,713 persons arrived in San Francisco by sea from 1849 to 1857, while 144,100 departed by sea in the same period. We must add to the number of arrivals by sea the far less accurate estimate of those who came overland, a slightly smaller number. Very few who took the transcontinental route to California wished to repeat the experience by returning overland. See Bancroft, *History of California*, pp. 623-624; Wright, *Cosmopolitan California*, Part I, pp. 341, 342.

90. *The Autobiography of Lincoln Steffens* (New York: Harcourt, Brace, 1931), p. 4.

91. Robert Louis Stevenson, *The Silverado Squatters* (London: Chatto & Windus, 1901), pp. 19, 3.

92. John E. Baur, *Health-Seekers in Southern California, 1870-1900* (San Marino, Calif.: Huntington Library, 1959), p. 116.

93. Newmark, *Sixty Years in Southern California*, pp. 527, 379.

94. J. M. Guinn, *The Great Real Estate Boom of 1887* (Los Angeles: Historical Society of Southern California, 1890).

95. Glenn S. Dumke, *The Boom of the Eighties in Southern California* (San Marino, Calif.: Huntington Library, 1944), p. 116.

96. Kathleen Norris, typed manuscript of a tape-recorded interview conducted by Roland E. Duncan (University of California, Bancroft Library Regional Oral History Office, Berkeley, 1956-1957), p. 1.

4

Europeans in California

THE FIRST WAVE of foreign immigrants, the majority of whom came from Germany and the British Isles, particularly Ireland, became assimilated quickly in the post-Gold Rush society. On a frontier where so much was needed, some of these pioneers proved extraordinarily inventive. Adolph Sutro, born in Prussia of Jewish ancestry, while selling merchandise to mining towns, conceived a brilliant plan for boring a tunnel in the Comstock Lode silver mines to facilitate the removal of the ore and improve the safety conditions of the miners. Levi Strauss, a Bavarian Jew, patented an invention for reinforcing with copper rivets the pockets and seams of work clothes that he manufactured —a stratagem devised by a Virginia City tailor, whose clients were so constantly ripping out the pockets of their pants in the mines that he bought rivets from a harness-maker to hold them together. Andrew S. Halladie, who was born in London, used the wire rope he manufactured in his San Francisco factory in his invention of the cable car, which was tried for the first time on the hills of San Francisco in August of 1873. He was impelled to the experiment after seeing a team of horses injured in pulling a too-heavily laden street car up a steep grade.

The Hanoverian, Claus Spreckels, ran a brewery after his arrival in San Francisco, but soon switched to sugar refining. He sold his first business in order to go back to Europe to study the entire sugar manufacturing process, serving an apprenticeship as a workman. On his return to the West Coast, he developed thousands of acres of land in Hawaii for sugar-cane cultivation, as well as beet sugar fields in California, and built refineries for processing sugar. He also acquired an interest in the steamship lines that carried his produce. When he tried to build a rival railroad to the Southern Pacific into the Central Valley, he ran into difficulties with a fellow countryman, Heinrich Alfred Kreiser from Wurttemberg, who had assumed the name of Henry Miller when he bought a friend's ticket to California.

While Spreckels was known as the "Sugar King," Miller was called by a later historian the "Clemenceau of the Plains," because of his opportunistic negotiations for land.[1] From a modest butcher shop in San Francisco he branched out into buying cattle and sheep in the Central Valley and then acquired land to pasture the animals at very advantageous prices. Through the Federal Swamp Land Act of 1850 "swamp and overflow" lands could be purchased at one dollar and a quarter an acre. In California this land was dry and usable most of the year because of the peculiar rain cycle. To reinforce his claim that the land belonged in the "swamp and overflow" category, Miller had himself pulled in a boat by a team of horses. Eventually, he and his Alsatian partner, Charles Lux, owned over a million acres of range land in several Western states, incurring the animosity of the smaller landowners whom they swallowed up and of the farmers who were barred from access to river water. The partners took advantage of the tradition that granted riparian rights to those whose land was contiguous to the streams.

When Miller returned to his native land on a visit, he

was treated as a celebrity. It was remembered that as a boy he had had a prophetic dream of seeing vast herds of cattle.

Stimulated by the enterprise of a Hungarian exile, Agoston Haraszthy, many Germans were infected by "the wine fever" of the early fifties. Some of them were experienced viticulturalists. The best known among them developed vineyards in the Napa and Sonoma valleys, where they found growing conditions similar to the home terrain where they had learned their skills. The group that formed the nucleus of the grape-growing colony of Anaheim in Southern California were not farmers, but included a gunsmith, an engraver, a bookbinder, a poet, a brewer, a hotel-keeper, a miller, a teacher, a shoemaker, a hatter, and several merchants, teamsters, carpenters, blacksmiths, and watchmakers. Prudently waiting two years until the vines planted by their leader were ready to bear, the colonists came down from San Francisco to San Diego by ship in September 1859, were carried ashore on the backs of Indians, and proceeded by wagon to the land near the Santa Ana River, which had been purchased from a *Californio*. The vineyard enterprises that flourished in the sandy soil irrigated by the river were a combination of Teutonic and Hispanic methods, appropriate to the bilingual name of the colony. The *zanjeros* and other laborers were Indians, Mexicans, and Chinese. When disease destroyed the vines in the 1880s, the adaptable group converted the land to orange and walnut orchards.[2]

At the other end of the state George Fredrick Schuler, a Bavarian who arrived in Shasta County in the 1870s, immediately established his place in the community by introducing a new variety of clover and taking charge of a volunteer company organized to punish Indians accused of killing a settler's wife. The Germans rather promptly became naturalized citizens, and along with the Irish voted the Democratic ticket in opposition to the anti-Catholic, anti-foreign Know-Nothing party. At the same time they enjoyed their beer gardens and *turnverein*, and created national cultural and benevolent societies, which provided a cushion for the transplanted life in the New World.

The history of the other early immigrant groups to California follows somewhat the same pattern. Cornishmen lived together, often in communities close to the mining areas, where they followed a traditional occupation. Some Scottish immigrants worked as lumbermen and millhands in the redwood forests of the Santa Cruz Mountains. Near the town of Ben Lomond, named for a mountain in Scotland, their descendents are living today. The Welsh seem to have preferred to settle near neighbors from home, yet were soon adapting to changes in occupation and participating in regional affairs.

William Powell, the previously mentioned Welsh immigrant, brought his family up the Sacramento and Feather rivers to a place near Sweetland in Nevada County in the summer of 1855. As they looked at the house rented for eight dollars a month, which was to be their future home, Powell confided in his diary, "My family saw this place lonely, not possessing enjoyment yet." In the next few days, working to make the dwelling habitable, wondering whether there would be profit or even employment for him in the hydraulic mining operations in the vicinity, he confessed that he was "very much dejected and exhausted by the appearance of the present times." After laying out a great deal of money to reach the promised land, perhaps there would be no prospect of earning a living. He and his eighteen-year-old son took the first jobs offered them and were paid six dollars a day apiece.

The early difficulties were soon over, however. In Wales he had expressed his dissatisfaction at "living under the oppressive yoke of strangers." In California he found freedom to pursue his religious and patriotic traditions. He once preached a sermon to a group of Indians who came to his door. (He reported that they laughed.) He joined a society of fellow countrymen who were raising money to establish a Welsh colony in Patagonia. "I am too old to go," he wrote.

Yet within a very short time after Powell's arrival, he was commenting on the state elections of 1855 and a year later was applying for his certificate of naturalization. He successfully welded the old and the new life, keeping his pride in his heritage, helping to start a language school and a church, and at the same time becoming a part of the mobile frontier society, adopting the local customs of changing jobs and speculating in land and mining claims.

Powell's chief reason for coming to America had been "much anxiety of mind about the prospects of my children." In 1882, writing home to Breconshire a year before his death, he was able to report that his oldest son had an eight-hundred-acre farm, a second son "has been an expert in obtaining cheap land to raise sheep," a third was a lawyer in San Francisco, and a fourth a doctor in Marysville.[3]

The Irish in California were the largest, and in many ways the most successful, group from the British Isles. Though some of the immigrants settled on farms, the majority congregated in the cities, particularly San Francisco, where they formed a solid nucleus of workingmen out of which would emerge the leaders of the labor union movement which had its origin in that city. Some of those who had fled from starvation never moved beyond the shanties on Telegraph Hill where they lived, surrounded by "the crooning and keening of women still mindful of famine, civil rebellion and death."[4] In 1895 an observer contrasted the lot of the proportionately large number of Irishwomen discovered in an almshouse in the city with the careers of their more successful compatriots who "rise to thrift, competence, political power—even greatness."[5]

From the early years of statehood, Irishmen plunged

into the rough and tumble of public life and rose quickly to positions of leadership. With their talent for oratory and political organization, they achieved a celebrity which in the East would have required several generations. On the California frontier there was nothing comparable to the Boston Brahmin tradition to hold them back.

David C. Broderick brought his experience in Tammany Hall politics West with him and in the pre-Civil War era shared power in the state and in the Democratic party with his arch rival, William Gwin from Tennessee. Both men had come to California with the express purpose of being elected to the United States Senate. When Broderick died in a duel at the hand of one of Gwin's allies, he was hailed by his partisans, who hoped to play upon national sympathies, as a martyr for the Union.

John Mackay, James G. Fair, William S. O'Brien, and James C. Flood, who were known as the "Silver Kings" because of their successful, and occasionally nefarious, dealings in Comstock Lode mining stock, launched their partnership after O'Brien and Flood made use of the tips they heard from customers in the bar they operated. (In their time, saloon-keeping was a springboard into public life, while later generations of Irish descendents would serve their apprenticeship at St. Ignatius High School and the University of San Francisco.) After Flood had become a millionaire in short order, he followed the custom of the wealthy by building a mansion in the suburbs of the San Francisco peninsula, to the discomfiture of the "first families." Gertrude Atherton, who had married into one of the established clans, wrote, ". . . for weeks the leading topic on the verandah was whether or not the Floods should be called upon when they moved in." The consideration of "business reasons," urged by the husbands, proved stronger than social pretensions and visits were exchanged.[6] The "Irish four" were in competition for control of the Comstock mines with William Chapman Ralston and William

Sharon of the Bank of California, both of whom had estates nearby.

Conditions in that period were too constantly changing, with instant millionaires rising from humble origins and established financiers like Ralston plunging to disaster, to permit the evolution of an elite class on a par with New York's "Four Hundred." Richard Henry Dana reported that people who had come to the state before 1853 could join the Pioneer Society and become "antiquaries of a ten or twelve years' range." [7] Twenty-four Germans and several English-, Scottish-, and Irish-born citizens were included in a biographical volume on California's "representative men" in 1881.[8]

The French, too, were among the earlier immigrant settlers. Though engaged to some extent in farming, particularly in viticulture, and with the Basques in sheep-herding, they seem to have had more successful careers in the cities. Through their occupations, especially in merchandising and restaurant ownership, they maintained a strong national identity, which gave them a special distinction; they enjoyed a position of esteem as representatives of a country known for the cultivation of the amenities, particularly valued on a raw frontier.

A French immigrant in Los Angeles, where there was at one time a small *quartier* near Alison Street, said, "The best ambassadors that France has had in America are the chefs and the milliners." [9] Two Parisian-style department stores, the White House and the City of Paris, were the pride of San Francisco. In both cities the French built hospitals and established cultural societies.

The success of these first immigrants was demonstrated by a brief revival of anti-foreign sentiment in the mid-eighties, when a group which called itself the American Party asked for a repeal of the naturalization laws and a ban on alien ownership of land. Concern was expressed that foreigners had acquired large tracts of land—an

English syndicate in Fresno County and a German who had become a millionaire through transactions in San Francisco real estate were cited by a spokesman, who aroused fears that absentee landlords in London, Paris, Vienna, and Berlin might control land in California.[10]

The brief flurry of this successor to the Know-Nothing party was soon forgotten, however, while the contribution of alien artists and naturalists in immortalizing the beauty of the California landscape demonstrated that foreigners came to the state with motives that were not exclusively mercenary. The most influential of these was the Scottish-born John Muir, who made the Sierra Nevada range his home. As a young man in 1863 he had walked from Oakland to Gilroy, across the Pacheco Pass, on through the Central Valley, and into the Yosemite Valley, a transcendent experience. He never lost his religious awe of the grandeur of the mountains and devoted his life to recapturing it in prose and to campaigning to preserve the wilderness. In his book, *My First Summer in the Sierra*, he contrasted the impact on the environment of the Indians, who "walk softly and hurt the landscape hardly more than the birds and squirrels," with "the white man's marks made in a few feverish years." [11] He founded the Sierra Club in 1892 and with fellow conservationtists succeeded in preserving Yosemite as a permanent national park.

Muir's Scottish friend, William Keith, put his impressions of the Sierra onto canvas, as did the Westphalian artist Albert Bierstadt, whose paintings of Yosemite and other California views hang in the Oakland Museum. The fact that contemplative men were seeking out scenic grandeur in an area that had so recently been the scene of frenzied fortune-hunting marked a change in the life of the state, as did the progression by which the sons of the successful pioneers, including those of foreign birth, grew up to become philanthropists and civic leaders.[12]

The Second Wave of Immigrants

In California, as elsewhere, the status of the first wave of Europeans was improved when immigrants from Eastern and Southern Europe began to arrive in considerable numbers late in the century. This movement was encouraged by the Immigrants Union, organized by Leland Stanford, Mark Hopkins, and other prominent businessmen. They dispatched agents to Copenhagen, Bremen, and Hamburg, as well as to the eastern United States to stimulate the arrival of colonists to occupy state land that was newly accessible as the railroad built lines into hitherto isolated regions.[13] The California Labor and Employment Exchange was started by entrepreneurs in Sacramento and San Francisco to weaken the bargaining position of labor by encouraging new settlers to come and, also, to colonize land in the interior. This second wave of immigrants dispersed north from San Diego, with a concentration in Stockton, Sacramento, and San Francisco.

The San Joaquin Valley was described as a "laboratory of races," where colonists from Portugal, Germany, Syria, Denmark, Sweden, Armenia, Switzerland, Finland, and Italy tamed the former range land to field crops and orchards.[14] Cattlemen tried to frighten away a group of colonists, mainly of Scandinavian origin, who came to Fresno County in 1875 to grow grapes and figs. They were told the temperature rose to 130 degrees in the shade, that birds dropped from the heat of the sun, and that fruit, if it grew at all, baked on the trees! They were warned about "fever & ague," with some basis in fact, since malaria was endemic in the San Joaquin Valley, but the settlers refused to be discouraged.[15] A few early Dutch colonies failed when their members could not cultivate the hardpan soil they had chosen to farm, though one Hollander reclaimed several thousand acres in the Sacramento Delta by constructing a polder, copying a technique used in the Low Countries in Europe.[16]

On the delta there was ethnic diversity in agriculture; at one period the Portuguese grew most of the truck vegetables, Italians raised beans and barley, and Japanese and Chinese planted potatoes and onions. They lived on separate islands, and crops were rotated when the tenants changed. There were national specialties in other areas as well. Scandinavians, Swiss, Dutch, Greeks, and Portuguese from the Azores dominated the dairy industry. Italians, Yugoslavians, Armenians (and Japanese) went into fruit raising, viticulture, and truck farming. To some extent the immigrant groups were following traditional occupations, seeking a climate and a setting as much as possible like the home countryside. The California coast recalled the Adriatic to the Italian and Dalmatian fishermen who plied their boats out of the San Diego harbor alongside the tuna boats of the Portuguese from Madeira and Pico Islands. In San Francisco Bay, where the Italians used their *felluca* boats for crab fishing, the oystermen at one period were Swedish and the shrimp fishermen were Chinese.[17]

The new immigrants worked very hard. Khatchik Minasian, who grew up in Fresno with his cousin William Saroyan, labored every summer as a boy in the San Joaquin and Imperial valleys "picking grapes, turning grapes, making boxes, doing all kinds of menial labor long hours in the heat. This is what life was in the Valley for most of the Armenians—in fact, for most of the people who were willing to work." [18] Yet he has written poetry of singular gentleness,[19] just as William Saroyan in his books expressed joy in the rich variety of life, growing up amidst fields, orchards, animals, and eccentric relatives, though he recently confided that the only way he survived his boyhood was to turn it into a beautiful myth.[20]

Both boys were fatherless and Minasian's mother, after becoming a widow, worked in a fruit-packing shed, a com-

mon means among the immigrant wives of augmenting
meager incomes and an employment that was closely tied
to the orchards that occupied their men. The European-
born wives frequently put in twelve-hour working days,
whether in their own kitchens or in food-processing operations near home. They were not parlor ornaments, yet they
were highly prized because women were scarce in all the
nationality groups.

An old resident of the Danish colony of Santa Ynez
Valley recalled that "whenever a new girl came to Solvang
. . . all the bachelors fell all over each other trying to meet
her." [21] The story is told that curious neighbors called from
a distance to have a look at the wife of a wheat grower
because she was the first Portuguese woman in Tulare
County. Another Portuguese wife in the valley sent her
husband off to cultivate his fields of sweet potatoes, set
her bread to rise, and all alone and unassisted gave birth
to a girl child, an experience she took as a matter of course,
since the family lived too far away to call on the help of
neighbors.[22]

Many immigrants considered it mandatory to marry
within their own group. If suitable girls were in short supply in California, they might send for one from home after
an exchange of photographs and after formal arrangements
had been made between the families. The husband-to-be
usually paid for his bride's passage to America, sometimes
giving her an escape clause. If on arrival she changed her
mind about marrying him, she or her family could repay
him the money he had advanced. Usually the couples went
ahead with the match, weighing whatever disillusionment
they might experience at the first sight of each other against
the prospect of establishing a family with their own cultural
roots in the new land.

Many Greeks and Italians, whose motive for immigration was economic, came to California alone, expecting to
return home to marry or leaving their wives behind. The

Greeks tended to marry late, since the head of the household had to provide a dowry for his unmarried sisters before he could establish his own family. The result was that the wives were sometimes five, ten, or even fifteen years younger than their husbands. Some Greek immigrants never sent for their wives. The Greek Benevolent Society of Los Angeles paid the traveling expenses of a few men who wished to be repatriated.[23]

Immigrant remittances were constantly flowing to Europe. Thousands of dollars of carefully accumulated small savings were sent home each year from California to ease the lives of relatives, build up retirement capital in the old country or, as the new Americans put down roots, the money was used to bring over kinfolk to join them. It was generally assumed that they would be sheltered on their arrival until they became used to the new life. In the viewpoint of older people from small villages, America was a very hazardous place and they would need the protection of relatives. When a young man—who later lived in San Diego—left his native Dalmatia in 1906, his grandfather told him, "You must remember that you are going to a strange country which is ten times larger than Olib, and a land full of godless and dangerous people; so carry with you at all times a scapular around your neck and a knife in your pocket." [24]

The different nationality groups formed benevolent societies for aid and assistance at times of financial or family crises. A typical society for the Danes of California and Nevada had a sick-and-mortuary fund, an aid fund, and an old-age fund, to which members paid fifty cents six times a year.

In a rural Mennonite community in the San Joaquin Valley one man who owned three hundred acres of land helped his brethren with small interest-free, short-term loans so that they could make a down payment on land, pay medical bills, and cope with other emergencies. This leader, Alfred Koehn, kept a revolving fund going for eighteen years, assisting 183 families. When he reached the limits of his lending capacity, he signed notes at the bank for other families. He said, "As I prospered I reached out, sharing with other people." It is a Mennonite tradition that if newly arrived families are needy, the other members of the sect give them a grocery shower and collect furniture for them. Elderly people live in cottages near the church or, if they need care, at a nursing home erected by the membership.[25] The first Mennonite families had come to Merced County in 1911, and through intensive irrigation converted desert land into orchards. In the Livingston-Winton area they prospered and retained their customs among neighbors of many different racial and ethnic groups. While there has been some defection among the young people, the traditional rural orientation of the group helped to keep them together.

The availability of land in California was a means to prosperity for immigrants of European peasant origin, as demonstrated by the history of a group of Spaniards and Portuguese who arrived after the turn of the century "by the back door." They had originally left the Iberian Peninsula to become contract laborers on sugar plantations in Hawaii. After arriving on the West Coast, many of them worked as migrant agricultural laborers as well as in the canneries and packing sheds, traveling to Rio Vista for the asparagus season and back to the Santa Clara Valley, where they were able to buy ranches and raise their own tree crops. With the enormous appreciation of land values they have achieved a modest prosperity. Other members of this group settled in Stockton, Vacaville, and in cities in the East Bay area near San Francisco.[26]

Italians, Yugoslavians, and Armenians have also climbed the ladder from farm labor to ranch ownership, in some instances with spectacular success. Members of these nationality groups have played an important role in the development of agribusiness in California. This has been a peculiarly New World development for men who were born, or whose fathers were born, on small survival farms in European villages where their forebears lived in feudal vassalage to a rich landlord. In the American West they found "the fulfillment of every peasant's dream," a place where "he who sows may expect to reap." [27] When they acquired land, they started with the frugal methods of the old country, thriftily saving their gains, building a nest egg.

A young Yugoslavian who arrived in San Francisco around the end of the last century was typical of this group in his attitude toward the land. Paul Mariani, at seventeen, followed his sweetheart to California, emigrating from a rocky island off the coast of Dalmatia, where, in his son's words, "There was hardly enough dirt for a family to survive on." Seeing miles and miles of rich earth in the Santa Clara Valley, his reaction was, "Whenever he had fifty cents, he put it down on a piece of land." Soon after he came to Cupertino in 1910, before he was able to invest in land himself, he began buying fruit crops—apricots, prunes, peaches, and pears—for drying, thus building up a business on faith and very little cash while the farmers trusted him over a bad year. He constructed the first dehydrator in the state, was the first to fly cherries East, and was the first to process soft prunes. "He built himself a very interesting empire with a third-grade education and a lot of native intelligence and sweat," said his son. The Yugoslavians who were buying land, growing soft fruit in the Santa Clara Valley and apples in the Pajaro Valley near Watsonville "worked like they were going to live forever and played like they were going to die tomorrow." They had come from a country where "if they had three acres of rock, that was something." [28]

The first small group of Armenians arrived in Fresno in 1885, the vanguard of the great number of refugees from the Turkish massacres, who by the early twenties made that city the largest Armenian center in the United States. On the surrounding ranches they grew pomegranates, figs, and raisin grapes, while the Italians developed truck crops, including their native eggplant and broccoli, in other parts of the state. The California soils and sun were congenial for the cultivation of these products of home.

For many years Italians have dominated the wine industry in California. The Italian Swiss Colony at Asti was formed in the 1880s by Andrea Sbarbaro and Pietro C. Rossi as a collectivist colony based on the theories of John Ruskin and Robert Owen. Louis Martini and the Mondavi family (Charles Krug Winery) have located vineyards in the Napa and Sonoma area, and Ernest and Julio Gallo produce wine grown from grapes in the San Joaquin Valley, in their output rivaling the Petri family.

The Gallo brothers and Louis Petri are typical of those successful Europeans who have converted to the California pattern of large land holdings, a carry-over from the days of the thousand-acre *ranchos*. The pioneers of giant corporation farming were two Italians, Mark J. Fontana and Joseph Di Giorgio. Fontana in 1889 founded the California Fruit Packing Corporation (Calpac), which was to become the largest fruit and vegetable canning enterprise in the world. With another immigrant from Ligurgia, Fontana produced canned goods under the brand name Marca del Monte, later shortened to Del Monte.

Joseph Di Giorgio came to California in the early years of the twentieth century after importing bananas on the East Coast. He purchased the Earl Fruit Company in 1910 and began to ship fruit East, starting a winery to process the grapes he could not ship. He then acquired a large tract of undeveloped land for about ninety dollars an acre near Bakersfield, the nucleus of an agricultural empire that eventually included holdings in several counties as well as in other states. Di Giorgio and his brother developed a complete operation from the field through all the stages of food processing. Their canned goods were packed under the S&W label. In 1939 Joseph Di Giorgio, testifying before a congressional committee, said: "There is a lot of labor propaganda in this part of the country that tries to make people believe that I am not a farmer. . . . I was born and raised on a farm. I came to this country when I was a young man about 14 years old and I worked for $8 a month. Even if I am the largest grower in the United States, I worked for it." [29]

A. P. Giannini, the founder of the Bank of America, was also a central figure in the development of agribusiness, and in his career he demonstrated a similar adaptation of European traditions to Western opportunities. He launched what has become the largest banking system in the world by conducting modest transactions with small investors. When he opened the doors of his Bank of Italy in 1904, he announced, "I'll start a clean bank, run for the little fellow." Heretofore, many banks in California had been tied to speculations in silver and gold mining.

Born in San Jose in 1870 to a farming family, Giannini grew up assisting his stepfather in produce merchandising, and while still a youth rubbed elbows with stevedores, farmers, and merchants of all nationalities. Following this apprenticeship, he began to lend money to growers.

At the time of San Francisco's earthquake and fire, Giannini piled the assets of his two-year-old bank—about three hundred thousand dollars—into two wagons under some crates of produce, and drove to the safety of his San Mateo home. But he was soon back in the city, conducting his business from a desk on the docks. Just before the turn of the century he had been instrumental in delivering the North Beach Italian district vote to help elect James Phelan as mayor when that reformer cut short the career of another son of Ireland, Chris ("Christ Himself") Buckley.[30]

Giannini became a power in California and in world bank-ing circles a quarter of a century later after a gubernatorial candidate he supported permitted the proliferation of branch banking in the state.

A winegrower explained Giannini's unique contribution: "Financing of agriculture was always thought of as a gamble. You name the family in agriculture north or south and it probably got its original financing from the Bank of America. . . . They would carry them over a bad year." [31] Now almost every small rural town in California has a branch of Giannini's bank. In communities near college campuses, however, they have been smashed and burned, and are now rebuilt like stone fortresses to withstand the attacks of disaffected young people who see them as a symbol of vested interests. As the world's largest agricul-tural lender, the Bank of America can exert a great in-fluence over the increasing industrialization of agriculture in California. A present-day successor to Giannini favors the expansion of giant agricultural corporations and the phasing out of "uneconomic" small farms. [32] Joseph Sartori and Andrea Sbarboro headed important banks in Cali-fornia, but most of the Italians in the state remained "little fellows." Some were stonecutters, others worked in the lumber business in Humboldt and Mendocino counties. There were small colonies of Italians in the Gold Rush country; some in Hornitos, where Domingo Ghirardelli, a forty-niner, had kept a store until he started the chocolate factory in San Francisco which is today a tourist attraction.

In the wake of ethnic rivalry with the Irish in the cities, an accommodation was worked out. A newspaper publisher in Los Angeles noted that "the Irish ditch-diggers were making a big fuss because all the Italians were coming into this country. But what did the Italians do? They only lifted the Irishmen out of the ditches and onto the police force." [33] In San Francisco members of the Catholic clergy, the fire department, and the police force have been predominantly Irish, while the later-arriving Italians developed a monopoly on garbage collection, which in Los Angles has been shared by several different racial and ethnic groups. The Irish dominated politics in San Francisco up until the turn of the century. More recently, other nationality groups, particularly Italians, have been equally important in the affairs of the city.

City life was sometimes difficult for new immigrants whose customs were radically different. In marked contrast to the ease of adjustment of the Mennonites in the San Joaquin Valley, another sectarian pacifist group, the Molokans, who fled from Russia and began settling on the West Coast in 1905, experienced great difficulty in making the transition from peasant life in Europe to existence as workingmen in California cities. They settled near Potrero Hill in San Francisco and in the Boyle Heights section of Los Angeles, where they remained unassimilated and out of harmony with their surroundings during their early years. Their sense of controlling their own lives was undermined by working for wages and buying food at a store instead of providing directly for their own subsistence by tilling the soil. Though no one interfered with their observances and they expressed gratitude that they did not have to produce a passport when leaving the city as they would have had to do in Russia, they felt that it was difficult to pass on their traditions to their children while surrounded on every side by alien influences. An elder mourned, "Our customs and city customs do not rhyme." [34]

Another entirely different group of Russians, the refugees from the tsarist era, began to arrive in the 1920s from France, Constantinople, and China, where they had fled from Siberia. Cultivated, many of them highly educated, they also settled in the cities, where their chief problem was in finding suitable employment. They had been army officers, lawyers, engineers, professors, members of the Imperial Opera Company, dancers, and actors in the

Imperial ballet, as well as members of the nobility with no particular occupation. In California they became janitors, elevator men, gardeners, shoemakers, and restaurant proprietors, though some of them continued to practice old professions or prepared themselves for new ones.[35]

Boris Shebeko, who arrived in the San Francisco Bay area in 1923 after a harrowing escape through China, took what jobs he could get in a pineapple packing house, a steel plant, a tannery, an ink factory, a cement plant, and on an automobile assembly line—each venture more discouraging than the last. He washed cars in a Southern Pacific Railroad yard with some former Russian generals who addressed each other as "Your Excellency" as they passed sandwiches back and forth at the lunch break. He concluded, "Life is impossible, absolutely impossible. I'm not going to stay in this country." But he was able to enroll at the University of California for training as an engineer, a favored occupation with Russian emigrés and their children.

Before they learned to speak English, some of the Russians in San Francisco moved close to the shops run by Polish Jews on Fillmore Street, in order to make their needs understood.[36] They have since dispersed throughout the city, though many are in the Richmond and Sunset districts.[37] In Southern California they settled mainly in Hollywood, where they were able to start retail businesses with a Russian flavor or where they found jobs in the motion picture industry. There is some similarity in the experience of the Russian intelligentsia and the French in California. Both have generally remained outside the large power struggles in the state in which other ethnic groups have taken leading roles; both have retained a distinctive cultural identity which is valued in social and artistic circles. The French also found a niche in the film studies as couturiers, hairdressers, fencing masters, and language teachers.[38]

Many of the management positions in the film industry

were filled by Jews—Samuel Goldwyn (Goldfish), Marcus Loew, Adolph Zukor, Lewis J. Selznick, William Fox, Louis B. Mayer, and Carl Laemmle—who had been jewelers, furriers, or garment manufacturers in the East. Some got their start in a business that became one of the most lucrative and influential in the nation by showing ten-minute reels in penny arcades. A recent study suggests that these men were successful because similar talents were required for mass-producing clothing and entertainment.[39]

Anti-Foreign Feeling

The film industry, where exotic antecedents and strange accents were valued, was a cosmopolitan world far removed from the Jewish colony in Boyle Heights and from the "foreign quarter" near the Macy Street School in Los Angeles where the poorer immigrants had crowded together at the time of the First World War.[40] The second generation of children growing up there was sensitive about the contrast between the culture of their parents and the American ways they observed outside the home. One of the Molokan girls said, "I don't blame any Americans for not wanting to get mixed up with a family like this." The girls with whom she worked "don't suspect that I am Russian. I never tell them about that." [41] Italian girls during the same period, though they did not repudiate their heritage, were disguising their names at work to avoid contemptuous slurs.[42] In 1910 about a third of the population of the city was foreign-born.

Even in San Francisco, where the immigrants and their descendents constituted over two-thirds of the population, and where different nationalities lived in separate areas of the city, children of foreign background were occasionally humiliated by their teachers.[43] At this period Stockton, Sacramento, and smaller valley towns had immigrant enclaves, while Fresno's population was one-half foreign-

born. It was reported that forty-eight different nationalities
had children in the city's schools. The Southern Pacific Railroad tracks constituted a racial "pale," with the immigrants
and dark-skinned groups living mainly on the west side of
the tracks; the Armenians were the first to break through
the barrier.[44]

The treatment of the Armenians in Fresno is an example of the nativist sentiment of the time before and
after World War I. In 1923 a young political refugee from
Turkish persecution wrote, "The Armenian immigrant is
here. He cannot go back to his native land. His homeland
is destroyed; his property gone; his relatives massacred. He
is going to stay here permanentÍy. . . . If that is the case,
then what are Americans going to do about it?" [45]

The Armenians, who were a proud people, had the
temerity to ignore the suggestions that they were not the
equals of their American-born neighbors. They were com-
petitive in business affairs and refused to be segregated to
a special neighborhood. A Fresno citizen complained to a
researcher, "They ought to be put in a part of town separated from us as the Russians and the Chinese who at least
are keeping their places." "They are the only foreigners . . .
who think they are as good as we are," said another commentator, while a third added, "My personal objection is
based on Anglo-Saxon prejudice (Nordic supremacy) to
people of another race." [46]

Though they were law-abiding, hard-working Christians
and imposed no moral or economic burden on their community, they were described in the most derogatory terms
by the Americans with whom they came in contact. In an-
alyzing this antipathy, which seemed to have so little basis
in behavioral or cultural differences, Richard La Piere, who
studied the relationships in the late twenties, suggested that
the previous experiences of the Armenian families had
conditioned them adversely. In a new setting the refugees
from horror at the hands of the Turks demonstrated "the

social anticipation of persecution which made, in time, for the very conditions, or somewhat similar ones, from which they were trying to escape." [47]

Armenians in Fresno were frequently compared to Jews in a disparaging way. Yet Jews, in fact, were integrated into the commercial and civic life of California communities from the early days. In clubs and social organizations little, if any, exclusion seems to have been practiced until a later generation.[48] Harriet Lane Levy, who grew up in San Francisco at 920 O'Farrell Street around the turn of the century, described the relationship between the Jews on the north side of the street and the Gentiles on the south side as "a pleasant dissociation . . . which no one wished to change." When in her teens, she was called upon to debate the question, "Are Jews Responsible for the Prejudices Against Them?" she answered, "I have never encountered prejudice against the Jews from without, only having observed the cleavage within the Jewish social body itself." She may have been particularly sensitive, because she was of Eastern European background, and Eastern European Jews were considered inferior to German Jews. "On the social counter, the price tag 'Polack' confessed second-class," she wrote. "No Baiern [Bavarian] marries a Pole unless he is *krumn* or *lahm* or *stumn* [crooked or lame or dumb]." [49]

French Jews, who were the elite in San Francisco, evidently felt some contempt for "Polacks." In a French history of the city, these immigrants from the Balkans were criticized for a lack of scruples and for the vulgarity of their women.[50]

The mistrust of foreigners recurred as a minor motif in the success story of European immigrants in California. A brief eruption of the Ku Klux Klan in various parts of the state in the 1920s revealed some of the issues that provoked native-born Americans to persecute aliens. The local Klans were not primarily concerned with racial minorities, but with Catholics and foreigners and those whose behavior violated current standards of public morality. In Western vigilante tradition, a Kern County chapter banished card-players, prostitutes, and others charged with "improper conduct." The most notorious action in Los Angeles was the "Inglewood Affair" of April 22, 1922, which involved a raid on the home of two brothers of "Spanish descent" accused of being bootleggers.[51]

The Eighteenth Amendment opened an area of conflict between the "drys," characteristically white Anglo-Saxon Protestants, and Europeans, to whom a ban on alcoholic consumption was incomprehensible. "Prohibition was a catastrophe, a disaster," said the Napa Valley winemaker, Louis Martini.[52] California wineries survived the era by diverting grapes to other uses, one of which was to sell them to people who made their own wine at home. Distinct from those citizens who disregarded the law, more or less with impunity, were a profiteering group of rumrunners and operators of clandestine stills who were of various nationalities. The Elduyan brothers of Inglewood were commanded by the Klan raiders to cease bootlegging and go back to farming.

The most memorable part of the affair, however, was the fact that a number of prominent local citizens were discovered beneath the white robes and hoods. This should not have been surprising in an era and a place where the average resident was "an aggressive Puritan," to quote Bruce Bliven,[53] who had found several hundred thousand former fellow Iowans in Southern California.

The Klan platform coincided with the doctrine of Americanism which enjoyed a vogue nationwide in the post-World War I era, when public opinion had turned against experiments abroad. The emphasis on "the limitation of foreign immigration" and the denouncement of "unwarranted strikes by foreign labor agitators" [54] may have been inspired by the reaction throughout the state to a series of dynamitings and bombings in public places during labor strife in which innocent people had been killed.

Anti-alien sentiment had played a part in labor controversies in California ever since European immigrants and their descendents became leaders in the workingmen's battles for better conditions, particularly in San Francisco, where the most successful union organizing took place. From Denis Kearney, whose activities will be treated in the next chapter, to Thomas J. Mooney, who was imprisoned for twenty-three years on a charge of complicity in a Preparedness Day Parade bombing in 1916, Irish names have predominated in the state's labor history. Frank Roney, who dominated the labor movement from 1881-1886, had taken part in the Fenian uprising before immigrating to California. He was succeeded in San Francisco by Alfred Fuhrman, one of the labor leaders who emerged from other nationality groups.

A Norwegian, Andrew Furuseth, as head of the Sailors' Union of the Pacific, was instrumental in correcting flagrant abuses in hiring practices and shipboard treatment. In the early days San Francisco's waterfront lodging houses were run by crimps who victimized the seamen who fell into their clutches. The crimp advanced credit to the seaman in port and acted as a middleman in arranging his next berth. The shanghaiing of sailors—who were dumped, drugged and bloodied—aboard ships was a fairly common practice until after the turn of the century. If the seaman wanted to quit, he was charged with desertion. Despite the federal laws against flogging, he was liable to physical abuse aboard ship. Furuseth is credited with instigating the reforms embodied in the La Follette Seaman's Act of 1915, which helped to break the power of the crimps and the tyranny of ships' officers.

These benefits were won after a period of strikes on the waterfront in which violence had erupted—the sort of unrest that would reoccur when another immigrant, the

Australian-born Harry Bridges, as head of the West Coast Longshoremen's and Warehousemen's Union, succeeded in organizing union-controlled hiring halls, despite continued efforts to deport him.

But in the post-World War I period there existed a more profound antiforeign prejudice, which was not provoked solely by external events, such as labor unrest, but was absorbed unthinkingly by the average American. As the early observers had judged the Indian and Hispanic societies of California with unselfconscious, unquestioning belief in the superiority of Anglo-Saxon standards, later commentators expressed the implicit judgment that Nordic peoples were of a higher order than others. The San Francisco-born novelist Jack London, a proclaimed socialist and passionate spokesman for the working class, paradoxically created heroes patterned on the Nietzschean ideal of the blond conqueror,[55] writing disdainfully of the "mongrel-bloods" of Southern and Eastern Europe. Most readers of his era would have accepted this view uncritically. Nativism was a doctrine that was subscribed to proudly by those who felt themselves to be among the elect. Its chief victims on the West Coast were not Europeans, however, but those who came from a different quarter of the globe.

1. Carey McWilliams, *California: The Great Exception* (New York: Current Books, Inc., 1949), p. 97.

2. Dorothea Jean Paule, "The German Settlement at Anaheim" (M.A. thesis, University of Southern California, Los Angeles, 1953).

3. *Diary of William Powell,* entries of April 30, July 12, July 19, July 28, August 1, August 19, September 5, 1855; January 6, October 13, 1856; January 20, 1858; letter dated November 12, 1882.

4. Quoted in James O. Clifford, "Irish Had Tough Going in Early California Economy," Palo Alto *Times,* September 9, 1972.

5. Mary Roberts (Coolidge) Smith, *Almshouse Women* (Boston: W. J. Schofield, 1895), p. 14.

6. Gertrude Atherton, *Adventures of a Novelist,* p. 63.

7. Dana, *Two Years Before the Mast and Twenty-Four Years After,* p. 401.

8. Alonzo Phelps, *Contemporary Biography of California's Representative Men* (San Francisco: A. L. Bancroft, 1881).

9. Mildred Stella Rubin, "The French in Los Angeles: A Study of a Transplanted Culture" (M.A. thesis, University of Southern California, Los Angeles, 1936), p. 31. (Translation.)

10. "Declaration of Principles of the American Party," in speech delivered by Hon. P. D. Wigginton, Fresno City, May 27, 1886 (Roy J. Woodward Memorial Library of Californiana, California State University, Fresno).

11. John Muir, *My First Summer in the Sierra* (Boston: Houghton Mifflin, 1911), pp. 54-55.

12. In the stormy politics of the earthquake era in San Francisco, Rudolph Spreckels, the son of the "Sugar King," allied himself in a reform movement with another wealthy and independent man, former mayor James D. Phelan, of Irish ancestry. They were bent on exposing the corruption of the city administration under the current Irish-German mayor, Eugene Schmitz, and his mentor, "Boss" Abraham Ruef, whose family were French Jews. These collaborators used their ethnic ties—Schmitz in seeking votes among San Francisco's German and Irish population, and Ruef by advertising his services as a lawyer in the French press.

13. For pro and con discussions of the Immigrants Union, see *Appendix to the Journal of the Senate and Assembly*, vol. 3, 19th Sess., 1872, pp. 1-5, 24, 42-48.

14. Wallace Smith, *Garden of the Sun: A History of the San Joaquin Valley 1772-1939* (Los Angeles: Lymanhouse, 1939), pp. 412-446; Virginia E. Thickens, "Pioneer Agricultural Colonies in Fresno County," *California Historical Society Quarterly*, vol. 25, March 1946.

15. Thickens, "Pioneer Agricultural Colonies in Fresno County."

16. Henry S. Lucas, *Netherlanders in America* (Ann Arbor: University of Michigan Press, 1955), p. 393.

17. "Commonwealth Club Tenancy Studies, April–June 1922," reported by R. E. Adams, *Survey of Race Relations: A Canadian-American Study of the Oriental on the Pacific Coast, 1920 ff.*, Ray Lyman Wilbur Papers, Hoover Institution Archives, Stanford, Calif.; William Figari, "San Francisco Bay and Waterfront, 1900-1965," tape-recorded interview conducted by Ruth Teiser (University of California, Bancroft Library Regional Oral History Office, Berkeley, 1969), p. 8.

18. Interview with Khatchik Minasian, Palo Alto, Calif., May 5, 1970.

19. David Kherdian and James Baloian, eds., *Down at the Santa Fe Depot: 20 Fresno Poets* (Fresno, Calif.: Giligia Press, 1970), pp. 103-107.

20. Peter Collier, "I'm the Same, but Different," *The New York Times Book Review*, April 12, 1972.

21. Margaret Wulfe's reminiscences, *Santa Ynez Valley News*, September 22, 1961.

22. This pioneer woman died at the age of eighty-four in 1970. From an interview with Mrs. John Sequeira, Livingston, Calif., February 24, 1970.

23. Mary Antoniou, "Welfare Activities among the Greek People in Los Angeles" (M.A. thesis, University of Southern California, Los Angeles, 1939), p. 79.

24. Gerald Gilbert Govorchin, *Americans from Yugoslavia* (Gainesville: University of Florida Press, 1961), p. 54.

25. Interview with Alfred Koehn, Livingston, Calif., February 24, 1970.

26. Interview with Mrs. Josephine Monge-Rodriques, Sunnyvale, Calif., June 29, 1972; interview with Gerald Fernandez, Sunnyvale, Calif., August 30, 1972; Gerald Fernandez, "By the Back Door," (California History Center, De Anza College, Cupertino, Calif.)

27. Angelo Pellegrini, *Americans by Choice* (New York: Macmillan Co., 1956), p. 140.

28. Interview with Paul Mariani, Jr., Los Altos, Calif., May 3, 1972.

29. Andrew Rolle, *The Immigrant Upraised: Italian Adventurers and Colonists in an Expanding America* (Norman: University of Oklahoma Press, 1968), pp. 273-274; Hans C. Palmer, "Italian Immigration and the Development of California Agriculture" (Ph.D. thesis, University of California, Berkeley, 1965); *Violations of Free Speech and Rights of Labor*, hearings before a subcommittee of the Committee on Education and Labor, United States Senate, 76th Congress, 2nd Sess., San Francisco, Calif., December 14, 1939, p. 17658.

30. Julian Dana, *A. P. Giannini: Giant in the West* (New York: Prentice-Hall, 1947), pp. 40-44, 54-55.

31. Louis A. Petri, "The Petri Family in the Wine Industry," typed manuscript of a tape-recorded interview conducted by Ruth Teiser (University of California, Bancroft Library Regional Oral History Office, Berkeley, 1971), p. 45.

32. Rudolph A. Peterson, speaking before the California Canners and Growers, San Francisco, November 25, 1968, *California Farmer Consumer Reporter*, December 1968.

33. Interview with T. M. McClennan, publisher of the Los Angeles *Ledger*, July 1924, *Survey of Race Relations*.

34. Pauline Vislick-Young, "Assimilation Problems of Russian Molokans in Los Angeles" (Ph.D. thesis, University of Southern California, Los Angeles, 1930), p. 90.

35. George M. Day, *The Russians in Hollywood: A Study in Cul-*

ture Conflict (Los Angeles: University of Southern California Press, 1934), p. 14.

36. Boris Shebeko, "Russian Civil War, 1918-1922 and Emigration," typed manuscript of a tape-recorded interview conducted by Richard A. Pierce (University of California, Bancroft Library Regional Oral History Office, Berkeley, 1961), pp. 252-260 *passim*.

37. Jon Stewart, "The Largest Russian Colony in America and How It Grew," *San Francisco,* vol. 14, no. 1, January 1972.

38. Rubin, "The French in Los Angeles," p. 31.

39. Max Vorspan and Lloyd P. Gartner, *History of the Jews of Los Angeles* (San Marino, Calif.: The Huntington Library, 1970), p. 133.

40. 1917 Report of the California Commission of Immigration and Housing, cited in Olive Putnam Kirschner, "The Italians in Los Angeles" (M.A. thesis, University of Southern California, Los Angeles, 1920), p. 8.

41. "Jennie's Story," *Survey of Race Relations.*

42. Kirschner, "The Italians in Los Angeles," p. 20.

43. Kathryn Forbes, *Mama's Bank Account* (New York: Harcourt, Brace, 1943), pp. 51-59.

44. *Survey of Race Relations.*

45. Aram Serkis Yeretzian, "A History of Armenian Immigration to America with Special Reference to Conditions in Los Angeles" (M.A. thesis, University of Southern California, Los Angeles, 1923), p. 95.

46. Richard Tracy La Piere, "The Armenian Colony in Fresno County, California: A Study in Social Psychology" (Ph.D. thesis, Stanford University, Stanford, Calif., 1930), pp. 342, 346.

49. Harriet Lane Levy, *920 O'Farrell Street* (Garden City, N.Y.:

48. Newmark, *Sixty Years in Southern California,* p. 383.

49. Harriet Lane Levy, *920 O'Farrell Street* (Garden City, N.Y.: Doubleday, 1947), pp. 16, 130, 212.

50. Kahn, Jules, *Histoire de San Francisco, 1776-1906* (Paris: Editions Sansot, 1927), p. 178.

51. Robert Lee Salley, "Activities of the Knights of the Ku Klux Klan in Southern California, 1921–1925" (M.A. thesis, University of Southern California, Los Angeles, 1963), pp. 13, 14, 15, 89, 90.

52. Pellegrini, *Americans by Choice,* p. 52.

53. Bruce Bliven, "Los Angeles, the City That Is Bacchanalian— in a Nice Way," *New Republic,* July 13, 1927.

54. As printed in the *Sacramento Union,* April 29, 1922, quoted in Salley, "Knights of the Ku Klux Klan," p. 60.

55. Philip S. Foner, *Jack London: American Rebel* (New York: Citadel Press, 1947), pp. 34-36.

5
Immigrants from Asia

✦

THERE ARE SOME SIMILARITIES in the experience of the Europeans and immigrants of other races, but in general the darker-skinned newcomers from Asia and Mexico began their lives in California at the lowest rung of the social and economic ladder and had more difficulty climbing upward. They played a major role in the development of the state, not individually, but as gangs of faceless men who arrived at a period of rapid industrial and agricultural expansion to build the railroads, contour the land, and harvest the crops. Regarded by employers as a useful source of cheap labor, they were resented by white workingmen, particularly those from other immigrant groups with whom they competed for jobs.

They accepted a *peon* status because they came to California with the intention of returning home with whatever money they could accumulate. Though opportunities were better than in their own countries, for the most part they were not planning to stay and were willing to live frugally in order to help support the families they had left behind. In their position as sojourners they had little recourse to the institutions that protected citizens, and were vulnerable to the attacks of various groups in the society. When they were no longer wanted, laws were enacted to restrict their immigration and those who did remain were prevented from enjoying the rights guaranteed to other immigrant people in the state.

The Chinese, as the largest racial minority up until the Chinese Exclusion Act of 1882, set the pattern for interaction between Caucasians and nonwhites in the labor market. In these relationships economic considerations were as important as racial differences. At first the Chinese excited only interest and amusement. Their appearance to the Western eye was more foreign than that of any of the other nationalities who arrived during the Gold Rush. Their "yellow" complexions were noted and their slanted eyes "most unexceptionably turned up at an angle of about forty-five degrees." [1] The costume of the men, usually consisting of blue trousers and loose blouses, broad-brimmed hats, with long hair queues hanging down behind, seemed as exotic as their speech was unintelligible. They were regarded as curiosities rather than as human beings.

This stereotyping had the effect of isolating them and exposing them to shifts in public opinion. The amused tolerance accorded the first "Celestials" who appeared on the streets of San Francisco gave way to hatred and fear when Chinese workers became pawns in the struggle between employers and organized labor. It was then that their peculiarities were pointed out with alarm. The habits and customs that set them apart from the rest of the community were discovered to be sinister and contaminating. The racial antipathy was a corollary of the feeling against them as competitors.

In an earlier chapter we noted the treatment of Chinese in the mining camps as reflection of both the nativist spirit and the resentment among the groups of independent miners of "hired serfs." The Chinese who were banished to picked-over diggings and forced to pay a foreign miners' tax were immigrants who had put themselves under a labor contract in order to have their passage paid to California.

There were precedents for this sort of arrangement in earlier eras. Before the American Revolution, impoverished Englishmen had worked off their passage to the colonies as indentured servants. Later immigrants from Europe and the Middle East would employ a similar system: Syrians supplying fellow-countrymen with peddler's equipment; Greek owners of shoeshine parlors bringing over young boys to work for them; Italians assuming the role of *padrones* over men recruited in villages in the old country. The 1864 federal law which permitted contract labor was revoked by the Foran Act of 1885. However, the practice has continued in California in one form or another, openly or clandestinely, up until the present day.

In 1848, before the first Constitutional Convention met in Monterey and when there were only a few Chinese merchants in San Francisco, a correspondent opposed to the importation of black slaves to California wrote to a newspaper in that city: "If white labor is too high for agriculture, laborers on contract may be brought from China, or elsewhere, who if well treated will work faithfully for low wages." [2] Governor John McDougal, in his annual message to the legislature in January 1852, favored the settlement of Chinese to reclaim the tule lands of the San Joaquin Valley. He spoke of them as "one of the most worthy classes of our newly adopted citizens—to whom the climate and character of these lands are peculiarly suited." [3] Twenty thousand Chinese arrived in California in that year.

A bill introduced in the legislature to enforce contracts made outside the state had the purpose of encouraging Chinese importation and excited much debate before it was defeated. One of its critics favored allowing the Chinese to engage in such enterprises as draining swamps, cultivating rice, raising silk, and planting tea, but opposed their competition in the "free labor market." [4] In the decades to come this note of alarm swelled to a chorus as thousands more Chinese were brought in for work which their employers claimed no white man would accept.

The Chinese question was argued with particular heat in California, as the chief port of entry and the gathering place for the shiploads of immigrants brought from the Far East, but anti-Chinese demonstrations occurred in other parts of the country as well when contract workers were sent out to meet regional demands for cheap labor or to act as strikebreakers.[5] The agitation at first developed along class lines.[6] Employers favored the importation of Chinese, as did the diplomats concerned with international amity. The United States was anxious to continue the remunerative trade with China which had been opened by negotiation in the 1840s. The attitude of many Californians and others who feared an inundation of "Mongolians" was expressed in an early legislative report, "We want the Chinese *trade*, but we do not want her surplus *population*." [7]

Conditions in Asia contributed to this movement of people. Natural disasters and political unrest in the southeastern Kwangtung provinces had uprooted young and old alike. Men who were unable to eke out a living in their depressed villages crowded into the port cities to create an available labor pool for the foreign shipowners and for Chinese crimps who were looking for workers to send abroad. Kidnapping, coercion, and slavery were employed in the traffic of human beings to Southeast Asia, Cuba, and South America, and in a scheme to import replacements for the freed slaves on plantations in the American southern states.[8]

On the other hand, the men who went to California generally were not forced against their will, but came by a credit-ticket system. Their fare was advanced by associations of kinsmen. Frequently, merchants who had prospered during the Gold Rush, when ships from Chinese ports had supplied San Francisco, would recruit young men from their native villages or men who had taken refuge in Canton, Hong Kong, or Macao. Transporting them was a profitable enterprise. A Sacramento newspaper carried a story about a ship arriving from Hong Kong with 369 passengers whose fare brought in forty thousand dollars and who were fed en route on the ninety-day voyage for $4.83 apiece.[9] Clipper ships owned by Americans, British, Dutch, and Chinese made the voyage from Hong Kong carrying up to five hundred passengers who paid an average of fifty dollars each for a voyage usually lasting two months that was passed below decks in closely confined quarters.[10]

On their arrival in California the immigrants would be met at the dock, taken to a hostel run by one of the Chinese associations, and supported until they went out to work, their indebtedness charged against their wages. Unlike the coolie laborers in the West Indies and South America, whose services were sold by the brokers, the immigrant to California might choose his employer as long as he paid off his obligations.

In fact, the laborer usually found employment through the association which had sponsored him, and he was closely controlled by the groups that made his immigration possible.[11] He accepted his position in a hierarchical structure that was familiar to him. The powerful *hui kuan* was a New World adaptation of Chinese institutions based on clan and district origin in the home country where, by tradition, the individual played a subordinate role in relation to his family or village. He was accustomed to being represented by a geographical or tribal group to which he gave up a certain amount of autonomy in exchange for protection.

His motive in emigrating was to support his family, which he could not do at home. He hoped to pay off his indenture, acquire enough money to send home, and eventually return himself to live a life of ease and honor. Before leaving for overseas he may have obeyed a family edict to choose a wife who would remain at home to look after his parents while he made a pledge to send remittances to help them. The associations in California would see that he fulfilled his promise. They might require him to pay initiation fees, building assessments, legal fees for representation to the American agencies and, finally, bones fees so that his remains could be shipped back to China if he were unable to make the return voyage during his lifetime. The merchant authorities could refuse him a passport to go home if he had not taken care of his obligations.

He was willing to submit to their edicts because, as a temporary resident, he needed their services. Both in outlying communities and in the larger cities of California, the district or clan associations acted as bankers, lending agencies, employment offices; they built joss houses for worship and provided social centers. The opium parlors, gambling houses, and brothels run by Chinese secret societies diverted the lonely exiles and gave them a brief respite from daily drudgery, but also increased their debt bondage.[12]

In the absence of consular representatives, the chief merchants who were the leaders in Chinese California enjoyed a prestige accorded mandarins in China.[13] Often they lived in anonymous splendor, entertaining key personages at magnificent banquets or traveling abroad in luxury. They preferred behind-the-scenes maneuvering and private negotiations with trusted lawyers who represented their interests to public notoriety. Occasionally the internecine warfare between rival groups or the aggressions of secret societies (tongs) that challenged the power structure demanded the intervention of American law enforcement agencies.[14] For the most part, however, the California courts and police did not interfere with the internal activities of the Chinese community unless Americans were involved. The Chinese, as aliens ineligible for citizenship, had few civil rights and, indeed, did not ask for these rights. Men who were primarily dedicated to working for the welfare of their distant families were willing to put up with abuses, as the early Protestant missionaries, who tried to move the Chinese into the American mainstream, discovered. The laborers were not generally interested in becoming Americanized, though a few were glad to be offered the opportunity to learn English. They did not lose their thralldom to the hierarchy that controlled their migration unless they cut themselves off from Chinese enclaves and even from their family ties (since their families were in effect hostages), and few were willing to do this.

Most of the movement of the Chinese workers was controlled by the associations as intermediaries in the labor market. Many stayed on in the mining areas in the Sierra, patiently sifting the debris left by the departed white adventurers and then following whites to new mining frontiers in Oregon, British Columbia, and eastward to the Rockies. Their presence as a majority in any mining area was a sign that it was on the decline, for they seem to have been the scavengers of the picked-over claims that others left.

This patient burrowing in the earth was put to use in another project. More than ten thousand Chinese were recruited or especially imported to lay the track for the Central Pacific Railroad that was being built eastward from Sacramento in the late sixties in furious competition with the Union Pacific, which had gangs of Irish laborers working west from Omaha. Charles Crocker, one of the "Big Four" who controlled the Central Pacific, a man six feet tall and weighing 260 pounds, urged the experiment of hiring 110-pound Chinese for the pick-and-shovel and earth-moving work after he discovered that the Caucasian hands he had hired were only interested in taking a free ride down the track to get to the Washoe silver mines.

His army of Chinese workers fulfilled his boast that since their ancestors had built the Great Wall of China, they could construct a roadbed across a seemingly impenetrable barricade of mountains to the desert in Utah.

The difficulties were enormous, particularly in the Sierra peaks in winter, where snowsheds had to be built to keep the tracks from being buried. Drilling through granite to bore a tunnel at the summit, the workers progressed less than a foot a day, but during the final spurt—six years after the first construction had begun—when they were rushing toward Salt Lake City to meet the Union Pacific, they were averaging a mile of track a day. Crocker drove them onward. "I used to go up and down that road," he said, "and went backwards and forwards . . . like a wild bull, and everybody was afraid of me. . . . The only way to do was to rule them with an iron hand." [15]

The Chinese gave him little trouble. A group once conducted a strike for a twelve-hour working day and forty dollars a month, but backed down when threatened with the loss of their jobs. Labor contractors who were American or Chinese merchants deducted the supplies they brought to them from the wages paid in coin—an efficient system praised by Leland Stanford, the president of the Central Pacific, who denied charges that "Crocker's pets," as they were called, were held in a state of virtual slavery.[16] The Chinese brought their own cooks and performed this feat of building a railroad across some of the world's most formidable obstacles on a diet chiefly of dried fish, rice, and tea. They also used some of their own equipment and methods, such as hanging from wicker baskets to chip ledges in the sheer vertical cliffs, and carrying the black powder used for blasting between bamboo poles. Many lost their lives in explosions of nitroglycerin; others died of over-exertion. As some fell by the wayside, temporarily or permanently, the contractors made sure that there was a sufficient labor pool so that another crew would be ready for the next shift.

At the completion of the project, when the two railroads met at Promontory, Utah, in May, 1869, "a picked squad of Chinese, their denim pantaloons and jackets newly scrubbed, their pigtails neatly braided and tied," [17] carried in the final rail and the ceremonial spikes and ties.* They went on to lay tracks in other parts of California when Crocker, Stanford, Huntington, and Hopkins created a network of rail lines north and south. At an 1876 ceremony at Newhall, commemorating the completion of the roadbed to Los Angeles, thousands of Chinese, according to one witness, "lined up on either side of the track, each at full attention and all presenting their—*shovels!* . . ." [19]

Reclamation work in the tideland areas of the San Joaquin Valley absorbed a smaller number of workers who did not, however, receive grants of land in exchange for draining the swamps, as Governor McDougal had suggested in 1852. A recent study documents their labor in the delta: "Using only shovels and wheelbarrows, working in waist-deep water, they dammed sloughs, cut drainage ditches, built floodgates and piled up levees. . . . Since wages were figured from the cubic yards of dirt moved, the bosses scrambled over the levees measuring the work completed. . . ." [20] Irish and Swedish workers were brought in to handle heavy horse-drawn scrapers. More permanent flood-resistant levees were later built with machinery, but again the Chinese were hired to do the handwork. [21] When they died on the job, their bodies were occasionally buried in the dikes, their skulls unearthed a century later. [22]

Some Chinese found in the Sacramento Delta a reminder of their native Pearl River Delta, and from the 1860s came there to pick fruit or raise potatoes or onions as tenants on land owned by Caucasians who were glad to have men of another race occupy the low country. (Chinese were considered to be not so susceptible to malaria as whites.) They

* At the 1969 centennial celebration on the same spot, Federal Transportation Secretary John Volpe angered the Chinese delegation by asking: "Who else but Americans could drill ten tunnels in mountains thirty feet deep in snow and who else but Americans could chisel through miles of solid granite?" Ms. March Fong, a California assemblywoman, sent a telegram to Volpe demanding that he publicly correct the record. [18]

occasionally worked on a partnership basis. Their sacks of potatoes were hauled down-river by steamer, the pilots often routing out a bunkhouse full of sleepy and half-clad Orientals in the middle of the night when they pulled up at a potato landing.[23] The Chinatowns that sprang up in the small river towns provided a community life of a sort for both the Chinese and for the transient laborers of Japanese, Filipino, and East Indian origin who came to work in the asparagus-growing enterprises after the turn of the century.[24]

However, most Chinese, though they had rural origins, tended to congregate in the cities of California where they found employment as vegetable and fish peddlers, in laundries, and as servants. A Chinese cook become almost a necessity for an affluent family as well as a requisite for any expedition organized for work or pleasure in the field. One of the earlier historians of the Chinese in California explained his usefulness: "He was a gap-filler, doing what no one else would do, or what remained undone, adapting himself to the white man's tastes, and slipping away, unprotestingly, to other tasks when the white man wanted his job." [25]

Friction developed, however, when Chinese workers began dominating cigar-making, shoemaking, and clothing manufacturing in San Francisco. When they went beyond service and domestic occupations or heavy construction work, they encroached on the interests of white workingmen. Because they were willing to labor long hours for low wages, businesses that employed them could undercut their competition by setting their prices low.

Some Easterners congratulated West Coast businessmen on importing a source of cheap labor that would not only enable them to develop the resources of the state but also undersell rivals in the marketplace. Others warned prospective settlers against coming West to compete with the Chinese. Californians were increasingly agitated about the problem. To pleas that their Sinophobia would injure trade with the Orient, they pointed out that the huge sum in remittances that the Chinese were sending home, allegedly running into millions of dollars, accounted for a considerable percentage of the American exports to China.[26]

Not only did their earnings not benefit the local economy, but the Chinese accepted a standard of living that Westerners would not tolerate. While their frugality, thrift, patience, and docility were praised by employers, Caucasian workingmen felt themselves at a disadvantage in relation to people who had so few wants and demanded so little. The Chinese did not bring over their families as did the other immigrants. Between 1850 and 1882 when 100,000 men arrived, only 8,848 women came to the United States.[27] Many of them were imported by the Chinese organizations as prostitutes.

Only a few years earlier women of other nationalities had arrived in California to fulfill the same function in the predominantly male Gold Rush society. The bordellos, gambling houses, and bars of San Francisco's Barbary Coast were perennially popular. Girls from different countries or races were grouped together and the clientele also tended to follow ethnic lines.[28] The continuous arrival of sailors and other adventurers kept alive the roistering spirit of the early years both in the Bay Area and other places, but the sentiment of the day increasingly idealized family life. Protestant ministers espoused the cause of respectable women. One of them said, "If a man cannot bring his family with him, let him remain where he is." [29] American and European settlers who did bring their families could not understand the resignation of the Chinese who would accept a lifetime's separation from their wives and children to stay on year after year as transients, as "strangers in the cities," in the words of Stanford M. Lyman.

Their relationship to their organizations tended to keep them from direct contact with the larger society. Even those who went out into Caucasian homes as servants returned, when they could, to the familiar, protective atmosphere of the nearest Chinatown. There they lived within an ethnic enclave that was infrequently visited by outsiders. The few reporters who penetrated behind the storefronts and curio shops came back with stories of underground labyrinths that never saw the light of day; of dark, dank dormitory cells, where men slept in closely packed tiers of bunks and the sick were hidden from view. In such an atmosphere contagious diseases might fester and spread to areas beyond the ghetto, the visitors warned.

"Vice dens," which not only kept the Chinese in thrall but threatened the health and morals of whites, lay hidden behind many doors like some primordial evil. The Chinese narcotic, opium, which was permitted though heavily taxed in customs until 1909, seemed far more sinister to Americans than their own anodynes. The Oriental opium-smoker lay in a trancelike state, while the Western man who drank liquor acted out his feelings in a democratic, if often noisy and violent, fashion for all the world to see. The clandestine quality of Chinese enterprises frightened Californians. They suspected a decorous facade that disguised abuses. It was known that girls in Hong Kong and other cities were kidnapped or persuaded by false promises of marriage to come to America, where they were bought and sold for large sums into concubinage or prostitution. Unwary girls in the United States had also been lured to California by procurers to work as "servants" at fantastic wages, but this practice, though long-lived, never achieved the notoriety of the Chinese traffic in "slave girls." [30]

The public response was expressed in legislative proposals "for the suppression of Chinese houses of ill fame" (1866), "to restrict the importation of Chinese females" (1870), and "to prevent the importation of Chinese criminals and to prevent the establishment of Coolie slavery" (1870). An "Act to Protect Public Health from Infection

Caused by Exhumation and Removal of the Remains of Deceased Persons" challenged the Chinese custom of shipping the bones of the dead to the homeland. San Francisco introduced an act defining the border of Chinatown, a queue-cutting ordinance, and a "lodging house" ordinance which stipulated that each person in such a building must have five hundred cubic feet of air space.

Much of this legislation was unenforceable and met with passive resistance on the part of the victims, the Chinese crowding the jails more densely than their lodging houses, but it was symptomatic of the harassment which the group had to endure. A San Franciscan commented on the change of attitude in the city: "In 1852 the Chinaman was allowed to turn out and celebrate the Fourth of July and it was considered a happy thing. In 1862 they would have been mobbed. In 1872 they would have been burned at the stake. . . ." [31]

Though this interpretation of the current mood is no doubt exaggerated, the Chinese were frequently subjected to physical abuse. On the streets they were roughed up by roving bands of whites while the police looked on indifferently. Mark Twain claimed it was because of an impassioned article he wrote about such an incident—the stoning of a laundryman—that he was fired from a San Francisco newspaper. His crony, Bret Harte, published an essay entitled "John Chinaman" in the *Golden Era* of April 4, 1863, in which he denounced the "vulgar clamor about servile and degraded races." [32] The two contributed, however, to the popular caricature of the Chinese, which was to be sentimentalized later by Vachel Lindsay, when they collaborated on a stage adaptation of Harte's poem, "The Heathen Chinese." This poem about the wily Ah Sin, who beat a white miner in a card game, provoked such a widespread and "hilarious" reaction that President Ulysses S. Grant decided to omit a reference to Chinese immigration in a message to Congress. In the opening-night curtain speech, Mark Twain explained: "The Chinaman is going to become a very frequent spectacle all over America, by and by, and a difficult political problem, too. Therefore it seems well enough to let the public study him a little on the stage beforehand." [33]

Another author of the period observed the current prejudice with the impartial eyes of a foreigner. Crossing the country by railroad in 1879, Robert Louis Stevenson marveled at the stupidity of the behavior of "my fellow-Caucasians towards our companions in the Chinese car . . . . They seemed never to have looked at them, listened to them, or thought of them, but hated them *a priori*. The Mongols were their enemies in that cruel and treacherous battle-field of money." [34]

The decade of the 1870s saw the greatest outbreak of Sinophobia in California, partly as a result of conflicting national and regional enactments. New federal laws introduced after the Civil War were contrary to local discriminatory measures. The Civil Rights Act and the Fourteenth Amendment to the United States Constitution overturned the state ruling that Negroes, Indians, and Asians were not allowed to testify in cases involving white citizens. This was dropped from the California code in 1872. There was a strong regional reaction against the Burlingame Treaty negotiated between the United States and China in 1868, which recognized "the inalienable right of man to change his home . . . and the mutual advantage of the free migration and emigration of their citizens . . . for purposes of curiosity, of trade or as permanent residents" and pledged to immigrants "the same privileges, immunities and exemptions as citizens" except in the matter of naturalization. An anti-Chinese convention was held in San Francisco in 1870, and soon afterwards the Anti-Coolie Club agitated against the upsurge of immigration from the Far East which was occurring.

This was a peak period of arrivals from the Orient:

twenty-two thousand laborers disembarking in the single year 1876 contributed to a total of at least sixty thousand Chinese in the state. Nearly a third of them were crowded into an area of about nine blocks in San Francisco. The city was also a gathering place for workingmen of other races, many of whom were unemployed. Unfortunately, the increase in Chinese immigration coincided with a serious state-wide depression. As the jobless drifted in from the mines and other failing enterprises, San Francisco become, as one historian wrote, not a melting pot, but a pressure cooker.[35]

When the protestations of the Anti-Coolie Club provoked hoodlums into destroying some Chinese laundries and trying to burn the docks of the Pacific Mail Steamship Company, old members of the Vigilance Committee of 1856 mobilized again to prevent violence. This was interpreted as the alignment of merchants against the common people. The businessmen and "the great landowners" profited from Chinese immigration, said the workingmen, noting that a lobbyist who went to Washington represented both the Chinese Six Companies and the "agricultural interests." [36]

The discontent of the unemployed against this coalition crystallized in a movement to form a Workingmen's party, opposed to both "coolie labor" and corporations. The president of the new Party, Denis Kearney, a drayman from County Cork, aroused crowds in the sandlots of the city with his powerful oratory, proclaiming the slogans of the hour, "Four Dollars a Day and Roast Beef," "The Chinese Must Go!"

Kearney's two enemies lived not far apart: the mansions of the rich industrialists, including those of Stanford, Crocker, and Hopkins, looked down Sacramento Street onto the Chinese quarter below. On the night of October 29, 1877, Kearney gathered a crowd of more than a thousand followers on Nob Hill and denounced the abuses of the capitalists whose monuments lay all around.

Alarmed city officials voted through an ordinance against inciting to violence and for a brief time Kearney and some of his associates were arrested and jailed. But this only served to strengthen his following, for he was the spokesman for widespread discontent. The frustration of the unemployed workingmen who swelled the ranks of his party was somewhat appeased by success in municipal and state elections. As a result, many laws and ordinances were introduced to impose handicaps on Chinese enterprises in San Francisco, Los Angeles, and other cities. Special taxes were imposed on vegetable peddlers and laundrymen (tradesmen who carried their goods between poles or made deliveries without a horse or vehicle) and fishermen (those who cast shrimp nets). A blanket "police tax" was exacted of Chinese in non-mining, non-agricultural occupations. The victims responded by going on strike or assessing themselves for funds to challenge the laws in court, often successfully.[37]

Denis Kearney's group carried their concerns to the convention which was called in 1878 to write a new state constitution. By joining the farmers—who were fighting the railroads—against the lawyers and legislators who represented the businessmen and large landowners, the Workingmen's Party succeeded in writing into the document articles regulating the monopolistic practices of corporations, as well as discriminatory measures against the Chinese. The two were dealt with together. An article stated that Chinese could not be employed in any corporation or "on any State, county, municipal, or other public work, except in punishment for crime."[38] (Though later declared unconstitutional, the anti-Chinese rulings remained in the constitution until the 1950s.)

The following year a new section was added to the State Penal Code. It threatened a fine up to a thousand dollars and a jail sentence to any person who employed Chinese to work in a corporation, and a penalty up to five thousand dollars for a corporation that employed

Chinese; the first to forfeit its charter if it were found guilty twice.[39]

This ruling was later declared to be unconstitutional. Many of the "reforms" wrought by the coalition of farmers and workingmen, the economic boycott against the Chinese as well as the attempts to curb monopolistic practices of the Southern Pacific and other corporations, were eroded by later court decisions. The end of the convention marked the decline of the Workingmen's party. One of its constitutional enactments that had more lasting significance was the official sanction given to the cities and towns of the state "for the removal of Chinese without the limits of such cities and towns, or for their location within prescribed portions of those limits. . . ."[40]

Anti-Chinese agitation was an essential ingredient of the success of the short-lived Workingmen's party for the reason that its appeal was emotional and broad-based, touching groups that had no economic stake in the question. Henry George, who as a journalist in San Francisco enjoyed a ringside seat at all the spectacles of civic unrest, noted the provocative, anti-Chinese speeches of prominent men who were in the political camp opposite Kearney.[41] Among the virulent written attacks that appeared in book form were the following titles: *Chinese Immigration and the Physiological Causes of the Decay of a Nation* (1862), *The Chinese Invasion* (1873), and *Short and True History of the Taking of California and Oregon by the Chinese in the Year A.D. 1899* (1882).

Other ethnic groups besides the Irish joined in the popular outcry, "attempting to keep in step with the mood of the day," as a historian of the Italians described their role.[42] The Indians, like the Mexicans, had singled out Chinese miners in the goldfields for persecution.[43] Legislative enactments provoked by Indian-white conflict declined as anti-Chinese legislation consumed more hours of discussion and reams of paper in Sacramento.

Representatives of the black people, the minority race with the smallest number of individuals in the state at this time (about four thousand in 1860), seem to have had a mixed response to the Chinese. A reporter for *Frederick Douglass's Paper* denounced them, but Douglass himself was chiefly opposed to the system by which they were exploited as being too reminiscent of the condition of his own people in the South.[44] Among whites, also, the Chinese question had been compared to the slavery issue that divided the nation.

Eventually, the Sinophobia on the West Coast was heeded in Washington for practical reasons: in close elections California's vote was critical, and Californians endorsed the candidates who promised to help stop the flow of immigration from Hong Kong. In 1876 the Congress sent a special committee to San Francisco to make a study of Chinese immigration. The following year a new treaty was negotiated with China, permitting the United States to "regulate, limit, or suspend" the immigration of Chinese laborers. After the State Democratic Convention had passed a resolution in favor of limitation, the California governor called a statewide holiday on March 4, 1882, in order that each community should indicate its opinion. An earlier polling of the citizenry conducted by the legislature indicated overwhelming support of a ban.

President Chester Arthur responded by signing a bill that excluded Chinese laborers for ten years, but admitted merchants and professional men, and their families. The Chinese Exclusion Act of 1882 was renewed for another ten years in 1892 and again for an indefinite period in 1902. Its passage marked the first restriction imposed by the federal government on unlimited immigration to the United States.

During the period 1880 to 1882 the Chinese, fearing that a cutoff policy was imminent, entered in larger numbers than at any time in the previous thirty years. By the

1890s, however, the effect of the restriction was evident in the declining population. The original laborers, not permitted to bring their wives or to re-enter the country if they left, remained as single men or returned permanently to China. Illegal immigrants were smuggled in, but not in sufficient numbers to offset the total of those who were dying or departing. The effect of the exclusion law was to postpone still further Chinese family settlement and to encourage illicit practices which separated the Chinese ghettos from the daily life of the communities outside.

The Chinese could not vote (they could not become naturalized), yet at one time they were required to pay a poll tax. They were also assessed for roads and schools for which they had little need, yet they were generally unprotesting. In circumventing discriminatory rulings, they might use such tactics as noncompliance, boycott, bribery of officials, or taking the matter to court, but they were rarely aggressive. For if they defended themselves against physical attack or if Caucasians were accidentally hurt in altercations between Chinese, the retaliation was apt to be swift and violent. In Hornitos, in the mining country, a group of old-timers recollected that when some children tormented "a Chinaman . . . down in the creek," he lost his temper and hurt one of them. The townsfolk "put him in jail, and that night, some of the men in town . . . went and got the Chinaman to come to the window and they got hold of his queue and they just battered his brains out." [45] One of the worst mob actions against the Chinese occurred in Los Angeles in October 1871, after a quarrel between two factions in the Chinese quarter in the Calle de los Negros erupted into violence. When a white citizen was killed during the attempted arrest of the principals, a mob gathered and surrounded the block, pulling the men, women, and children from their hiding places in the building. They were kicked, beaten, and dragged with ropes "around the neck, just like animals." [46] Nineteen were killed. When the sheriff took away the survivors for safe-keeping, the crowd plundered the vacated buildings. Even in a town where in the early days homicide was almost a daily occurrence, this massacre was long remembered.

A similar triggering action, in which a white man was killed in the crossfire during a battle between rival tongs, resulted in the banishment of the Chinese from Humboldt County in 1885. The Oriental laborers had come north to engage in mining, fishing, railroad construction, and work in the canneries and logging camps. Citizen indigation mounted following the establishment in the Eureka Chinese quarter of brothels, gambling houses, and opium dens run by a criminal element who brandished firearms and failed to heed the orders of local lawmen that they should temper their quarrels. After the fatal shooting, all Chinese were given twenty-four hours to leave town. Three hundred people, including four merchants who had been in the city a decade, were loaded aboard two steamers and shipped to San Francisco. Only a few men, married to Indian women, who lived a three-days' distance on horseback from the coastal towns were not disturbed.

The merchants sued for their losses and property damage but Eureka was absolved of all charges by the courts. The rallying cry in the county became "The Chinese Must Never Return." Later attempts through the years to bring in Chinese laborers were checked—at times, forcibly. When two Japanese tried to start an art goods store in 1909, it was dynamited. As late as 1930 when the Japanese ambassador was touring the redwood country, he was met by a local delegation south of Garberville who escorted him to the Del Norte county line without allowing him to stop. A historian of the northern counties found that longtime residents attributed this anti-Oriental prejudice to the ingrown clannishness of the early lumbermen leaders, many of whom came from Nova Scotia.[47] In 1937 the *Humboldt Times* boasted: "Humboldt County has the unique distinc-

tion of being the only community in which there are no
Oriental colonies. . . ." A section of the Eureka city charter
of 1941 forbad Chinese employment and the sale of Chinese articles. This was revoked in the post-World War II
era, when a few Orientals came to settle without incident
in the county which had achieved an international reputa-
tion for its exclusion policy.[48]

Other towns in California followed the mandate of the
1879 constitution to banish the Chinese. The citizens of
Redding held an anti-Oriental meeting in January 1886.
They pledged "no trouble, no violence, no resistance, no
gore" and ordered the Chinese evicted.[49] Anti-Chinese riots
occurred sporadically over a period of thirty years in such
diverse places as Santa Ana, Martinez, Truckee, and Napa
as well as in cities of the Northwest and western Canada.[50]

In communities where the Chinese were permitted to
remain, they were generally relegated to their own ghettos.
San Francisco's Chinatown was at times literally sealed off
by health officers when there was a smallpox epidemic or
an outbreak of bubonic plague. White women and children
were indoctrinated to beware of contamination in that
sector. The earthquake of 1906 violently dislodged its residents, some of whom, it was popularly believed, had long
remained hidden from the light of day in their subter-
ranean cells. Like the other refugees from that April holocaust, they fled from the burning city with their possessions
stuffed into pillowcases. An observer who watched them
get off a train in Berkeley remembers "those poor Chinese
women with their 'lily feet' walking along as if they were
on stilts." Even in that time of emergency, other homeless
people objected to having the Chinese camp near them.[51]

As for the controversies within the enclave, the local
police continued to adopt a policy of noninterference unless
Caucasians were involved. In the isolation from the larger
society, there is some similarity between the tongs and the
operation of the *Comorro,* or *Mano Nera* (Black Hand),

an extortion ring run by a group of Neopolitans at the expense of prosperous members of the Italian colony in San Francisco around the turn of the century. The extortionists assumed, usually correctly, that their victims would not take their threats to the city police. It was a matter for Italians to settle among themselves.[52]

As the *Mano Nera* was an American adaptation of an Old World organization, so the Chinese tongs, which had carried on a type of guerrilla warfare against the government in China, changed their function in California to one of helping members of small clans to hold their own against the larger groups, occasionally employing "selective violence" as a method. "We call it murder," said a policeman in Los Angeles, "but they call it 'settling with the tong.'"[53]

Police in West Coast cities were reported to be inclined to ignore gambling and prostitution, both in the Chinese quarter and elsewhere in town. Some of them, it was suggested, were paid to look the other way, with the result that an indignant member of the clergy or a crusading editor might conduct an exposé or undertake to rescue the girls. Inspector John J. Manion of San Francisco, who was called "the Irish overlord of Chinatown," took credit for eliminating tong wars, gambling, opium dens, and "slave girls" during his years in the city.[54] He had the help of an intrepid Scottish lady named Donaldina Cameron, who worked under the aegis of the Presbyterian Church to free hapless prostitutes and abused children forced to labor as indentured servants. She conducted sudden raids, breaking down doors and escaping with her quarry before the outraged owners could protest the loss of their valuable property.[55] This was an ethnic conflict with deep cultural impications. The owners, feeling unjustly defrauded, appealed to the courts, usually in vain. American moral standards came down on the side of the rescued girls.

The woman believed to be the first second-generation

Chinese of her sex to vote in a presidential election, was, in 1910, given asylum by Miss Cameron at her mission home after she refused to go through with an arranged marriage planned by her family.[56] Despite missionary efforts, however, the isolation of West Coast Chinese broke down very slowly. The stereotypes which alarmed Caucasians were perpetuated for commercial profit. Chinatowns, one observer said, were "looked upon as a commercial asset—a sort of human zoo—which becomes a point of attraction for tourists." [57] Exhibits of opium-smoking became a popular publicity stunt, said a Chinese writer. When the old Chinatown in Los Angeles was razed to make way for Union Station, curious onlookers were disappointed that there seemed to have been no secret passages or underground cellars.[58] By this time the Chinese "menace" was receding and a new race of Orientals was agitating Californians.

The Japanese Arrive

The Japanese, who inherited the role and the prejudice accorded to the Chinese, were a small minority on the West Coast until the end of the nineteenth century. Like the Chinese, they had left their home villages in rural areas because of poverty and overcrowding. Young men, part of the "surplus population," had gone out in the late 1860s to work as contract laborers on the sugar plantations in Hawaii and some had come to the West Coast under the indenture system. A group of about 1500 students arrived to pursue their education in the United States, and some of these "schoolboys" supported themselves by domestic service. Most of the 17,700 Japanese who arrived between 1898 and 1900 were from farm families who had a certain amount of status in Japan—they were young, robust, trained to till the soil. Some of them were skilled fishermen. They arrived as independent workers, but unable to speak English. Intending to return home with the money they earned, they, like the Chinese, hired themselves out in gangs under bilingual bosses. The agitation that developed against them in San Francisco had a familiar aspect. When a group of fifteen were hired clandestinely to work as cobblers at depressed wages in a shoe factory, Caucasian union members discovered them and drove them from their benches. A Japanese restaurant was picketed by members of the cooks' and waiters' union. A new slogan, "Japs Must Go" was attributed to Dr. Charles O'Connell, who at the height of his activities with the Workingmen's party some years earlier had uncovered what he believed to be a case of leprosy in Chinatown and had driven the victim through the streets as a warning to the community. When bubonic plague broke out in Chinatown in 1900, a program was launched by the city to round up and inoculate all Asians, to the acute distress of the Japanese, who called on their government to intervene. At the meetings that were being held around this time to discuss the renewal of the Chinese Exclusion Act, resolutions against the Japanese were drafted, stating that "the assumed virtue of the Japanese—i.e., their partial adoption of American customs—makes them the more dangerous as competitors." [59]

In their response to the New World, the Japanese more closely resembled the European immigrants than other Asians. They soon left San Francisco to take the place of the Chinese in farm labor and other enterprises requiring gangs of men. However, they tended to be less inclined to accept the lower standards of wages and working conditions offered to nonwhites. When they occasionally called strikes or walked off the job, the surprised employers wistfully recalled the docile Chinese.

Many of the immigrants from Nippon were not content to remain indefinitely as field hands. Like the Europeans, they were attracted by the availability of land. They saved their wages, and by enterprise and self-denial began to buy or lease acreages, generally preferring to rent land since they did not intend to stay in the United States. They were willing to acquire plots that were too small or too difficult to interest other growers, applying methods of intensive cultivation learned in Japan where farms were subdivided between family members. Like the Armenians, Yugoslavians, and Italians, they introduced products from home to American soil, improvising techniques to meet the special problems of farming in the West. In some areas they had to use dynamite to blast holes in the hardpan earth before they could start orchards. In the semidesert country near Livingston, where some Japanese Christians formed an agricultural colony in 1906, they had to dig away the drifting sand that constantly threatened to bury seedling trees. They experimented with rice-growing (considered "not a white man's job") in Colusa County, and drained swamps in the San Joaquin Delta to create islands on which they planted potatoes. Here George Shima, who was called the "Potato King," developed such a successful enterprise that he brought over fellow-countrymen in considerable numbers to assist him.

Working with small allotments, the hard-working Issei (the first generation) brought a great quantity of unimproved land into cultivation. As they moved from farm labor to entrepreneurial status, they returned home to choose wives or sent for "picture brides" by mail, a method of courtship that was well adapted to the traditional system of arranged marriages. The husbands, who had had to wait to acquire a nest egg, were often considerably older than the kimono-clad girls who awaited them with their proxy marriage certificates at the immigration station. Once on American soil, the Japanese wife and the children she bore became laborers in the family business of farming enterprise. Caucasians were shocked that new mothers would get up soon after childbirth to go back to work, leaving the baby alone or carrying it with them to the fields. Their help was needed to achieve the margin of success which made it possible to work for oneself rather than for others.

The effort required to get ahead in America postponed the dream of returning to Japan. Though many of the Japanese immigrants remained bachelors and day laborers, those who had families and enjoyed the profits of their own labor had more of a stake in the new land than the Chinese. They also had closer ties with the home country through cultural and economic exchanges (children were often sent to Japan for education), and through the active intervention in their affairs of consular representatives and the Japanese Association, which had been created to be an intermediary at the time of the bubonic plague incident. West Coast racial discrimination toward the expatriates provoked a strong response from Japan, an aggressive world power, which served to convert local incidents into international crises. The actions of Japan, in turn, increased the prejudice against the Issei. They were seen as agents of the Japanese Imperial Government on American soil, and accusations about spying were relayed from the early years of their settlement.[60]

One of the first incidents in which the president of the United States was forced to intervene occurred soon after the San Francisco earthquake in 1906, when the corrupt city government tried to create a diversion from its own misdeeds by ruling that Japanese children, some of whom were overage for their classes, should be sent to a separate Oriental school. There had been no Asian segregation in the first city schools. In a group of seventy-five foreign pupils (among thirty-eight Americans) enrolled at the Happy Valley Free School which met in the chapel of the Howard Street Presbyterian Church in the 1850s, was one Chinese among children from England, Ireland, Scotland, Spain, Germany, and Chile, and a large contingent from Australia and New Zealand.[61] In 1854 the black community formed a separate school, also in a church building, with twenty-three students.

The Political Code of the state first stipulated that "the education of children of African descent and Indian children must be provided for in separate schools." [62] In 1872 blacks successfully petitioned the state supreme court to have their children admitted to the public schools. Later state laws gave school trustees "the power to exclude children of filthy or vicious habits, or children suffering from contagious or infectious diseases, and also to establish separate schools for children for Indian children and children of Mongolian or Chinese descent." [63] In 1902 the Chinese brought an unsuccessful suit to desegregate the schools throughout the state. Four years later, President Theodore Roosevelt arbitrated in the San Francisco case by negotiating a settlement with Japan. Through a Gentlemen's Agreement the distasteful ruling was abolished and in exchange for this concession, Japan agreed to restrict the emigration of laborers.

But soon the Imperial Government protested a much more serious act of discrimination against the Issei, aimed at curbing their competition in agriculture. Caucasian small farmers complained that the Japanese were taking away the best land and driving them out of business by unfair methods, working longer hours, living at a lower standard than white men could tolerate, and raising large families to help them take over yet more land. Like the Workingmen's denunciation of the Chinese, this cry of a threatened economic group won a sympathetic response from a cross-section of the population who believed that California was a racial frontier, a battleground between Oriental and Occidental.

Aside from the "invasion" of agricultural lands, the issue of racial purity was evoked. A spokesman for the California Progressive party, which was trying to surpass the Democrats in anti-Asian agitation, wrote: "Race . .

counts more than anything else in the world. It is the mark God placed on those whom he put asunder. It is grounded in the instincts of man, and is not amenable to reason . . . . So the line is biological, and we draw it at the biological point." He ventured the opinion that intermarriage between a Japanese and a white person would be a "a sort of international adultery." [64]

After the first California statute against miscegenation was passed in 1872, a judge testifying before a Congressional committee on Chinese immigration had given his opinion "that the Chinese are almost another species of the *genus homo*. I do not think they are another species, but they are a very wide variety. I think they vary so much [from the Aryan or European race] that the offspring of the Chinamen, united with the American race, would be infertile, or it would be imperfectly fertile." [65] Asians had intermarried with the native populations in other places where they had immigrated—Malaya, Borneo, the Philippines, Hawaii, Mexico, and Central America—but the "hybridization of races" was a spectre that continued to haunt Californians and was effectively utilized by special-interest groups who were promoting anti-Asian restrictions for other motives.

The politicians of the era, including Roosevelt and his later opponent, Woodrow Wilson, seem to have espoused an anti-Japanese stance for domestic consumption in California elections, while trying to forestall discriminatory legislation in the state that would call forth the anger of Japan or prevent the Panama-Pacific International Exposition from being held in San Francisco. [66] The United States had ventured into foreign affairs in the Pacific after the Spanish-American War and Roosevelt had acted as a mediator in the Russo-Japanese War. International relations might be undermined by West Coast actions against resident Asians.

Despite the interference of the federal government, the

California Legislature passed the Alien Land Law in 1913 which stipulated that only aliens eligible for citizenship could acquire, possess, enjoy, transmit, and inherit real property. Though Japanese were not mentioned, the intent of the new law was that they and other aliens who could not become naturalized, i.e., Asians, could not buy land or lease it for more than three years. A contemporary journalist who deplored what he called "Japanese agrarian aggression," wrote: "In vain for Exposition Directors to protest, in vain for Presidents to intervene. . . . When the issue was raised there were but five men in the whole Legislature who dared to go home to their constituents and say: *'The line was drawn between the white man and the brown and we voted for the brown.'* " [67]

Wilson's secretary of state, William Jennings Bryan, exchanged notes with Japan's outraged Count Chinda, attempting to allay the adverse effect of the regional action on the relations between the two countries. The Japanese Association in California tried to mollify the Californians' prejudice by making sure that the Issei were not an economic burden to their communities. The president of the Association wrote to President Wilson in 1919 that they were "advising" their members "as best we know how, not to work so hard as to cause their neighbors to criticize them, and to create some leisure for self-development." [68] Spokesmen for the Issei gave speeches and published tracts in their own defense and cultivated opinion-molders in their communities in an attempt to improve their group image.

But the restrictions imposed by the Alien Land Law forced them to fulfill the stereotype of the superefficient competitor. They had to work harder than ever to overcome the obstacles raised against their enterprise, controlling the marketing of their vegetables and fruits by cooperative arrangements between growers, wholesalers, and retailers which, to white rivals, "had many of the characteristics of a purposive economic grouping." [69] Loopholes in the 1913 law allowed them to expand by acquiring title to land through their American-born children or by forming corporations with Caucasians, of whom there were quite a number willing to be "front men" for prosperous Issei enterprises.

Plainly, the 1913 law was not as effective as its proponents had hoped it would be. In 1920 a public referendum was held on the question. After a strenuous campaign by rival candidates for the Senate, the Hearst newspapers, the American Legion, the State Grange, the Native Sons of the Golden West, and the California Federation of Labor, Californians voted three to one to tighten the restrictions of the Alien Land Law. All the states except Utah, where Japanese were engaged in agriculture, passed similar legislation.

The 1920 amendment was a severe blow to the Issei. Though they could own land through their citizen children, they were deprived of the use of more than 300,000 acres of leased land. To become sharecroppers or tenant farmers was a long step backwards. One of them wrote, "Materially and spiritually, the Japanese are, so to speak, sentenced to death by the land law, the enactment of which I regret for the United States as well. The Japanese are born expert in agricultural pursuits. If given full opportunity [they] would increase a great deal the wealth of California as well as of the United States. The progress of the Japanese farmers in this country is not for Japan but for the second and third generations." [70] A minority group of Caucasians, opposed to the ruling on the grounds that agriculture would suffer a setback if the Japanese farmers were prevented from having a financial interest in the crops they raised, were willing to help the Issei devise methods of continuing their entrepreneurship. Most of the Japanese stayed on the land, but some who had been fishermen in Japan resumed that career, moving to the fishing colony at Terminal

Island in East San Pedro, which was as isolated in its cultural life as a Japanese village, despite the competition of Italian and Dalmatian fishermen who lived nearby. Bills were introduced periodically in the legislature to prevent aliens ineligible for citizenship from fishing commercially. Rumors were circulated to the effect that the Issei were Japanese naval officers in disguise and that their boats were minelayers.

The Japanese managed to sidetract these laws through strenuous lobbying. Their leaders continued to counsel conciliation in the face of the puzzling behavior of antagonistic whites. In 1923 the president of the Japanese Association of Los Angeles advised "hardworking ladies" to avoid "improper attire or manners and displaying unwelcome old customs in the presence of Americans," and counseled their husbands to do their best "in keeping their premises always clean, and in keeping up good friendship with the American neighbors and even when there arises a misunderstanding, they must be always careful not to act foolishly out of their excitement. There is a marked tendency in Americans to do riotous things when excited and they are apt to do almost unreasonable things out of passion. It may be worthwhile to keep this particular fact always in mind," he wrote.[71]

At this time a campaign was underway in California to prohibit Japanese immigration by federal law. Its chief spokesman was a Sacramento-born newspaper publisher, V. S. McClatchy, who told a Congressional Committee on Immigration and Naturalization that the Issei had practiced a "determined utilization" of economic advantages "in securing a place for their race in this country through systematized plans of peaceful penetration." [72] In speaking of the West Coast Japanese, opponents often employed military semantics. The aggressive paternalism of the mother country, the attachment of the immigrants to their native culture—as expressed by their language schools and their Buddhist and Shinto shrines—convinced fearful Caucasians that their settlement was a plot to establish a Japanese beachhead in the United States. Even their high birthrate seemed subversive. In 1920 there were approximately 72,000 first- and second-generation Japanese in California, though emigration from Japan had been curtailed by the terms of the Gentlemen's Agreement and a 1920 ban on "picture brides." A formal exclusion policy would be more of a diplomatic affront than a practical deterrent.

The Chinese Exclusion Act of 1882 had first introduced the ethnic factor into United States immigration policy. In the same year, a head tax of fifty cents (raised to four dollars in 1907) was imposed on each new arrival from Europe and certain "undesirables" and paupers were excluded. A growing resentment of immigrants from Eastern and Southern Europe, coupled with a fear of foreign radicals and anarchists, was translated into new restrictions after the First World War. In 1917 a law, passed over Wilson's veto, subjected newcomers to a literacy test, doubled the entry fee, and excluded chronic alcoholics as well as tuberculars, imbeciles, and moral degenerates. "Immigration policy frankly founded on racial considerations" [73] was incorporated in the Johnson-Reed Act of 1924, which set an absolute ceiling on annual admissions. After 1927, 150,000 immigrants were to be admitted annually on the basis of quotas of 2 percent of the number of each nationality in the United States in 1890, which meant that twelve out of fifteen newcomers would be British, Irish, German, Dutch, and Scandinavian. [74]

In its Section 12C, which barred all aliens ineligible for citizenship, the 1924 law put the United States in the company of South Africa, Australia, and New Zealand in the matter of Asian exclusion. President Calvin Coolidge, in signing the measure into law, is reported to have said, "If the exclusion provision stood alone, I should disapprove

it without hesitation. . . ." [75] Again there was a strong
reaction in Japan. Prayer meetings, demonstrations, and
anti-American boycotts took place. The ambassadors in
Tokyo and Washington resigned. A newspaper contrasted
the new policy with the American treatment of oppressed
Armenians. "They called the Turks barbarous but the
Americans are the Turks now." [76]

Immigrants to New York's Ellis Island might hence-
forth think ironically of Emma Lazarus' words inscribed at
the base of the Statue of Liberty about "the golden door"
which was now partly closed. San Francisco's immigration
station was on Angel Island in the bay. Opened in 1910,
it had separate facilities for Asians. New arrivals complained of the jail-like atmosphere, the humiliating physical
examinations, the feeling of "indescribable oppression."
One man remembered the inscriptions, cursing the officers'
treatment, written in Chinese and Japanese on the walls
by those who had been detained.[77]

1. Description of a Chinese girl in San Francisco. *Alta California*, July 1, 1851.
2. G. C. H. in the *Californian*, November 4, 1848, quoted in
Bancroft, *History of California*, vol. 6, p. 290, fn. 75.
3. Gov. John McDougal's message, January 7, 1852, *Journal of
the Assembly*, 3rd Sess., 1852, p. 15.
4. Minority Report of the Select Committee on Senate Bill No.
63 for "An Act to Enforce Contracts and Obligations to Perform
Work and Labor," *Journal of the Senate*, 3rd Sess., Appendix, 1852,
pp. 669-675.
5. Stanford M. Lyman, "Strangers in the Cities: The Chinese
on the Urban Frontier," in Wollenberg, *Ethnic Conflict in California
History*, pp. 74-77.
6. McWilliams, *California: The Great Exception*, p. 140.
7. *Journal of the Assembly*, 6th Sess., Doc. 19, Appendix, 1855,
p. 7.
8. Lyman, "Strangers in the Cities," p. 70.
9. "An Act to Enforce Contracts and Obligations to Perform
Work and Labor," p. 673.
10. Gunther Barth, *Bitter Strength: A History of Chinese in the
United States, 1850–1870* (Cambridge, Mass.: Harvard University
Press, 1964), pp. 58-74.

11. Elmer Clarence Sandmeyer, *The Anti-Chinese Movement in California* (Urbana: University of Illinois Press, 1939), pp. 26-29.

12. George Chu, "Chinatowns in the Delta: The Chinese in the Sacramento-San Joaquin Delta, 1870–1960," *California Historical Society Quarterly,* vol. 49, March 1970, p. 30; Barth, *Bitter Strength,* p. 100.

13. Barth, *Bitter Strength,* p. 81.

14. *Ibid.,* pp. 105, 106.

15. George Stewart, *Donner Pass* (Menlo Park, Calif.: Lane Publishing Co., 1964), p. 47.

16. Oscar Lewis, *The Big Four: The Story of Huntington, Stanford, Hopkins, and Crocker, and of the Building of the Central Pacific* (New York: Alfred A. Knopf, 1938), p. 71.

17. *Ibid.,* p. 99.

18. *San Francisco Chronicle & Examiner,* May 18, 1969.

19. Newmark, *Sixty Years in Southern California,* p. 504.

20. Chu, "Chinatowns in the Delta," p. 24.

21. *Ibid.,* pp. 24-25.

22. Interview with Dr. Paul Barnes, Walnut Grove, Calif., May 9, 1970.

23. Jerry MacMullen, *Paddle-Wheel Days in California* (Stanford, Calif.: Stanford University Press, 1944), pp. 92-93.

24. Chu, "Chinatowns in the Delta," pp. 29-31.

25. Mary Roberts Coolidge, *Chinese Immigration* (New York: Henry Holt & Co., 1909), p. 22.

26. Sandmeyer, *The Anti-Chinese Movement,* p. 32.

27. Lyman, "Strangers in the Cities," p. 83.

28. William Figari, "San Francisco Bay and Waterfront, 1900-1965," typed manuscript of a tape-recorded interview conducted by Ruth Teiser (University of California, Bancroft Library Regional Oral History Office, Berkeley, 1969), pp. 44-45.

29. Rev. William Taylor, quoted in Curt Gentry, *The Madams of San Francisco* (Garden City, N. Y.: Doubleday & Co., 1964), p. 45.

30. *Ibid.,* pp. 44-45.

31. Testimony of John F. Swift, quoted in George Seward, *Chinese Immigration in Its Social and Economic Aspects* (New York: Charles Scribner's Sons, 1881), p. 250.

32. Duckett, *Mark Twain and Bret Harte,* pp. 22, 53-54.

33. *Ibid.,* pp. 56, 143.

34. Robert Louis Stevenson, *Across the Plains* (New York: Charles Scribner's Sons, 1897), p. 62.

35. Bean, *California: An Interpretive History,* p. 236.

36. Sandmeyer, *The Anti-Chinese Movement,* p. 33.

37. Lyman, "Strangers in the Cities," p. 95; William R. Locklear, "The Anti-Chinese Movement in Los Angeles," in Roger Daniels and Spencer C. Olin, Jr., eds., *Racism in California: A Reader in the History of Oppression* (New York: Macmillan Co., 1972), p. 101.

38. *Constitution of California,* Secs. 2, 3; Art. XIX, 1879.

39. *Acts Amendatory of the Penal Code Passed at the 23rd Session of the Legislature,* approved February 13, 1880, Chap. 3; Secs. 178, 179; pp. 1-2.

40. *Constitution of California,* Sec. 4, Art. XIX, 1879.

41. Henry George, "The Kearney Agitation in California," *Popular Science Monthly,* 7, August 1880, in N. Ray and Gladys Gilmore, *Readings in California History* (New York: Thomas Y. Crowell, 1966), pp. 204-205.

42. Rolle, *The Immigrant Upraised,* p. 259.

43. Barth, *Bitter Strength,* p. 145.

44. Leon Litwack, *North of Slavery: The Negro in the Free States,* *1790-1860* (Chicago, Ill.: University of Chicago Press, 1961), p. 167.

45. "Life in a Mining Town, Hornitos, California," typed manuscript of a tape-recorded interview conducted by Corinne Glib (University of California, Bancroft Library Regional Oral History Office, Berkeley, 1956), p. 22.

46. Statement of a Chinese merchant, Ferguson Alley, Los Angeles, July 29, 1924, *Survey of Race Relations.*

47. Lynwood Carranco, "A Study in Prejudice: The Chinese and Humboldt County, California," *The Redwood Country: History, Language, Folklore* (Dubuque, Iowa: Kendall Hunt Pub. Co., 1971), pp. 46-47.

48. *Ibid.,* pp. 45-46.

49. Edward Petersen, "In the Shadow of the Mountain: A Short History of Shasta County, California," typed manuscript, Public Library, Redding, California, 1965.

50. Lyman, "Strangers in the Cities," p. 94.

51. Interview with Mrs. Walter Sharp, Portola Valley, Calif., May 1970.

52. Bob Patterson, "The Mafia, Revisited," *California Living Magazine, San Franisco Sunday Examiner and Chronicle,* January 10, 1971.

53. Interview with an officer of the Los Angeles Police Force, Vice Division, July 29, 1924, *Survey of Race Relations.*

54. John J. Manion, "Reminiscences" (University of California, Bancroft Library Manuscript Collection, Berkeley).

55. Carol Green Wilson, *Chinatown Quest: The Life Adventures of Donaldina Cameron* (Stanford, Calif.: Stanford University Press, 1931).

56. Tye Schultze, who met her Caucasian husband when she was working as an interpreter at the immigration station on Angel Island, died at the age of eighty-four on March 10, 1972.

57. R. D. McKenzie, "The Oriental Invasion," *Journal of Applied Sociology,* 10, p. 126.

58. Wen-Hui Chung Chen, "Changing Socio-Cultural Patterns of

the Chinese Community in Los Angeles" (Ph.D. dissertation, University of Southern California, Los Angeles, 1952), pp. 377, 416.

59. Yamato Ichihashi, *Japanese in the United States: A Critical Study of the Problems of Japanese Immigrants and Their Children* (Palo Alto, Calif.: Stanford University Press, 1932), p. 231.

60. Kanichi Kawasaki, "The Japanese Community of East San Pedro, Terminal Island, California" (M.A. thesis, University of Southern California, Los Angeles, 1931), p. 38.

61. *Alta California*, March 4, 1851.

62. Political Code, Art. X, Sec. 1669.

63. No. 1662, *Statutes of California*, 30th Sess., 1893, p. 253.

64. Roger Daniels, "The Progressives Draw the Color Line," in Daniels and Olin, *Racism in California*, p. 119.

65. Judge S. C. Hastings testifying before the Congressional Committee on Chinese Immigration in 1877, *Survey of Race Relations*.

66. Daniels, "Progressives Draw the Color Line," pp. 116-134.

67. Peter Clark MacFarlane, quoted in Audrie Girdner and Anne Loftis, *The Great Betrayal: The Evacuation of the Japanese-Americans during World War II* (New York: Macmillan Co., 1968), pp. 58-60.

68. John Modell, "Japanese-Americans: Some Costs of Group Achievement," in Wollenberg, *Ethnic Conflict in California History*, pp. 112-113.

69. *Ibid.*, p. 107.

70. "Life History of a Japanese Man," Santa Paula, Calif., December 29, 1924. Translation in *Survey of Race Relations*.

71. Sei Fujii, president of the Japanese Association of Los Angeles, Calif., July 1923, *Survey of Race Relations*.

72. V. S. McClatchy before the House Committee on Immigration and Naturalization, July 13-14, 1924, *Survey of Race Relations*.

73. Michael Kraus, *Immigration, the American Mosaic* (Princeton, N. J.: D. Van Nostrand Co., 1966), p. 92.

74. *Ibid.*, p. 93.

75. R. L. Buell, *Japanese Immigration*, World Peace Foundation pamphlet, vol. 7, Boston, Mass., 1924, p. 371.

76. *Japan American News*, March 6, 1927, quoted in R. D. McKenzie, *Oriental Exclusion*, American Group, Institute of Pacific Relations (Chicago, Ill.: University of Chicago Press, 1927), pp. 48-49.

77. "Life History of Masao Dodo," *Survey of Race Relations*.

6

Later Migrations

AS THE CHINESE POPULATION in California declined and
no new Japanese immigrants were admitted, the role they
had filled after their arrival as laborers began to be taken
over by other Asians, and Mexicans.[1] The California climate with its rainless summers led to the development of
large-acreage farming, highly capitalized because of the
high cost of irrigation. To offset the expense of reclaiming
land, growers needed a cheap, itinerant labor supply "that
would take itself off and live contentedly on its earnings
between periods of demand." [2] The Oriental was considered
ideal in this respect. When the crops were ready to pick,
a bilingual boss would relay instructions from the grower,
who "merely left an order for a certain number of boys
(they were boys till they died of old age) to be at a certain
place on a certain day to do a certain kind of work." [3]

The Hindus, Koreans, and Filipinos

In the early years after the turn of the century a new
group of dark-skinned men was seen in the fields. The
turbaned East Indians were usually called Hindus by
Californians. The majority were Sikhs from the Punjab,

most of whom had come into the state from British Columbia around 1908. By 1920 there were between three and four thousand East Indians in California, some of them working in rice cultivation near Willows, or in the hop fields in Yuba County. (They did not seem to be allergic to the hops, which sometimes caused a skin rash among white pickers.) Others were in the fertile Imperial Valley, which had been created in southeastern California early in the century when Colorado River water was brought in from Mexico through the American Canal. Cotton, cantaloupe, citrus, and other profitable crops were grown in the former Colorado desert where summer temperatures rose to over 100 degrees. Some said it was not "a white man's country." [4] The East Indians who worked there would get up before dawn to start their labor while it was still cool.

They were experts in irrigation. When some farmers near Manteca in the San Joaquin Valley were having trouble with their young sugar-beet plants set out in a sandy stretch of land, they were persuaded to bring a group of Hindus to try to save the crop. One of them told the boss that the water ditches were laid out wrong. He showed how they should be arranged. "You get a tractor and drive behind me while I walk," he suggested. Though the boss said twelve men were needed for the irrigation job, six East Indians agreed to work "twenty-four hours and one hour for cook time, twenty-five hours a day!" By running the water day and night, not flooding anything, they saved the plants. [5]

This new group attracted attention through their distinctive appearance—their combination of dark skin and Caucasian features. "We are shocked to see a black white man," explained a resident of the Imperial Valley, [6] where East Indians were treated like Negroes by that part of the white population which was of Southern origin, and were relegated to the undesirable sections when they came to town. An East Indian seriously injured in an automobile accident was refused treatment by a doctor in Brawley. He could get no ambulance service to El Centro, so "they had to take him there in a Ford car." [7] Prejudice was widespread elsewhere as well. A member of the Asian Exclusion League reported that a Hindu camp on the upper watershed of the Russian River was causing typhoid fever among vacationers farther down the river. A commissioner of the State Bureau of Labor Statistics said that the Hindu was "the most undesirable immigrant in the State . . . unfit for association with American people." [8] After 1917 they were excluded under a "barred zone" provision in the immigration law, passed over President Wilson's veto.

Though an Indian scholar published a tract attempting to prove that his people were Aryans and hence eligible for United States citizenship (he wrote, "The Punjabis living at present in the Pacific Coast states are as pure Caucasians as the Germans"),[9] a legal decision upheld by the United States Supreme Court ruled that "a high-caste Hindu is not a 'white person'" within the definition of the Naturalization Act.[10] Some East Indians who had become naturalized lost their American citizenship. Under the Alien Land Laws, they, like the Japanese, were prevented from buying or leasing land directly. The decision in the naturalization case involving Takao Ozawa, in which the United States Supreme Court in 1922 ruled that an Issei could not be an American citizen, was cited in the East Indian case.

Some Koreans who arrived in the same period as the East Indians were actually confused with Japanese immigrants, a sensitive point, since many were resentful that their country had become a Japanese protectorate after 1910. Their numbers were always small (by 1930 there were 1,097 Koreans in the state), and they were never a significant group in agriculture. Though a few were involved in rice culture in the Sacramento Valley and in other enterprises using farm labor, they settled chiefly in the cities, with the largest concentration in Los Angeles.

Many had been converted to Christianity by missionaries in their own country and in Hawaii. "I first thought when I came to the United States that everyone was a fine Christian," said one immigrant, "but I soon learned better. I found out there are several kinds of Christians and you have to be careful." [11]

West Coast attitudes were a shock to the large number of Filipinos (over 31,000) who arrived in California in the decade 1920 to 1930. Many of them had been laborers in Hawaii, and before they had left their own islands for the Hawaiian sugar plantations, their hands had been inspected for calluses to be sure that they were real laborers.[12] Since their country had been under the American flag since the end of the Spanish-American War, they came to the United States without restriction, yet their status was ambiguous. In terms of passports and protection across foreign borders, they were considered to be Americans; yet only those who had served in the United States Army or Navy could apply for citizenship.

At first they were welcomed by growers. The dean of the State College of Agriculture expressed the opinion that compared with the average Japanese or Chinese "the Filipino is not particularly aggressive" and that they would probably not be "abandoning farm labor and competing with the white residents of California in the more lucrative professions." [13] The farm laborers were young men, some of them not yet twenty, "who came on a great adventure," according to one second-generation commentator. "They came because their buddies came and they were offered what seemed to them remunerative opportunities. They did make good money, no question about it. And I don't think they resented the work either. They worked hard. I don't think they came with any carefully laid out plans." [14] They worked at asparagus-cutting, fruit-picking, rice-harvesting, hoeing and topping beets, lettuce-harvesting, grape-picking, celery-planting, hop-picking, and general ranch labor.

When they got paid, they would go into town and spend

their money freely, outraging Caucasians who saw them in the company of white girls. The male-female ratio among Filipinos was fifteen to one in the first decade of heavy immigration. To offset the possibility of widespread miscegenation, a court in 1930 ruled that an American woman would lose her citizenship if she married a Filipino, a Los Angeles judge nullified existing Filipino-white marriages, and the California legislature in 1933 amended the state ban on interracial marriage to include "members of the Malay race." Filipinos married women from other immigrant groups—Mexican, mulatto, Hungarian, Spanish, and Italian—and a few Filipino-American marriages were arranged by legal subterfuge.[15] In the Filipino culture, racial intermarriage was approved.

In 1930 a justice of the peace in northern Monterey County launched some familiar charges: the Filipinos had unhealthy habits and debased the wage scale, slept fifteen in a room, and lived on a diet of rice and fish. He felt it was outrageous that little brown men but ten years removed from the loin and breechcloth were pursuing local girls.[16] The local chamber of commerce issued anti-Filipino resolutions which "set an attitudinal tone" for the whites in Watsonville in January of 1930, when a mob of five hundred men went on a rampage, raiding dance halls, destroying property, beating up Filipinos. When one was killed, the violence abated.[17] Some fled to the Turlock area where night riders warned them to evacuate in two hours. The Filipino center in Stockton was "blasted." [18]

Filipino farm workers were resented first by white laboring men and then by growers, when they formed a union and conducted a successful strike for higher wages in the lettuce fields of Salinas before vigilantes moved them out. The demand that their immigration be stopped, which had been articulated among labor groups before the Wall Street crash in 1929, increased with the onset of the Great Depression. In 1931, hoping to forestall an exclusion law, the Philippine Society of California proposed that volunteers among the unemployed immigrants be repatriated at United States government expense. This program, approved by Congress, was undertaken in 1934, just after the passage of the Philippines Independence Act inaugurated a Filipino exclusion policy which reduced the quota of entrants to fifty annually. The unemployed repatriated immigrants could then return to the United States only under the quotas. But to the surprise of the law's sponsors, only 2,190 took the opportunity for a free boat ride home. Why did they stay in a state where life had proved to be so different from the glowing promises of liberty and equality that were circulated in textbooks on American history used in schools in their native land? "[We] Filipinos are taught to regard Americans as our equals," wrote Carlos Bulosan. "The terrible truth in America shatters the Filipino's dream of fraternity. . . . I shall never forget what I have suffered in this country because of racial prejudice." [19]

A second-generation observer, Peter Jamero, thinks they stayed because during the Depression they didn't have any money to speak of and it would have been a disgrace to go home without some cash in their pockets. "The other factor was there was some real resentment at how they'd been treated and they vowed to do a lot better for themselves at that point." [20] Jamero's mother, Apolonia, who had been a teacher in her native land, came to the United States for further education in 1929, and was one of a very small number of Filipino women at that period who married after arrival. She and her husband Ceferino Jamero, all during the following years and up until the present day, have run a labor camp for bachelor fellow countrymen, charging them less than two dollars a day for room and board. Peter and his seven brothers and sisters grew up helping to cook and wash dishes for as many as a hundred "uncles" who joined the family periodically between trips to Stockton for the asparagus harvest. His father acted as a labor contractor, hiring out workers in the vineyards and fruit orchards surrounding his own forty acres. Some of the aging laborers still make the annual trek to the delta, figuring, "If you can't work, you might as well throw in your deck!" The next generation are not committed to agriculture. "We have never seen ourselves as being tied to the land," said Peter Jamero, who holds several academic degrees. All the Jamero children graduated from, or are attending, college, a characteristic pattern among Asians, even in rural communities where many of the Caucasians do not go beyond high school.

Except in a few places like Walnut Grove in Sacramento County, where the schools were segregated until World War II, the second generation of Asians went to school with all the other children in their communities in spite of the 1885 law (dropped from the Educational Code in 1947). Some teachers reported that social contacts were limited to the classrooms, that the children separated along ethnic lines on the playground. In other places there was a good deal of mixing, with the children hurling racial epithets at each other in a good-natured way. But there was at least one instance in which parents blocked the election of an Asian child to a position in the student government. A discouraged Japanese boy in a Fresno high school wrote an essay entitled, "What Is Wrong with Us?" complaining that his conditioning had started him out in life feeling he was "foredoomed to failure." But in the same city in the same period (the early twenties) a high-spirited Chinese girl was shocking staid members of the Chinese and American communties with her satires on both groups and her articles in the Fresno and San Francisco newspapers.[21]

The first Asian college students were immigrants who had come for the purpose of furthering their education. The Filipino *pensenados* who arrived in the early years of the century were chosen from the privileged classes, and many became political leaders on their return home. Other Asian students supported themselves with domestic work while they studied. They were disturbed by the contrast between their own cultural backgrounds and the treatment they received from West Coast Caucasians who made no distinction between one nationality or another, or between laborers and members of the professional class. The students complained of being turned away when they tried to rent rooms in private homes, of being refused accommodations at dormitories run by the YMCA. Some East Indians were denied service at the cafeteria run by the Associated Students of the University of California at Berkeley.[22] A house which served as a center for Indian students on the campus was financed by a group of Hindu laborers who met at the Sikh temple in Stockton. Most of the immigrants from the Punjab favored the independence of their country from Great Britain. (On the eve of the First World War, a small group of Indian revolutionaries on the West Coast was arrested for violation of the neutrality treaty in plotting the overthrow of British rule in India with the furtive support of the German government.) Similarly, many California Chinese supported the aim of the Nationalists to overthrow the Manchu Dynasty, as outlined by Dr. Sun Yat Sen on visits to the West Coast.[23]

By the time the American-born Asian students reached college age in the thirties, the atmosphere on campuses and in surrounding communities was more tolerant, but the Japanese and Chinese students, who generally had excellent scholastic records, were discouraged by counselors from preparing for careers such as teaching, for which they could never expect to be hired. The graduate engineer running a fruit stand became a standard wry joke among the Nisei (second-generation Japanese), many of whom had to go to Japan to find jobs commensurate with their education.

Japanese and Chinese families were forced by community pressure to live side by side in many towns, even though they did not understand each other's language or have much contact. In Walnut Grove the two races lived together until 1915, when a fire burned many houses, then most of the Chinese moved to nearby Locke.

"There seems always to be a demand, by the white population, that this element be segregated," wrote some San Jose real-estate brokers in 1924. "There is always the knowledge that they practice vices peculiar to their own people, and some peculiar to all people, which are a source of danger and contamination and especially so when practiced in close proximity to the white population." [24] A detailed study of arrest records and the nature of offenses committed by Japanese and Chinese in California in the years 1900-1927, however, indicates that there was a very low crime rate among Orientals; they committed very few offenses against persons or property, and the number of felons in the state prisons of either Chinese or Japanese ancestry was negligible.

A frequent charge of "vagrancy" brought against the Chinese suggests harassment by white law-enforcement officials. Other of their violations were not crimes in their own cultural milieu, as for example, gambling, running lotteries, practicing their own herbal medicine (which was an infraction of state medical laws) and, in one instance, exhuming a body. They were also arrested for violating immigration and narcotics laws. Both groups ran into difficulties with license ordinances, which may have been a matter of misunderstanding of local rulings or of ignoring rulings that were deliberately drawn up to curb their enterprise. The Japanese were most frequently cited for "gaming" and violating liquor laws—this last suggesting that their ties with the general population during the Prohibition era were closer than those of the Chinese.[25]

The Japanese associations in various California cities exerted pressure to close Chinese gambling operations and tried to indoctrinate their own members to avoid them, motivated in part, perhaps, by a desire to follow Caucasian standards. The Japanese were more inclined than the Chinese to leave the inner city racial enclaves to seek housing in suburban neighborhoods, despite the realtors' pledge to abide by restrictive covenants and the boast of many communities that they were 100 percent white American. In the twenties the Issei succeeded in building a Christian church in Hollywood in a "cosmopolitan" neighborhood which had Chinese, Serbian, and black families; but a proposal to build a Buddhist church in Pasadena was blocked by local opponents. This was the period in which members of the Anti-Oriental League sent threatening letters to Caucasians who patronized Japanese and Chinese markets, ending with the slogan "Help Keep California White." In 1920 the Chinese constituted less than one percent and the Japanese only a little over two percent of the state's population.[26]

North from Mexico

Among the 757,625 foreigners (excluding Asians) in California in 1920, the second highest number, after Italians, came from Mexico,[27] the result of the most active movement across the border since the Sonorans came during the Gold Rush. In the first thirty years of the twentieth century nearly 10 percent of the population of Mexico migrated to the southwestern United States—Texas receiving the largest number of immigrants, followed by California, Arizona, and New Mexico, in that order. In 1900 there were only about 8,000 Mexicans in California; by 1930 there were 368,013. [28] The Mexican migration was stimulated by adverse economic conditions, following a period of revolutionary unrest in Mexico after 1910, as well as by American recruitment. Agents crossed the border to hire road crews for the Southern Pacific and Santa Fe railroads. More Mexican workers were brought in to work in the cotton fields as the crop was moved west from Texas and Arizona to California. In the Imperial Valley, an estimated 21,000 Mexican immigrants had arrived by the mid-twenties to harvest the fields of cotton, lettuce, and cantaloupes. Like the East Indians, they were expert in irrigation and were willing to work in the desert temperatures. There was a local saying, "When there is no Mexican, there will be no Valley." [29]

Nineteen-twenty was the year of the first "Mexican harvest" in the San Joaquin Valley, where the acreage planted in cotton would increase more than thirty-fold in the next decade. As Mexican laborers followed the sugar-beet crop from California as far north as Ohio and Michigan, it was apparent that this new source of labor was to be an essential element in large-scale farming. The proximity of the border gave the grower considerable control in employment policies. The migration could be shut down temporarily or new workers brought in as needed. A seemingly unlimited supply kept the wages low. If the first men hired began to demand better working conditions and more pay, a fresh crew who were more desperate could be imported to take their places.

Since workers who returned home when they had enough money to satisfy them created a problem for the grower, he sometimes kept them on the job (as, for example, when a crew had contracted to block, thin, and harvest sugar beets over several months), by holding back part of their wages to make sure they would not leave before the final operation was completed.[30] Labor bosses sometimes took advantage of this system by pocketing the withheld wages themselves just as employment bureaus sometimes capitalized on the grower's need for large crews by bribing the foreman on a ranch to dismiss one group of men and hire another bunch, each one of whom paid a commission to the bureau. The "rapid turnover" method increased the profits of the middleman while costing the immigrant both his job and his cash.[31]

Ernesto Galarza, who worked in the Sacramento Valley as a youth shortly after the First World War, describes the system under which workers were hired: "Once we were in camp, owing the employer for the ride to the job, having no means to get back to town except by walking and no money for the next meal, arguments over working conditions were settled in favor of the boss." The contractor might cheat in weighing in each picker's amount or take off two or three lugs of grapes when figuring the day's record. He might sell soda pop instead of providing water. At the labor camp where young Ernesto lived, the main street was an irrigation ditch, which also supplied water for drinking, cooking, laundering, and bathing.[32]

Mexican workers were accused of being a menace to the health of the communities near their jobs, although almost invariably they were housed in quarters that made decent living difficult. An Imperial Valley grower said, "The only thing that saves us is the climate, the heat and the sunshine." [33] Labor camps were subject to inspection by the Commission on Immigration and Housing, created after the opening of the Panama Canal, when a large influx of new immigrants was expected. Just about that time, 1913, the "Wheatland riot" on the Durst hop ranch in Yuba County exposed conditions under which migrant workers lived. Twenty-eight hundred people—men, women, and children —slept on straw, and awaited their turn at about ten privies. There was no garbage disposal. The pickers spent long hours in the Sacramento Valley heat without any drinking water provided in the fields. After an investigation, the commission set up standards for labor camps, requiring a bunk for each worker, good latrines, clean water, and screened kitchens.[34] But in spite of mass periodic inspections, many of the labor camps in the state continued to be a disgrace.[35]

When a child, stricken with a gastrointestinal infection, died at a camp where he worked, Ernesto Galarza went to Sacramento to appeal to Simon J. Lubin of the commission's board of directors. An investigation revealed that the water supply for the workers and their families was polluted from a stable. Lubin told the young Mexican to get the workers to organize to improve their living conditions but Galarza was fired from his job. The first secretary of the commission had indicted farm managers who refused "to meet the social responsibilities which come with the hiring of human beings for labor." [36] But the California grower had an entirely different relationship to his temporary work crew than did the middle-western farmer to his hired man. He was inclined to regard the Mexicans "as a necessary evil," or at best as an item in his cost versus profit inventory.[37]

There was a real cultural disparity between the two groups, as an early observer noted: "The American employer cannot understand why, when the Mexican has a chance to earn a dollar or two he will not avail himself of the opportunity. The Mexican laborer cannot understand why there should be such a mad rush all day, every day, when all that is gained in the end is fatigue and darkness." [38] For the immigrants, California offered material attractions and some security, as compared with chaotic economic conditions at home. One said, "They told me in Mexico that if you have no money in the United States that people will not let you starve." [39] The American interpretation was: "When they offer their labor, this country is the 'Land of Hard Knocks.' When they offer their woes in the charity market, it is the 'Land of Easy Beans.' " [40]

Those who crossed the border had such strong roots in the homeland that they generally accepted only the "utilitarian symbols" of America, buying cars and appliances, when they could afford them, to take back with them. They were insulated from any real relationship to life north of the border by the nature of their contacts with it, moving around in the company of fellow countrymen, not having to learn English because a middleman interpreted between them and the Anglos.

Their transient status put them at a disadvantage as far as community benefits were concerned. If they brought their wives and children, they were often traveling around so much following the crops, with the whole family working, that it resulted in their not staying long enough in any one school district for the children to benefit from the universal free public education offered. When the children did go to school, they were put into special "Americanization" classes, which had a social, as well as a professional, connotation of inferiority. Teachers did not think it was worth while to give Mexican children serious attention. The attitude of school trustees in the Imperial Valley was reported to be, "Let them come in and sit, but don't waste time teaching them." [41]

Not intending to stay permanently, Mexican families would settle in *colonias* or *barrios* where cheap rentals were available. They were almost invariably located, as Carey McWilliams wrote, "on 'the other side of' something: a railroad track, a bridge, a river or a highway." [42] It was psychologically comfortable to live in a *colonia* amidst *chicanos* (unskilled workers just arrived in the United States) and *pochos* (those who had grown up in California). The culture was transplanted. "I never lost the sense that we were the same, from Jalco (Jalcocotán where he was born) to Sacramento," wrote Ernesto Galarza. In the *colonias* newcomers could puzzle over the strange ways of the Americans, find out what they needed to know about the local scene, and give and receive *asistencia,* an arrangement "on trust . . . between people who had plenty of nothing. . . ." [43]

The physical surroundings aggravated serious health problems, such as tuberculosis, which the families often brought with them. Their houses would often be located in unincorporated areas where there were no zoning requirements, no sewers, no hard-surface roads or street lighting. Cesar Chavez lived in such a *barrio* in Santa Clara County, which was referred to by the inhabitants as "Sal si puedes!" ("Get out if you can!") His family had come to California in 1937, long after the first wave of immigrants, after they lost the farm they owned in Arizona. They began following the crops on an annual circuit from the Imperial Valley to Marysville, pausing at times at places such as Oxnard, where they spent one rainy winter in a tent; in Delano; and in Brawley, where, as Chavez remembers, "the cops wouldn't let us into Anglo Town." [44]

As family immigration increased a few Mexican groups, who felt some degree of permanence, wanted to move to the higher rent areas near their towns in order to get city services. Some became naturalized citizens, though many were reluctant to take this step because they felt they might change their minds about returning home later. One man who was asked whether he wanted to become an American, replied, "What is the advantage? We cannot go around wearing our citizenship papers on our sleeves. If we did, that would make no difference. We would still have to go upstairs in the movie houses, live in the low parts of town, send our children to the old and ugly schools. . . ." [45]

In Santa Ana, where this man lived, Mexicans planted, cultivated, and harvested the sugar-beet crop, and hauled the beets to the factory door; but they were not employed in the sugar refinery. The field work with the sugar beets was "brutal," Cesar Chavez once said, rejoicing that harvesting had been mechanized. "That was work for an animal, not a man. Stooping and digging all day, and the beets are *heavy.* . . . And then to go home to some little place, with all those kids, and hot and dirty—*that* is how a man is crucified." [46]

In 1927 when Simon J. Lubin accused the growers of treating Mexicans like peons corralled in barbed-wire stockades, he was addressing groups who thought that their workers were satisfied with simple things like a few tortillas and driving around "beautiful California" in a "battered flivver" and "doing the homing pigeon stunt back to Mexico with more money than their neighbors dreamed existed." This stereotype of the Mexican drifting and enjoying the sunshine on an adobe wall [47] was rudely shattered that same year, when Mexican workers in Southern California formed a union, the Confederación de Uniones Obreras Mexicanas, with twenty locals, and the following year called a strike in the Imperial Valley cantaloupe fields at harvest time. They wanted more pay. The average wage for Mexicans in 1928 was thirty-five cents an hour, or three dollars a day. One of their objectives was to prevent the *patrón* from taking a cut of their wages. When they stopped picking just as fourteen thousand carloads of melons were ripe for shipment, the growers threatened to bring in replacements from Texas and Arizona. The local district attorney called on the help of law enforcement officials to prevent the strikers from assembling, and through arrests and threatened deportation, they were forced to return to the fields. They did, however, win some concessions in a more successful attempt two years later.

The increased display of dissatisfaction by Mexican laborers, added to the decline in farm prices following the Stock Market crash in 1929, forced growers and community leaders in California to take a different view of Mexican immigration. During the twenties there was some attempt to impose a head tax on new entrants, but with less than one hundred men patrolling the boundary on the United States side before the establishment of the border patrol in 1924, the majority of Mexicans entered illegally, simply by climbing over a fence. In 1928, before the cantaloupe strike, California growers joined with those in Arizona and Texas to fight a bill introduced in Congress to apply the restrictions of the 1924 immigration quota system to Mexico.[48]

From time to time there had been talk of "enforced rotation" and the deportation of unemployed aliens by taxpayers who objected to supporting "indigents," when the farm workers from the San Joaquin Valley would come down to Los Angeles between jobs to live on the county, or as one woman called the welfare service, the "court." She said, "I have for shame to eat the flour of the 'court' in my tortillas." [49]

With the onset of the Depression, the problem of people on relief became critical in Los Angeles and other counties of the Southland, where Mexican families accounted for between one-fifth and one-third of the case load. A repatriation program was begun in 1931. Thousands of *repatriados* (the figure is variously estimated at between 50,000 and 80,000), including a few naturalized citizens caught in the roundup, were forcibly shipped home, an episode reminiscent of the expulsion of Sonorans from the goldfields in 1852. This was not a voluntary program as was the Filipino repatriation, in which only a little over two thousand souls elected to leave the West Coast. The Mexican deportation was on such a large scale that one spokesman guessed that of the seasonal labor force that had been coming into the state from the time of the First World War, only 10 percent remained. [50] A few years later, when agricultural workers were needed again at the time of the Second World War, the United States launched the *bracero* program to bring them back.

The Dust Bowl Migrants

In some respects the history of Mexican farm laborers is similar to that of the Dust Bowl migrants who were entering California just as many of the *repatriados* were leaving. Charles Wollenberg has pointed out that the migrants' situation was unique in that they were the first Anglo-Saxon Protestant group coming into the state whose social and economic position subjected them to the prejudice, discrimination, and exploitation that had heretofore been reserved for racial minorities. The terms "Okie" and "Arkie," which were fastened on them, took on connotations similar to the familiar racial epithets "nigger" and "greaser." [51]

Even before the migrants arrived, not all farm workers in California had been Asians, Mexicans, or Europeans. In periods of economic depression, unemployed white Americans became agricultural laborers. On the Durst hop ranch at the time of the "Wheatland riot," pickers of twenty-seven different nationalities had been counted, and among the Americans were two categories in particular, hoboes—many of whom were IWW members who helped to organize the discontented—and "vacation laborers." It was a custom for some families to combine camping out in the country with earning extra cash picking crops, particularly during the war years when manpower was scarce. Seasonal work in orchards, packing sheds, and canneries was a favorite means of augmenting income for college students and housewives, as well as small farmers and orchardists who hired out in their spare time away from their own land. As soon as cotton was planted in the San Joaquin Valley in the twenties, carloads of "tourists" from Oklahoma and Texas started driving over to pick it.

These casual laborers blazed the trail for the desperate migration of the thirties, when over three hundred thousand native white Americans came to California from the south central states, more than eighty thousand of them from Oklahoma. Many of the Dust Bowl migrants were tenant farmers—not usually farm owners—some of whom had spent a number of years moving around at home in Texas or Oklahoma, Arkansas or Louisiana, trying to improve their lot on one depleted acreage after another. The boll weevil, the Depression, and six years of drought finally brought them to the point of deciding to move out for good, selling "crop, stock and farming tools." [52] Some of the Texans had been "tractored out" as the price of cotton sank and landlords and foreclosing mortgage companies consolidated small farms into larger holdings that could be run more economically by machines. Like the Joads in Steinbeck's *Grapes of Wrath*, the tenant farmers sold what they could not take, piled the family and everything they could get into and on top of a car, turned their backs on what was left of their dust-eroded farms, and started off. Their vehicles, loaded like "mechanized burros," inspired the border inspectors to call them "tin-can tourists." [53]

The migration was a movement West, first to Arizona, where growers had advertised for cotton pickers. There the seasonal workers encountered the sort of large-scale, irrigated farming that was typical of California but so different from the small operation—one man and a team—to which they were accustomed. Arizona, however, was just a temporary stopping place. Californians wondered if they proceeded to the Coast because they had heard of Depression-born panaceas like the Townsend Plan, which proposed giving everyone over sixty a pension, and Upton Sinclair's program EPIC (End Poverty in California).

The state had already attracted an enormous number of people of all ages and from all walks of life who simply "took to the road" when the Depression hit and headed West under the illusion that conditions would be better there. They arrived in caravans of cars, hitchhiked, or took freight trains, "hopping the blinds." The rumors of jobs being available in building canals, bridges, and dams proved illusory; there were no jobs until the federal government created them under the WPA. The wanderers who had come to Los Angeles, which was called the "transient capital of the world," went from the twenty-five-cent hotels to the ten-cent flophouses, and finally, to the park benches, until the police told them to move on. Emergency help was provided through the Federal Transient Service. After November 1935, the policy was to give these visitors carfare and to send them home.[54]

Nineteen thirty-five was the year that the Dust Bowl migrants began to arrive in considerable numbers. Dorothea Lange, who took memorable pictures of these people for the Farm Security Administration, remembered the weekend when the first wave arrived in Southern California. "It was as sharp and sudden as that when I was there. . . . And we said, 'What is this? What is this?' And from that time on it came like a deluge. . . . A month later they were trying to close the border." [55]

Throughout the state, farm income had sunk to almost half of its 1929 level, thousands of people had lost homes and farms, and in 1934 about one-fifth of the population was on relief. Los Angeles had been the mecca of earlier transients. Fearing another mass invasion of indigents, the Los Angeles Police Department, with the approval of the mayor and the city council, set up a "border blockade" to discourage people who looked as if they might add to the welfare burden of the city. Sixteen stations were set up at various points along the state line in Southern California to stop incoming cars, buses, and trains. Those who failed to pass the inspection were to be ordered to leave the state or go to jail. Though it was a clear violation of the rights of citizens, the "border blockade" was, in fact, not a serious deterrent. After the first flurry of activity, only a few cars a week were stopped. Altogether, a little under fourteen hundred people were turned back and some five hundred arrested, presumably for refusing to leave, before the blockade was declared illegal by the state attorney general and lifted in mid-April, 1936.[56]

The new migration was geared to the harvest seasons. The newcomers looked for work in the Imperial Valley or traveled up Highway 99 to the San Joaquin Valley. If lucky, they found tent space in an auto camp, with water and electric light, for a dollar a week. Sometimes they just squatted by the side of the road, as did a family of Texans encamped near Wasco: "They chase them out of one camp because they say it isn't sanitary—there's no running water —so people live out here in the brush like a den o' hogs or pigs." [57]

In Marysville during these years there seemed to be more migrants and derelicts camping in the river bottoms in the summer, waiting for the fruit to ripen, than there were permanent residents in the town.[58] Some of the earlier comers had better arrangements. A large clan from Oklahoma, whose oldest members had come into Tulare County in 1913 and had tried and failed at independent farming and sharecropping, lived in a dilapidated former hotel in a town near Fresno and followed a six-months' crop circuit around the state. From their wintering place near Fresno, they went to Marysville in May to pick cherries, spent June in Modesto and Patterson counties in the apricot orchards, and from July to September were in Yuba City and Marysville picking peaches, followed by hop-picking, after which they returned to Fresno for the cotton season. When there was no work from December to May, they went on relief. Their cars were their only real property.[59]

There just was not enough work for everyone. Migrants would flock to the places where it was rumored that people were being hired, only to find dozens who had arrived before them already being turned away. When they went to the Arakalian Vineyards at Livingston in the early morning hours, the foreman, who could take only a few men, would keep out of sight.[60] A carrot puller in the Imperial Valley said men were sleeping in the field rows to hold a place in order to earn sixty cents a day.[61] Most families were able to work only about half the year and earned from one hundred to four hundred dollars.

"We like to work and not just set around," said a migrant in Kern County. "I'd rather do anything but set around, but they just ain't no chance here in California, seems like. You wait for work 2 weeks," then "fight like flies for the work. You eat it up faster than you can make it." [62]

During this period growers occasionally let the fruit drop and the vegetables rot in the field because they could not afford to meet a payroll; or they would cut wages to the bare minimum, taking advantage of the large labor pool, in order to make a profit. The economist Paul S. Taylor commented before a congressional committee, "It seems easier for large agricultural employers to organize to control wages than to organize to revise other costs to meet fluctuating economic conditions." [63] Farm wages decreased by 25 percent from 1930 to 1935.[64]

A young Greek immigrant was shocked when he came into the San Joaquin Valley at this period. In Europe he had known times of drought and flood and wars when everybody suffered; in California he saw poverty in the midst of plenty—young girls in dresses made of gunny sacks, desperate men sifting the riverbeds for gold, while an orchard owner sat with a shotgun across his knees to keep away the hungry people who might try to eat the apricots he could not sell.[65]

It was a situation that invited the intervention of labor organizers to precipitate an unleashing of anger and frustration such as was described by John Steinbeck in his novel, *In Dubious Battle*.[66] Between 1933 and 1938 there were 180 agricultural strikes in California, more than in any other state. Many involved violence, damage to property, evictions, and deportations; some were organized by members of the Communist party, others by affiliates of the AFL and the CIO.

The growers joined together to meet the crisis. The Associated Farmers, formed in 1933, had widespread support from business, banking, and railroad interests, and local law enforcement agencies. The conflict was seen as one between outsiders—radical organizers and transient laborers—against the established communities. During a lettuce strike in Salinas in 1936 the sheriff commanded all able-bodied citizens to report to the City Hall for an emergency and furnished them with ax handles to drive the pickets from the streets. Undercover agents were recruited and townspeople were deputized in other places.[67]

Public sentiment, as expressed in the press, was mainly on the side of the growers, who were trying to hold on in the Depression and were now threatened with disastrous labor problems. Dr. Taylor pointed out that among the "embattled farmers," as they were sympathetically called, it was the large-scale growers who were the chief employers of labor;[68]

the relationship was similar to that of the employer and employee in industry. The retaliation of the growers and their partisans was expressed in antipicketing ordinances and mass arrests. Union organizers who were avowed Communists were convicted under the State Criminal Syndicalism Act. Other protesters were denounced as subversive. A former Oklahoman made over one hundred speeches, trying to organize the Tulare County cotton pickers who averaged one-dollar-a-day earnings in 1932. He was opposed to outside agitators and testified in one of the criminal syndicalism trials in 1935, but after his own organizing efforts resulted in a strike, he was thrown into the Hanford jail. "They put me in jail for thinkin'. Kind of a distinction, bein' in jail these days." [69] Government relief agencies were regarded with suspicion by the growers because of their sympathetic treatment of the migrants. The growers feared that newly constructed government camps for migrant families might turn into trouble centers, since there was no policy about evicting tenants who were associated with the strikes.

These issues exploded before the whole nation with the appearance in 1939 of John Steinbeck's documentary novel about the Dust Bowl exodus to California, followed a few months later by Carey McWilliams' *Factories in the Field.* While congressional committees urged by groups of liberals took up the migrant problem, Kern County banned *The Grapes of Wrath.* Its allegations against growers were hotly denied by the Associated Farmers. Members of the clergy denounced its "immorality" and a Congressman from Oklahoma protested the "slander" of the tenant farmers of his state. The attention of the country was focused on California just as several communities were prosecuting individuals for violating a law which made it a misdemeanor to bring indigent persons into the state. They reasoned that the relatively high welfare payments, almost double the allowance in Oklahoma, would continue to attract those who were down on their luck unless the door were closed. A test case involving Fred W. Edwards from Marysville, who brought his brother-in-law from Texas, was carried all the way to the United States Supreme Court by the American Civil Liberties Union. The indigent law was declared unconstitutional in December 1941.

By that time the migrants had begun to sort themselves out. Some of the families went home. Others continued to follow the crops around California, creating a problem for school districts in different areas where the children came into classes for a month or two at a time and then were withdrawn to work in the fields. Teachers were urged to offer the children as much as they could for as long as they had them,[70] but some of the tax-paying permanent residents of communities which received a sudden influx of transient families were less than enthusiastic. Other migrant families, however, fulfilled a long-wished-for dream of settling down, sometimes transforming the places where they had first put up a temporary shelter into permanent communities. Promoters bought unincorporated land and sold them cheap lots where they built subdivisions. On these properties could be seen the different stages of their lives in California: at the back of the lot, the remains of the family car that brought them West; then a chicken shed which had been their first home; and in front, the new house in which they were living.[71]

World War II, which brought full employment and higher farm income to California, eased the economic problems of the migrants. Some of them went to the cities for defense-industry jobs, but the majority stayed in rural areas where some gradually moved up the ladder to entrepreneurial status while others were active on the side of labor in the post-World War II agricultural strikes.[72]

The Evacuation of the Japanese

The war was responsible for the banishment of another group of Californians. Approximately ninety-four thousand people of Japanese ancestry, two-thirds of whom were

American-born, were evicted from their communities and incarcerated in relocation centers. This unprecedented roundup of citizens and aliens was ordered during a time of mounting hysteria in the weeks following the surprise attack by Japanese planes on the American bases at Pearl Harbor. Public officials predicted that the resident Japanese would commit acts of sabotage and espionage, and urged that they be placed under the jurisdiction of the army. Although "military necessity" was given as a justification for overriding constitutional guarantees, the evacuation demand was conveyed to President Franklin D. Roosevelt by West Coast legislators, whose constituents had for years been trying to eliminate the competition of the Japanese in agriculture, produce-marketing, and fishing. The war emergency provided an opportunity.

The immigrant descendents of other Axis nations with which the United States was at war were not disturbed, except for individuals arrested by the FBI for suspected disloyalty who were given a hearing to prove guilt or innocence. The entire West Coast Japanese population from California, western Oregon and Washington, and a part of Arizona was ordered, without any trial, to be placed in "protective custody." The war in the Pacific was more threatening to people along the West Coast than the European war, but there is no doubt that the relative position of the immigrant groups in the society was a major factor in the difference in treatment. The Italians in California were represented by such well-known men as A. P. Giannini, San Francisco's Mayor Angelo Rossi, and the DiMaggio brothers. The German group had among its spokesmen prominent refugees from Nazi persecution, such as Thomas Mann. An early plan by the military men of the Western Defense Command to detain German and Italian aliens was dropped as soon as the Japanese were behind barbed wire.

A familiar sight in California cities in the spring of 1942 was the evacuation orders posted on telephone poles, ordering Issei and Nisei to settle their affairs and report with their luggage to depots and loading zones at a certain time. The army urged their leaders to cooperate; the alternative, they were told, would be a forced removal at bayonet point. The evacuees came conscientiously with their families and possessions, were checked aboard buses and trains, and carried sometimes four hundred miles to the other end of the state. More often, however, they were taken only a few miles to the nearest fairground or race-track that had been hastily converted into a camp community, where some of them were housed in the stables and slept on mattresses stuffed with straw. For several months they lived surrounded by high fences and armed guards in facilities they had known in a different context in their days of freedom. They could look outside and see a familiar world, "so near and yet so far."

Then they were moved again, this time to ten relocation centers in wilderness areas in six Western states. Two of the camps were in California—one, called Manzanar, was near Lone Pine in the Owens Valley in the eastern part of the state; the other was far to the north at Tule Lake near the Oregon border. Rumors of dissension among the inmates of these centers were deliberately distorted by California newspapers as the incarcerated Issei and Nisei were identified with the enemy in the Pacific in a vicious propaganda campaign.

Until January 1945, when the West Coast was reopened, there were no free Japanese-Americans in California except for a few servicemen on furlough or attached to the Western Defense Command, and a few Japanese wives of Caucasians who were released early. The mass exodus had resulted in a certain amount of economic dislocation as the Japanese left truck farms and nurseries. By and large, however, their prewar competitors profited from their absence. When the word came that the evacuation orders were rescinded, groups of Caucasians, masking their self-interest in a cloak of indignant patriotism, armed themselves to stop the Japanese from coming back. It was a frightening situation. The hatred had grown to alarming proportions after two and a half years of war propaganda, particularly in communities where families had lost sons in battles of the Pacific theater. In Salinas, where a local National Guard unit had been decimated in the Death March on Bataan, the returned Japanese could not come into town. Caucasian friends who brought them supplies were threatened. Night riders and bomb-throwers attacked them in Central Valley communities; some of the vigilantes were in the employ of respectable citizens who had an economic interest in discouraging the returning farmers.

A determined campaign by state officials to protect the families who were coming out of the camps was joined by sympathetic civic groups. The appearance of wounded Nisei veterans who had proved their loyalty to the United States by their exploits on the battlefields of Europe helped to change public opinion. The former evacuees ignored the excitement and quietly set about picking up the pieces of their disrupted lives, pruning neglected orchards, repairing vandalized buildings, searching out missing possessions. The active opposition died down before the end of the war in August 1945.

For those who had no place to go to, hostels, run by government agencies and civilian volunteers, were set up in Japanese churches. Some elderly unattached Issei had to be forced to leave the relocation centers, and on their return were dependent upon the security of the hostels. One center in Stockton stayed open until 1967, when the last resident went to Japan after the others had all died. Many of the Nisei, on the other hand, had left the relocation centers to scatter all over America. They did not come back immediately. Some never returned.

California had undergone another population boom during the war years, and housing was in short supply. The Japanese evacuees came back to find that black people were living in the "Little Tokyos" of Los Angeles and San Francisco. There had been a tremendous influx of Negroes from the South into California to work in the shipyards and defense industries during the war. Between 1940 and 1950 the black population of San Francisco increased from four thousand to forty-five thousand, and in the same period it went up by 168.8 percent in Los Angeles. Two-thirds of the newcomers came from Arkansas, Louisiana, Oklahoma, and Texas, the states from which whites had fled during the Dust Bowl years. But the black migrants, born and bred in rural areas of the southwest central states, went to the West Coast metropolitan centers where war industries were located.

A farm laborer, who had been getting $1.25 credit at a plantation store for chopping cotton back in his home community near the Mississippi River, found himself earning $10 a day as a welder in a shipbuilding company in Richmond, California. This good employment lasted through the war, but after the first layoffs the next jobs paid only a little more than half as much, after which the former defense workers found they could only get the "hot, heavy and dirty" jobs or the ones in service occupations.[73] They stayed on, hoping that the employment situation would improve, for California had fewer discriminatory restrictions than the communities of the South. Court rulings in the forties were opening up public facilities, theaters, swimming pools, and restaurants to all races. There was no poll tax or intimidation at the voting booth. In 1943 at least ten bills were introduced in the legislature to outlaw discrimination on the basis of race in areas of work and places of public accommodation. The real barriers were in equal employment (most unions were closed to blacks) and in housing.

In San Francisco black migrants went into housing projects in Hunters Point or crowded into the Fillmore District, where landlords charged them high rents "for makeshift apartments bootlegged in sagging, unpainted

Victorians." [74] In Los Angeles, they went to those parts of the city where black people were already living.

There had been Negroes in Los Angeles from its beginnings as a Spanish *pueblo*. Two among the original twenty-three adult settlers were Negroes,[75] and interracial marriages took place freely. The friendly relationships of the pioneer community changed as the population increased. Up until about 1910 the small number of black residents lived in every district in the city. In the twenties and thirties, as their numbers increased, they began to be segregated into particular neighborhoods. There were quite a number of Negro professionals who were fairly prosperous—about one-third of the black population owned their own homes. Dining-car waiters and Pullman-car porters settled their families in the city to be near the railroad terminus. Occasionally, as the residential patterns became stratified, black people who could pass for white would buy into a new neighborhood. The Caucasians resisted these "invaders," shoring up "front-line trenches" on certain streets and boulevards. Both black and white businessmen manipulated this neighborhood checkerboard play to reap profits.[76]

Black Los Angelenos, who in 1921 had taken issue with the Ku Klux Klan over the release of D. W. Griffith's pro-Klan film, *The Birth of a Nation*, struggled with Klan factions in Compton on questions of local government control in nearby Watts. Since before the First World War, there had been Negro families in a section of the Watts subdivision called "Mudtown." It had been sold to black people because it was considered "undesirable"; it was low, sandy, and damp, and flooded during the rainy season.[77] Cows and ducks contributed to a rural atmosphere which had a certain charm; as a Negro writer in 1931 described it, it was "like a tiny section of the Deep South literally translated." [78] Before World War II, blacks were concentrated in the southern section of Watts, with Anglos and

Mexicans to the north. By the time the war began and the new black population arrived from the South, Los Angeles was a "thoroughly segregated city." [79]

The old residents in the black ghettos had to make way for the stream of newcomers (by 1956 they were arriving at a rate of seventeen hundred a month), most of them moving into new public-housing projects erected in Watts. This physical crowding bred the tensions which exploded in the summer of 1965. In the next chapter we will consider some of the other factors involved.

1. In 1880 the 75,000 Chinese constituted 15 percent of the population of California; only 86 Japanese were recorded. In 1890 there were 72,472 Chinese and 1,147 Japanese in the state. In 1900 there were 45,753 Chinese and 10,151 Japanese. In 1910 there were 36,248 Chinese and 41,356 Japanese. In 1920 there were 28,812 Chinese and 71,952 Japanese.

2. A grower quoted in *Survey of Race Relations.*

3. Curtis Smith, "Personal Experiences with the Orientals," *Survey of Race Relations.*

4. Interview with Dr. E. E. Chandler and William C. Smith, *Survey of Race Relations.*

5. From an interview with G. S. Sahi, Livingston, Calif., February 23, 1970.

6. Interview with Chandler and Smith, *Survey of Race Relations.*

7. *Ibid.*

8. Willard A. Schurr, "Hindus in Los Angeles," *Survey of Race Relations.*

9. Dr. Pardaman Singh, Ph.D., *Ethnological Epitome of the Hindustanees of the Pacific Coast* (Stockton, Calif.: Khalsa Diwan Society, 1922).

10. *United States vs. Bhagat Singh Thind,* decided February 19, 1923, *Supreme Court Reporter,* vol. 43, no. 10, April 1, 1923, pp. 338-342.

11. Quoted in *Survey of Race Relations.*

12. Interview with Mrs. Apolonia Jamero, Livingston, Calif., February 1970.

13. Letter from E. D. Merrill to Eliot Mears, March 18, 1925, *Survey of Race Relations.*

14. Interview with Peter Jamero, Menlo Park, Calif., May 18, 1970.

15. Valentin R. Aquino, *The Filipino Community in Los Angeles*

(M.A. thesis, University of Southern California, Los Angeles, 1952), pp. 69, 71; Marcos Pera Berbano, "The Social Status of Filipinos in Los Angeles County" (M.A. thesis, University of Southern California, Los Angeles, 1931), pp. 62, 69.

16. H. Brett Melendy, "California's Discrimination Against Filipinos, 1927-1935," in Daniels and Olin, *Racism in California,* p. 145.

17. *Ibid.,* p. 148.

18. *San Francisco News,* January 29, 1930.

19. Melendy, "California's Discrimination Against Filipinos," p. 141.

20. Peter Jamero interview, May 18, 1970.

21. *Survey of Race Relations.*

22. Schurr, "Hindus in Los Angeles."

23. Interview with Ping Lee, Walnut Grove, Calif., May 9, 1970.

24. Report by a San Jose Realty Board Committee, July 29, 1924, *Survey of Race Relations.*

25. Walter G. Beach, "Oriental Crime in California: A Study of Offenses Committed by Orientals in That State, 1900-1927," *Stanford University Publications, History, Economics, and Political Science,* vol. 3, no. 3, 1932.

26. *Ibid.*

27. The figures given are: Italy, 88,502; Mexico, 86,610; Germany, 67,180; Canada, 59,562; England, 58,572; Ireland, 45,308; Sweden, 31,925; Russia, 27,224; Portugal, 24,517; France, 20,387; Denmark, 18,721; Scotland, 16,597; Switzerland, 16,097; Austria, 13,264; Spain, 11,123; Greece, 10,313; Yugoslavia, 7,277; Poland, 7,082; Finland, 7,005; Armenia, 5,687; Hungary, 5,252; Czechoslovakia, 3,377. *Fourteenth Census of the United States,* Government Printing Office, Washington, D.C., 1922, p. 109.

28. Carey McWilliams, *North from Mexico: The Spanish-Speaking People of the United States* (New York: Greenwood Press, 1968 [orig. pub. 1948]).

29. Kathryn Cromp, Louise F. Shields, and Charles A. Thomsen, "Study of the Mexican Population in Imperial Valley, California" (University of California, Bancroft Library Manuscript Collection, Berkeley).

30. McWilliams, *North from Mexico,* p. 180.

31. Helen Walker Douglas, "The Conflict of Cultures in First Generation Mexicans in Santa Ana, California" (M.A. thesis, University of Southern California, Los Angeles, 1928), p. 32.

32. Ernesto Galarza, *Barrio Boy* (South Bend, Ind.: University of Notre Dame Press, 1971), pp. 266 ff.

33. Cromp, Shields, and Thomsen, "Mexican Population in Imperial Valley."

34. The commission recorded the inspection of 1,400 camps

throughout the state, housing an estimated 75,000 people of over forty different nationalities who worked for the railroads, in the oil fields, and in agriculture (the majority, Mexican and Southern European), whose average earnings were $1.51 a day after 70¢ had been deducted for board. California Commission of Immigration and Housing, *2nd Annual Report,* 1916.

35. National Labor Board, *Report of Special Commission on Imperial Valley Farm Situation,* February 11, 1934.

36. Charlton Parker, "The Wheatland Hop Field Riot," *California Outlook,* March 14, 1914.

37. Cromp, Shields, and Thomsen, "Mexican Population in Imperial Valley."

38. Douglas, "Conflict of Cultures," p. 19.

39. *Ibid.,* p. 38.

40. California Commission of Immigration and Housing, *2nd Annual Report,* 1916.

41. Cromp, Shields, and Thomsen, "Mexican Population in Imperial Valley."

42. McWilliams, *North from Mexico,* p. 217.

43. Galarza, *Barrio Boy,* pp. 201, 236-237.

44. Peter Matthiessen, *Sal Si Puedes: Cesar Chavez and the New American Revolution* (New York: Random House, 1969), p. 223.

45. Douglas, "Conflict of Cultures," p. 7.

46. Matthiessen, *Sal Si Puedes,* p. 228.

47. McWilliams, *North from Mexico,* p. 190.

48. Charles Wollenberg, "Conflict in the Fields: Mexican Workers in California Agri-business," in Wollenburg, *Ethnic Conflict in California History,* pp. 140-141.

49. Douglas, "Conflict of Cultures," p. 38.

50. McWilliams, *North from Mexico,* p. 193.

51. Wollenberg, "Conflict in the Fields," p. 152.

52. Sign on a barn in Oklahoma County, August 12, 1938, from Dorothea Lange and Paul Schuster Taylor, *An American Exodus: A Record of Human Erosion* (New York: Reynal & Hitchcock, 1939).

53. Joseph P. Zeronian, "A Narrative History of Migrating Oklahomans in California, 1935–1940" (M.A. thesis, University of Southern California, Los Angeles, 1965), p. 20.

54. Cheryl Beth Campbell, "A Study of the Federal Transient Program with Special Reference to Fifty Transient Families in Los Angeles" (M.A. thesis, University of Southern California, Los Angeles, 1936).

55. Dorothea Lange, "The Making of a Documentary Photographer," typed manuscript of a tape-recorded interview conducted by Suzanne Riess. (University of California, Bancroft Library Regional Oral History Office, 1968), p. 175.

56. Zeronian, "Migrating Oklahomans," p. 29.

57. Lange and Taylor, *An American Exodus*, p. 109.

58. Interview with Carlton Sheffield, Portola Valley, Calif., June 7, 1970.

59. *Migratory Labor in California, Special Surveys and Studies*, State Relief Administration of California, 1936, p. 135.

60. Interview with Alfred Koehn, Livingston, Calif., February 24, 1970.

61. Lange and Taylor, *An American Exodus*, p. 115.

62. *Violations of Free Speech and Rights of Labor*. Hearings before a Subcommittee of the Committee on Education and Labor, United States Senate, 76th Congress, 2nd Sess., San Francisco, Dec. 6, 1939, p. 17234.

63. *Ibid.*, p. 17218.

64. *Migratory Labor in California*, p. 121.

65. Interview with Gus Stamenson, Livingston, Calif., September 6, 1972.

66. The 1936 novel described the organization of a strike among fruit-pickers by labor agitators, based on Steinbeck's conversations with an organizer named Tom Collins.

67. *American Civil Liberties Union News*, San Francisco, October 1936; *Violations of Free Speech and Rights of Labor*, pp. 17500 ff.

68. *Violations of Free Speech and Rights of Labor*, pp. 17215, 17217. Over a quarter of the agricultural produce in California was produced by 2.6% of the farms.

69. *Migratory Labor in California*, p. 139.

70. *Teaching Children Who Move with the Crops: Report and Recommendations of the Fresno County Project, the Education Program for Migrant Children, 1955.*

71. Zeronian, "Migrating Oklahomans," p. 42.

72. Ernesto Galarza, *Spiders in the House and Workers in the Field* (Notre Dame, Ind.: University of Notre Dame Press, 1970).

73. Wilson Record, "Willie Stokes at the Golden Gate," *The Crisis*, June 1949.

74. "The Negro in San Francisco," *San Francisco Call-Bulletin*, December 4, 1961.

75. Theodore H. Hittell, *History of California*, vol. 1 (San Francisco: N. J. Stone & Co., 1897), p. 434.

76. J. Max Bond, "The Negro in Los Angeles" (Ph.D. thesis, University of Southern California, Los Angeles, 1936), pp. 69 ff.

77. *Ibid.*, p. 87.

78. Arna Bontemps, "God Sends Sunday," quoted in "Watts: Before the Riot" in Paul Bullock, ed., *Watts: The Aftermath—An Inside View of the Ghetto by the People of Watts* (New York: Grove Press, 1969).

79. *Ibid.*

7

Recent Developments

♆ ★ ♆

THE HOLOCAUST AT WATTS exploded in palm-lined neighborhoods of pastel-colored dwellings that, at a superficial glance, had none of the marks of a slum area. Further, it occurred during the administration of a governor committed to improving civil rights for racial minorities. The year after Edmund G. ("Pat") Brown took office in 1958, California became the fifteenth state to enact a fair employment practices law. Soon afterward the legislature passed rulings prohibiting real estate brokers and apartment house owners from practicing racial discrimination in the sale or rental of property.

These new fair housing laws chiefly benefited middle-class minorities. They were evoked in behalf of high-salaried black engineers and scientists brought to the West Coast by the booming aerospace industries under federal contracts. But before the effectiveness of the laws really had been tested, they were abolished by popular mandate. The California Real Estate Association sponsored a ballot measure that had the effect of nullifying existing fair housing legislation and prohibiting the enactment of similar measures in the future. Despite the active opposition of civil rights groups and other civic organizations, in the election

227

of November 1964, Proposition 14 passed by a vote of roughly two to one.

Although it was eventually declared unconstitutional (in May 1967) by the United States Supreme Court, which upheld a state court ruling, its passage seemed to indicate that, in the opinion of the electorate, the state administration was moving too fast in the field of civil rights. California voters went on record to assert that an owner's control over his private property was more important than the right of all men to enjoy freedom of choice about where they should live. The proposition was worded to suggest that the principle was one, not of racial discrimination, but of the property owner's prerogatives.

The passage of Proposition 14 had little direct impact on the people in the ghettos, since the benefits of the fair housing laws had hardly begun to reach them anyway. The proposition's chief significance lay in the fact that it was an endorsement of a long-standing policy of separation of the races which had created Watts and other areas of black urban concentration in the first place. Negroes in California, whose numbers increased seven-fold between 1940 and 1960, were excluded for the most part from the hundreds of new housing tracts that were erected to meet the postwar home shortage. When black people had followed whites to the suburbs, new ghettos were created to accommodate them.

In 1954, when a Negro family succeeded in buying a resale home in a moderate-priced neighborhood thirty-five miles south of San Francisco, real estate men promoted panic selling among the white residents to stimulate a rapid turnover of homes at immense profit to themselves. From the realtors' viewpoints, East Palo Alto–Belle Haven had the advantage of being cut off from the communities to the west by a freeway. The black families could be physically separated from all-white neighborhoods by the bay on one side and by the traffic artery on the other. During the period of transition the district school board made a fateful decision to build a new high school in the area, which was becoming almost entirely black, thus initiating an error that would be compounded over the years.

For the residents of East Palo Alto, San Francisco's Hunters Point, and Los Angeles' Watts, the promise of a better life in California seemed more hopeful than the existence in the rural South from which so many of them had migrated. Frustration was all the more keen when they found themselves with "increased economic means" (though in the early sixties many families in Watts had yearly incomes under four thousand dollars), yet "contained and restricted." [1] There was little industry in the ghettos; the schools seemed to offer no preparation for employment or social utility. With poor public transportation, people, when shopping, were dependent on neighborhood stores, where the merchandise was overpriced. They were far from the medical clinics, hospitals, libraries, and cultural centers located in the heart of the white communities outside. Their chief visitors from that world were policemen, social workers, collection agents, and profiteering salesmen. The isolation of the ghettos, the separation of the races, increased fear and hostility. On the San Francisco peninsula, the realtors, "the keepers of the wall," [2] adopted the creed: "They shall not pass!" In the Southland, a resident of a community near Watts told the Los Angeles City Council that Willowbrook would either stay lily-white or would run red with blood.[3]

In the early sixties the young men of Watts, caged in their south central downtown area, were becoming aware of the stirrings in the outside world, their expectations aroused less by the reforms of the progressive administration in Sacramento than by the civil rights movement in the national arena. "Blacks from different gangs, even from different sides of town, started to huddle together on the street corners and in the parks," wrote J. K. Obatala.

"They talked about the usual things—sex and violence and parties—but they also talked about Selma and Birmingham and Martin Luther King and James Meredith and Medgar Evers and Malcolm X and the members of their own gangs who had been felled by the bullets of white policemen." [4]

The group that met in an area called the "Parking Lot" were shaped by the social pathology of their environment; educationally, they were "dropouts"; occupationally, they were "obsolete." To counteract their feelings of being "powerless" and "invisible," they adopted their own codes for survival, developing highly stylized personal roles and engaging in activities that got them into trouble with the police.[5] They expressed their alienation in behavior that won them notoriety in the community. Habituated to violence, they felt no restraint in venting their hatred on the symbols of the apartheid society.

"Late one afternoon," wrote Obatala of those events in the summer of 1965, "a message flashed through the grapevine: 'The cops are at it again.' At *what*, few people knew and even fewer cared; whatever the police were doing, they had already done it one time too many. And so the anger and rage that had accumulated over the years erupted into open warfare between two kinds of Americans: the Outs and the Ins. For most of the youth gangs that had roamed and terrorized South Central Los Angeles, the riot was the Last Great Rumble." [6]

Significantly the youthful ringleaders were joined by a cross-section of the Negro community. Several thousand residents of Watts participated in the looting and burning; others expressed an "emotional identification with those who were rioting in the streets." [7]

The most serious civil uprising in the history of Los Angeles lasted 144 hours. Thirty-four people were killed, over a thousand were injured, and millions of dollars of property was destroyed. Though the violence seemed random to horrified spectators—most of whom watched it on television from the safety of their living rooms—the targets were symbols of the injustices that had long festered in the community. Homes, schools, libraries, churches, and public buildings were generally spared, as well as service stations and automobile agencies, while the rioters attacked "white-owned stores which charged outrageous prices, sold inferior goods, and applied extortionate credit arrangements." [8]

The "insensate rage of destruction" [9] finally died down, and when the governor lifted the curfew, called off the National Guard, and began to assess the damage caused by six days of burning and breaking, the Los Angeles community and the state, shocked into action, began pouring offers of help and relief money into Watts. Businessmen, writers, social workers, psychiatrists, and other professionals offered their services. A commission was appointed at a cost of a quarter of a million dollars to assess and interpret the disaster.

A lesser conflagration at San Francisco's Hunters Point the following summer elicited the same reaction. The black ghettos were invisible no longer. Job training programs and new businesses were started, the Office of Economic Opportunity and other agencies came in to help. The "poverty industry" was born, and many black residents found employment in setting up programs and dispensing the funds, the "conscience money" proffered to atone for previous neglect. Hunters Point began receiving three million dollars a year from the federal Model Cities Program. New industries, as well as credit unions and other benefits, were started in Watts. In spite of the changes, however, joblessness, crime, and drug addiction are continuing problems in urban areas of high black concentration. A reporter in Watts in the summer of '72 wrote of "deteriorating houses, empty storefronts and vacant lots strewn with broken bottles and twisted cans. . . . Would-be hustlers still hang around in vacant lots, learning the rules of the street from the reigning neighborhood toughs." [10] "Hustling" is a real, alternative lifestyle in an area of high unemployment. It's hard to "go straight" if you can't get a job; it's hard to get a job if you're an ex-convict. Many ghetto residents are trapped in this vicious circle.

In the opinion of a contemporary, the young rioters of 1965 "were trying to burn their way *into* the system, not out of it." [11] In personal terms, a year later they were able to achieve the same sense of fulfillment—which they had previously experienced in actions of mass destructiveness —in diametrically different circumstances, when they acted as guardians of public safety at a cultural festival held to commemorate the anniversary of the riot. On the recently rubble-strewn streets, which became the setting for musical events that attracted the greater Los Angeles community, the men who had committed arson and theft twelve months before became the guardians of law and order. From the Parking Lot gang was born the Sons of Watts Improvement Association. From a similar group of disaffected youths in San Francisco was born the Young Men for Action at Hunters Point.

Though many white Californians, individually and through organizations, had rushed in to proffer aid and to listen to the pent-up grievances released by the catalytic actions of August 1965 and later, a delayed negative re- action to the riots was expressed in subsequent elections. This Caucasian backlash was considered to be a factor in the defeat of Governor Brown in 1966 by his conservative Republican challenger, Ronald Reagan, though the Berkeley students' revolt of 1964, which had no racial overtones, was perhaps of even greater significance in the campaign. Three years later the mayor of Los Angeles, Samuel Yorty, defeated a moderate challenger, City Councilman Thomas Bradley, by arousing fears among the white electorate of a militant take-over by the black people in the city, who constituted about 18 percent of the total population. The following year, however, another personable black moderate, Wilson Riles, defeated a conservative, Max Rafferty, for the nonpartisan post of State Superintendent of Public Instruction. These political races reflect the wide divergence among the electorate, which makes it difficult to predict the outcome of elections in California. Bradley is preparing to challenge Yorty again in 1973.

The Watts riot took place at the end of a period of gradual advances in the field of civil rights that had first gained momentum at the time of World War II and had been the work of a coalition of white liberals and black moderates. The ghetto uprisings in the mid-sixties suggested that both the programs and their architects were not representing the needs of a large majority of black people in the state.

"Man, nobody speaks for me. I speak for myself," said a youth at Hunters Point in September 1965.[12] Quite suddenly at this time voices from the black urban ghettos began to express their feelings in their own words, with no attempt to conciliate white listeners or to play lip service to the old ideals of brotherhood and integration. The new harsh rhetoric came from the college campuses where minority recruitment programs had been launched and from the neighborhoods where housewives and mothers organized to improve the conditions of life on their own terms. The ideological movement toward racial separatism, that was expressed in the demand for black studies, black schools, and the exclusion of whites from local enterprises, was carried to its extreme by the Oakland-born Black Panther party. Through their use of militant symbols the Panthers reversed the stereotype of black political impotence, substituting a new image of blacks as aggressive revolutionaries.

Their armed stance inspired young black followers as well as young activists of other races while antagonizing Negroes of moderate views. Recently the Panthers have laid down their guns to run for public office, though in working "within the system" they have not renounced their goal of changing it to benefit blacks and "oppressed people." Bobby Seale, a veteran of court battles and altercations with the police, is campaigning to become mayor of Oakland, a city with a population that is one-third black. He hopes to "make it the first city in the country which can be used as a revolutionary camp." [13]

A number of more orthodox black politicians, who have come up through an apprenticeship in poverty agencies and local government, have scored a notable success in nearby Berkeley. Ronald Dellums went from a seat on the Berkeley City Council to running for Congress, and ousted a liberal white incumbent in the June 1970 primary. His victory was hailed as an index of the success of "the new politics"; an unprecedented 67 percent of the inhabitants of Berkeley registered to vote. This largely young white electorate, some of them veterans of the campus disturbances of the sixties, later put into office a self-styled radical slate of city councilmen with a black mayor. Dellums was re-elected in 1972.

Augustus Hawkins of Los Angeles has been in Congress for a number of terms. Yvonne Brathwaite Burke, who also represents Los Angeles' black population of over three-quarters of a million people, was elected to Congress in November 1972, after serving as one of three women in the California State Legislature. There are now six black assemblymen. Others among them have been prominent in Democratic politics. In April 1970, Assemblyman John Miller of Oakland was chosen by his colleagues to succeed Jesse Unruh as leader of the lower house. State Senator Mervyn Dymally represents a predominantly black constituency in Los Angeles, while Assemblyman Willie Brown is elected from a racially mixed district in San Francisco.

Brown, a strong McGovern supporter, and Yvonne Brathwaite Burke, who was co-chairman, played important roles in the 1972 Democratic National Convention. The multiracial harmony of the California delegates reflected the atmosphere of the convention but was symptomatic of an easing of tension within the state in the wake of the acquittal of Angela Davis and a recent urging by black spokesmen of a moratorium on violence.

Not all black people in California supported McGovern in 1972. Some joined Negro leaders nationwide, some of formerly anti-establishment orientation, who worked to re-elect Richard Nixon. They stated as a reason for their defection from the traditionally black Democratic position their confidence in the president's support of business.[14] On balance, in considering the turbulent decade of the sixties in California race relations, it appears that black capitalism, which is dependent on white monetary transfusions, profited from the consciousness-raising of that period, even as many white Californians voiced alarm at the new militancy and independence of people in the ghettos.

A barometer of the feelings of both races has been the emotional issue of school busing to achieve integration. Is "the mixing of bodies" in the classroom a desirable goal? As in other states, both blacks and whites have different answers to this question. The National Association for the Advancement of Colored People filed a suit that resulted in the attempt to correct racial imbalance in San Francisco's ninety-six elementary schools by a busing program started in the fall of 1971. This effort has been deemed successful by the judge who ordered it, despite vocal opposition from some of the parents which resulted in the firing of the superintendent of schools. Successful busing programs in Pasadena, Berkeley, and other cities have been implemented with less trauma.

Throughout the state, however, segregated education is increasing. More than one-third of all black pupils attend schools that are 90 percent black, and over one-half attend schools that are 50 percent or more black. One-third of the Spanish-surnamed children in California attend schools in which they make up half the student body.[15] This reflects the continuing flight of white families to the suburbs and the fact that minority pupil enrollment is increasing while the total number of school children statewide is declining. But in the November 1972 election, the majority of California voters indicated that they were opposed to busing: 62 percent favored Proposition 21, which would bar assignment of children to schools because of race, color, or creed, and repeal an existing state law which seeks to eliminate racial and ethnic imbalance in the public schools. After the election the NAACP announced that it would challenge the constitutionality of the initiative in the courts.

The hiring of black and Mexican-American teachers is not keeping pace with the increase of pupils from these racial groups, though among Asians the teacher-pupil ratio is in balance. The employment of Negro and Chicano teachers has increased by less than one percent since 1967. Overall, minority groups comprise slightly over 10 percent of the teaching force and 29 percent of the pupils in the state's schools.[16] At the same time, white teachers have complained that quota systems based on racial origin and the principle of "affirmative action," by which schools seek to provide ethnic models for children, have worked to their disadvantage. In the past decade black Californians have made their most notable gains in public positions as administrators in schools and colleges and in leadership posts in the West Coast branches of prominent religious denominations.

The Brown Renaissance

With the emphasis on black-versus-white urban confrontations in the post-World War II era, the Mexican-Americans, the largest minority group in the state, for a time played a secondary role. The 3.2 million Mexican-Americans in California constitute 16 percent of the total population of the state. In Los Angeles, where 1.1 million live, they represent one-seventh of the population. They account for more than 50 percent of the total number of people in San Benito and Imperial counties. Yet between 1900 and 1960 only one individual of Spanish surname sat in the legislature. Most of the group were nonvoters, with the result that they received little attention from elected officials. Their requests for city services were likely to be ignored. Health inspectors let them live in substandard houses, which were then razed when new freeways were routed through their neighborhoods.

In 1960 the "sleeping giant" began to arise.[17] An intensive voter registration drive, conducted throughout the state by the Community Service Organization in behalf of John F. Kennedy, brought many heretofore uninvolved residents of the *barrios* into participation in the political process. The enormously increased activism of Mexican-Americans has been expressed on many levels, ranging from street battles between police and angry Chicanos to a vocal demand for ethnic recognition in public life. From the Brown Berets to the *pachuco*-style street gangs to the nonviolent farm labor pickets, Mexican-Americans have made the headlines in California recently.

An earlier movement toward assimilation with Anglo culture, which characterized some of the upwardly-mobile second generation, has been replaced by strong 'ethnic pride and identification with the Indian rather than the European-Caucasian side of their genetic inheritance. This is connected with the rejection of the ideal of public education as a vehicle for Americanization. The Third World movement, in which minority groups unite to proclaim their separate identities, is a repudiation of the "melting pot." The young Chicanos who are playing successful roles in the Anglo world are loyal to the traditions of the *barrio*. Whatever success they achieve will be plowed back into the community. They are glad to accept the opportunities of the larger society, but are on guard lest achievement separate them from their origins. Like the blacks, they are critical of middle-class liberal causes which seem irrelevant to the problems of people of minority races.

They ask recognition of California's dual-language tradition, especially the abolishment of the literacy test in English as a qualification for voting. A law in effect since 1894 has been challenged in the courts and in a 1972 state ballot proposition. Bilingual classrooms are being started in a number of schools with a high Mexican-American enrollment. Chicanos want a correct interpretation of their culture, with Mexican stereotypes removed from advertising. The Anglo sociologists' view of Mexican-American life was attacked in the quarterly *El Grito*, published in Berkeley by Quinto Sol Publications. A group has suggested that the territory ceded to the United States through the Treaty of Guadalupe Hidalgo, called Aztlán, be restored to Spanish-Indian autonomy. A separatist political party, La Raza Unida, has taken away votes from more traditional Chicano Democrats.

In the federal census Americans of Mexican ancestry were listed as white and identified by Spanish surnames. In 1970 Chicano leaders challenged the census-takers, and demanded a recount on the ground that people who had difficulty with English were being overlooked. They argued that an undercount could cost the group heavily in government grants and programs based on numbers. Census figures indicate that one out of six Californians is of Latin origin, the majority being Mexican. The *Latinos* of San Francisco, concentrated in the Mission District, are from Central America, Puerto Rico, Cuba, Spain, and South America (only one-fifth are of Mexican descent) but Los Angeles has the largest Mexican population of any city in the United States.

At present there is one Congressman, Edward Roybal, and two Chicano assemblymen representing the huge Los Angeles constituency, but there is not a single member of the group on the Los Angeles City Council or on the County Board of Supervisors. In an August 1971 count, of the 15,650 elected officials on all levels in the state, it was discovered that only 310 were Mexican-Americans.[18] A new movement toward reapportionment promises to correct this underrepresentation. (In the November 1972 election, five Chicanos won seats in the legislature.) One of the prime movers in this as well as in the fight to extend voting privileges to non-English-speaking citizens is the Negro state senator, Mervyn Dymally, who practices "the politics of coalition," a departure from earlier hostility between Chicanos and black Californians.

In Stockton a coalition of blacks, whites, and Chicanos succeeded in the last few years in winning representation for the city's minority race population, about one-third of the total, who live on the southside. This was accomplished by passing an amendment to the city charter to permit voting by district rather than at large for city council and school board members.[19]

Recently Chicanos have won elections in many small San Joaquin Valley towns, where they constitute a sizable group. With the help of Fresno leaders of the Mexican-American Political Association (MAPA), Chicanos have become members of the city councils in Dinuba, Sanger, Huron, Reedley, Fresno, and Mendota. In the spring of 1972 Mexican-Americans won a majority on the city council in Parlier, where they represent 85 percent of the approximately two thousand people. The town had been rent with dissension, manifested by acts of vandalism and arson, since a previous council, without a single Mexican-American member, had appointed an Anglo newcomer as police chief over the head of a Chicano who had served on the force eighteen years. The Anglo police chief blamed

"Communist revolutionaries" for the trouble.[20] But Arcadio Viveros, the young leader who engineered the successful election, said, "All our lives we've been told that we don't have the intelligence to make our own decisions, that we're only good to work in the fields. We're going to show them we're not like that. We will work for the whole community. Racism is very strong here. Maybe by setting examples we can change people's minds." [21]

The new Chicano activism in the valley has been given impetus by the farm labor organizing movement of Cesar Chavez. Feliciano Urrutia, a young tractor driver at Gallo Vineyards and a representative of the United Farm Workers Organizing Committee, became the president of the Livingston Community Action Council,[22] which grew out of a strike by Mexican-American students at the high school. Under a board which represented a cross-section of the community—Anglo, Portuguese, Japanese-American as well as Chicano—the council started a day-care center and a clinic staffed by medical students from Stanford University.

Cesar Chavez was an apricot picker in the Santa Clara Valley when he was tapped for leadership training by a Quaker organizer, Fred Ross, and pressed into the political action campaign of the Community Service Organization, first in San Jose and later in the San Joaquin Valley. There he was brought into touch with migrant pickers whose plight seemed to him to be so urgent that he gave up his work with the CSO to devote his full time to labor organizing. "It is a great tragedy," Chavez said recently, "that in this land of plenty the men and women who work to feed us haven't enough to eat." [23]

The contest between the farm workers and the California growers has a special interest for ethnic history in that it is a conflict between groups of immigrants. Many of the growers are of Italian, Yugoslavian, Armenian, Swedish, and Japanese ancestry. Some of them represent the giant corporations that dominate the state's five-billion dollar agricultural industry, which is the base for the prosperity of the cities of Stockton and Fresno and the smaller valley towns.

The Mexican-American and Filipino farm workers were supported by a coalition of liberals and churchmen, while the growers hired a public relations firm to present their case to the public. "We fought it on economic grounds," said a small grower, Stephen Pavitch, "and the union—the union and the churches—fought it on moral grounds." [24] Protestant churches, through the National Farm Worker Ministry, have been closely involved on the side of the farm workers. Many of the growers, as well as Chicano and Filipino farm workers, are Catholics, and the Bishop's Committee on Farm Labor has acted as a mediator to bring both sides to the bargaining table. On the other hand both Protestant and Catholic churches, located in the areas where the strikes were occurring, were inclined to side with the growers who represented the business community.

The leader of the most successful farm labor union in the nation's history is seen by his opponents as a hardheaded labor organizer, and by outside religious and social action groups as a modern-day saint who has taken a vow of poverty and nonviolence to effect long-overdue social changes. His success has been partly a matter of time and place. In 1964 the internationally approved *bracero* program, under which Mexican aliens were imported on a temporary basis to work in the fields, was canceled, leaving the farm labor field to domestic workers and a smaller number of "green carders" imported under the Immigration and Naturalization Service. Agriculture produces more income in California than in any other state. Chavez concentrated on the multimillion-dollar table-grape crop, which required experienced hands several times a year for pruning and girdling vines and picking. He selected a relatively small target area around Delano in the southern San Joaquin Valley.

For a time the organizing activities followed a familiar pattern. When most of the workers at the Guimarra vineyards walked off the job, they were replaced with alien strikebreakers. The technique that made the organizing effort of the farm workers ultimately successful was a nationwide boycott against table grapes. This involved a slow, painstaking campaign carried on in cities thousands of miles from the Delano headquarters. After three years the publicity and the cumulative effect in the market brought the growers to the bargaining table. In July 1970, John Guimarra, Jr., and twenty-five other grape growers signed contracts with UFWOC which by then was affiliated with the AFL-CIO.

The three-year contracts provided wages of $1.80 an hour—fifteen cents above the state minimum—with a provision for an increase, incentive payments of twenty cents per box of grapes, ten cents an hour for a health and welfare fund, and two cents a box for an economic development fund to provide housing for elderly workers. A worker-grower committee was to regulate the use of dangerous pesticides. Strikes were prohibited during the three-year period covered by the contract.

Since that time a number of wine-grape and lettuce growers, as well as a few who market other produce, have signed contracts with UFWOC, which is competing in some areas with the Teamsters Union. The Teamsters have been represented by UFWOC as outsiders coming in to sign "sweetheart" contracts with the growers in order to undercut the bargaining position of the legitimate union. The 1970 contracts must be renegotiated in 1973. UFWOC claims that the growers have not been hurt economically, because the value of the table-grape crop has increased from 36.3 to 42.6 million since the first contracts were signed.[25] One grower described the settlement as an "armed truce." Another said, "We aren't enthralled with UFWOC, but we can live with them." [26]

Much more critical are various marketing groups, labor contractors whose role has been eliminated by the union hiring hall, and small growers who are caught in an economic squeeze. The independent growers, who own from forty to two hundred acres of land apiece, survive the competition of the giant corporations by their crop selection, by cooperative marketing and use of equipment, and by informal but often long-standing working arrangements with laborers hired at harvest time. Some feel that they cannot afford to operate under a union contract, arguing that the union has increased the cost of producing any one crop from 30 to 35 percent.[27]

Other small growers insist that the threat to their livelihood is not the union, but the conglomerates that can afford to undersell the market. "The small farmer has to get big or he has to get out. Nine times out of ten he gets out," said Gus Stamenson, a Greek immigrant who has been a leader in the National Coalition for Land Reform which seeks to enforce the 160-acre limitation on irrigated land.[28] He criticized government policies that subsidize "vertically integrated corporations" and the use of the taxpayers' dollars to support land grant colleges in their invention of machines that "replace workingmen who must have food and shelter regardless if they work or not." [29]

Japanese-American small growers opposed to UFWOC have organized a Nisei Farmers League that includes Scandinavians, Armenians, and other nationalities in its membership. In 1972 Nisei farmers picked grapes and donated their wages to nonstriking workers, in support of vineyard owners against whom a strike was in progress during the renegotiation of a union contract. The bitter recriminations made by the warring groups in this conflict recalled the labor troubles of the mid-thirties, when Japanese-American growers battled Mexican strikers. The Issei were also active in labor organizing at that time. In 1936, a year of labor unrest in California, the president of the California Japanese Labor Union was held for deportation.[30]

Another group that has moved from worker to employer status are the Sikhs. The East Indian peach growers, who play an important role today in the agricultural economy of Yuba and Sutter counties, employ Mexican farm laborers and learn Spanish so that they can speak to their help. The immigration of people from the Punjab is small but continuous. They begin by working as unskilled laborers, but save money to buy land of their own. One man who came in 1967 has already acquired a thirty-four-acre orchard, which he manages with his sons.[31] Pakistanis in rice-growing near Sacramento follow a similar pattern.

The Filipinos, like the Mexicans, have generally not gone into farm management, but have been very active in the farm labor movement since the thirties. UFWOC represents a merger of Chavez' United Farm Workers and the Filipino Agricultural Workers Organizing Committee. Chavez has insisted on the equality of the two groups against the advice of some Chicanos who want to assert the supremacy of *la raza*. His cooperation with Anglos, however, has created a problem with some of the Filipinos. Young, idealistic, middle-class whites have offered their services to the union. Many work in union offices around the country for ten dollars a week and five dollars for personal expenses, with housing provided. Others have advanced in the leadership circle around Chavez to the degree that Larry Ithiong, the Filipino former vice-president of the union, resigned because he felt that the cause was becoming too much concerned with long-range social change rather than with the immediate welfare of the workers.[32]

The opposition to the union is very strong. "We are in the same position the CIO was back in the thirties," [33] said Chavez shortly before California voters went to the polls to register their opinion on a November 1972 ballot referendum, sponsored by the growers, which would

have curtailed UFWOC's organizing activities and outlawed its most effective weapon, the secondary boycott.
Over $500,000 was spent by farm groups to qualify and
promote the measure, which was rejected by a substantial
margin. Farm spokesmen have announced that they will
try again. As the contest has become the focus of nationwide interest and is moving into other states, it has taken
on a political coloration. Prominent Democrats, notably the
Kennedy family, support Chavez, while California's Republican governor, Ronald Reagan, has been allied with the
growers.[34] With a membership of 40,000 out of approximately 96,000 permanent and 500,000 temporary farm
workers in California, the union has moved its headquarters
from Delano to Keene in Kern County.

The future relationship of farm management and farm
labor in California is unpredictable. There is the problem
of the small farmers who are being crowded out of operation
by the giant conglomerates. Though orchardists, including
Nisei and Punjabi entrepreneurs, are making a living on
less than one hundred acres, many feel that the unioniza-
tion of farm workers will put them out of business. As for
the factory farms, the question remains as to whether their
executives will try to avoid the problems and costs of
negotiation of labor contracts by phasing out crops that
require hand labor and converting to those that can be
handled by machine. Mechanical harvesting is on the increase. Foes of the union concede, however, that it has
improved conditions for all farm workers just by its existence.

Another problem, an old one in California, is the effect
on the labor market of the hundreds of thousands of aliens,
the majority from Mexico, who enter the state illegally. An
estimated 300,000 were living in the Los Angeles area in
1971. Over 120,000 people were deported from the state
the same year. They come to California—and other states
—because there are not enough jobs in Mexico. Country
people flocking to the cities are destitute. In the United

States, though the cost of living is higher, they can earn ten times as much as at home. Some, whose families have scraped together the money to send them north, pay as much $200 to be smuggled across the border. Others enter on a seventy-two-hour visitor's pass and then stay on. If they are caught, they get a free ride home after signing a "voluntary departure" form. Formal prosecution is reserved for those who are involved in the multimillion dollar drug traffic between the two countries. The border patrol agents, posted to check narcotics smuggling, sometimes catch illegal aliens being carried across the border by truck.

The illegal alien traffic concerns others states as well,[35] but one-third of the Mexicans who were deported last year were apprehended in California. One of the factors that increases the difficulty of handling the problem (which costs the United States around $35 million a year) is the eagerness of businessmen and growers to hire illegal aliens who work for less than legal residents and under conditions over which the employer alone has complete control. Worker protest is checked by the threat of exposure and deportation. Though illegal aliens are profitable for employers, they debase working conditions for the citizen labor force and contribute to welfare costs when domestic workers are deprived of jobs.

A bill introduced into the the California legislature in 1971 by a freshman assemblyman, Dixon Arnett, would penalize employers who knowingly hire illegal aliens *"if such employment would have an adverse effect on lawful resident workers."* [36] Like similar laws in the past (one was introduced in 1939), it was declared unconstitutional in a state court on the grounds that the federal government had preempted the field of legislation dealing with illegal aliens.

The illegal alien migration is profitable to many people. On the balance sheet, industry and agriculture are saving more by employing noncitizens than the cost to the state and federal government as a result of their residence in California. Mexican-Americans are involved in the problem in that some of them, like the recently appointed United States treasurer, Romano Branuelos, have been accused of hiring illegal aliens in their businesses. Chicano groups have complained of surprise raids by agents of the Immigration and Naturalization Service, protesting that American citizens who could not speak fluent English were mistakenly apprehended, that searches were conducted without warrants, and that Mexicans were being singled out, whereas illegal aliens from Canada and Europe were ignored. [37] On the other hand Mexican-Americans are the chief complainants about illegal aliens. In the 1971 registration, 387,155 *legal* Mexican aliens were recorded in California.

From the Orient

During the years when Chinese immigration was prohibited, coolie laborers were smuggled into California, but not in such large numbers as Mexican nationals. The Chinese population reached its lowest point in the 1920s. After alien wives were permitted to enter in 1930,[38] a second generation began to arrive, but many families were still separated, and a considerable number of older men returned to China during the Depression years. The outbreak of the Sino-Japanese War in 1937, followed by World War II, cut off movement in either direction. With the repeal of the Chinese Exclusion Act in 1942, a yearly quota of 105 immigrants was set.[39] After the war five thousand Chinese war brides of American servicemen, were admitted with their children, along with the other foreign war brides. Then the McCarran-Walter Immigration Act of 1952 lifted all restrictions against Asian immigration, and in 1965 the national origins formula of the 1924 laws was abolished, with the result that Asian quotas were put on the same basis as that of the European. Between 1950 and 1970 the Chinese population in California more than doubled.[40]

There is a substantial Chinese middle class who live

in the suburbs; they were among the first to profit from the relaxation of residential restrictions on race. Distinguished Chinese scholars and scientists have made outstanding contributions to American life. Chinese have achieved success in many fields, including architecture and the building trades. Some of the new immigrants are students and professionals from different parts of China who have found a place for themselves fairly rapidly in West Coast communities and institutions and became a part of this middle class, profiting from the favorable image of the Chinese that had developed during the war.

A larger group who came from Hong Kong, to which many of them had fled from other parts of China, have had to take refuge in the Chinese ghettos of the West Coast as did the immigrants of one hundred years earlier. Families with four or five children live in a single room, sharing cooking and toilet facilities with other people in their building. To make ends meet, both parents work— the father perhaps as a dishwasher in a restaurant; the mother in a nonunionized garment factory, with her preschool child under her worktable and the other children waiting for her in the street outside.

A Chinese-American writer described San Francisco's Chinatown with its sixty thousand people as the only pocket of poverty in the United States that is a major tourist attraction. In an area of fine restaurants, elderly people are undernourished.[41] Behind the colorful facade, maintained for visitors, are dwellings in which there exist serious health and social problems. The incidence of tuberculosis attests to the overcrowding. Young street gangs defy the stereotype of the well-behaved Chinese youth. The criminal activities of young immigrants from Hong Kong, which include extortion and murder, have alarmed the older generation, including the merchant-spokesmen for West Coast communities. The victims are Chinese, and in some cases city law enforcement agencies have not been called in lest the complex working relationships in the Chinese community be upset by outsiders. "The matter has not been brought to the attention of the police," said one spokesman in San Francisco. "It will be handled internally." [42]

This same spirit has caused Chinese parents to oppose the court-ordered busing of their children to schools outside Chinatown. Of all the groups in San Francisco that defied the busing order in the fall of 1971, the Chinese expressed the most intense emotion. New influences are changing some of the attitudes in Chinatown. Younger American-born Chinese, some based at California State University, San Francisco, have challenged the power structure and tried to bring some of the problems of the community into the open.

In 1969 a youth group formed a Red Guard patterned after the Black Panthers and ideologically committed to Maoist doctrine, an intentional affront to the conservative elders who were attached to the Taiwan government. Their disruptions were a threat to the tourist image of Chinatown. Significantly, they were an American-born group, whereas the young criminal gangs, who have shaken down local businesses and who allegedly been been hired to protect long-time gambling operations, are immigrants. It is expected that the shift in diplomatic relations between Peking and Washington will be reflected in the curio shops of Chinatown. As a living area, it is so crowded that people are moving to Los Angeles and other cities, but Los Angeles' Chinatown is just as densely settled. The California Chinese are a predominantly urban group. Only a few descendents are to be found in the former mining areas and in the towns of the Sacramento Delta, which now have historical significance. A joss house at Oroville will be preserved by the state after the death of the last worshiper.[43] Historical markers commemorate the site of the San Luis Obispo store owned by the labor contractor Ah Louis, as well as the locale of an early Japanese tea and silk growing colony at Gold Hill near Sacramento.

Second- and third-generation Chinese are marrying into

other races, but not with such frequency as the Sansei, the third-generation Japanese-Americans. In 1920 the Issei potato grower, George Shima, told a congressional committee, "In a hundred years when you come back you will see this warm Japanese blood mixed up with your race." [44] At that time no one dreamed how prophetic his words would be. California's miscegenation law was abolished by the state supreme court in 1948, almost two decades before the federal tribunal's ruling on interracial marriage. In 1949 eighty licenses were issued in Los Angeles to couples of mixed race. The majority were unions between white women and Negroes, Filipinos, Chinese, Malays, and Japanese. A smaller number of white men married women of the races listed above, the largest number being Japanese-white marriages. [45] A recent study in Fresno County and San Francisco showed that the same pattern holds today: Japanese-American women marry Caucasian men more frequently than the reverse. In 1971, in these two places, among the Japanese there were more racially mixed marriages than marriages within the race. [46] Asian parents often have been more reluctant than Caucasians to give their blessing to such unions, but the attitude is changing. Now, however, Japanese-Americans are asking what this trend means in terms of the perpetuation of their cultural heritage.

The high intermarriage rate is symptomatic of the changed situation of the *Nikkei* ("the Japanese") in the postwar years. Whereas before 1940 they had been largely frustrated in their careers, on their return from the relocation camps they were able to use their education and training in the expanding job market in which the racial barriers to equal opportunity were being removed. The Japanese-Americans were prime beneficiaries of the civil rights laws, many of which they helped to implement. They moved into the middle class and into the suburbs without leaving behind in the inner cities a core poverty group of any size. Los Angeles' Little Tokyo and San Francisco's Japantown are today mainly business communities, though they still contain residential neighborhoods where older people live.[47]

The prosperity of the Nisei has created identity problems for their children. The Sansei have repudiated to some extent the white middle-class orientation of their parents to proclaim common cause with other racial minorities. The racial separation which characterized the older generations, particularly the Issei, and which has been evoked by the Sansei poet, Lawson Inada,[48] has given way to participation in the Third World movements. Sansei joined black students in protest against Dr. S. I. Hayakawa, the Canadian-born Japanese philologist who became the president of California State University, San Francisco, during a 1969 strike. Chinese and Japanese have united in activist movements and in the publication of their own newspapers— *Gidra* in Los Angeles and *Rodan* in San Francisco.

The attitude of the younger generation seems to have influenced the Nisei, who have shown a willingness to challenge the establishment when an injustice was brought to their attention in a way that would have been unthinkable to the Issei. After a Negro newspaper in Los Angeles exposed the racial implications in the 1969 firing of the county coroner, Japanese-born Dr. Tsunetomi (Thomas) Noguchi, from the post he had held for two years, a Nisei committee raised funds for a reconsideration of his case that resulted in his reinstatement. Thoroughness and persistence characterize the campaigns in which Nikkei, through the Japanese American Citizens League (JACL), have worked to abolish discriminatory statutes, liberalize immigration laws, and finally to press successfully for the repeal, in 1971, of Title II of the Internal Security Act of 1950, which provided for detention camps for potential subversives at a time of national emergency. Though the law was inspired by fears of communism, to the Nisei it too closely resembled the emergency governmental orders under which they were interned in 1942. They had made its repeal a particular goal.

The Sansei have discovered the evacuation experience

of their parents as an example of persecution which links them to the other racial minorities who are presently engaged in direct confrontations with the white society from which the Sansei are insulated by their middle-class status. The evacuation years have been re-evoked and re-evaluated. The change in Caucasian attitudes toward Japanese-Americans in the last thirty years has been startling; yet some Nikkei feel that the favor they now enjoy is precarious. A number of "hate calls" were phoned in when California newspapers and radio stations publicized a traveling exhibit of photographs and paintings of the evacuation in 1972.

The Sansei are interested in Japanese culture, but do not look to Japan as a place of refuge and protection as their grandparents did. The sense of kinship with the peoples of the Third World was taken up by their elders who, at the 1972 convention of the Japanese American Citizens League, proclaimed a commitment to Pan-Asianism.

Asians have been less active in politics in California than blacks and Chicanos. The first non-European immigrant to serve in Congress was Judge Dalip S. Saund, an East Indian from the Imperial Valley, who won a seat in 1956 after campaigning intensively among Mexican-Americans in his constituency. He spent sixteen thousand dollars traveling throughout his desert district by car, while his opponent, the aviatrix Jacqueline Cochran Odlum of Indio, who was supported by wealthy friends in Palm Springs, did much of her campaigning by air. Judge Saund had come to the United States as a student in 1919 and had been naturalized thirty years later.[49]

A Chinese, George Chinn, has been appointed to fill a vacancy on the San Francisco Board of Supervisors, which is as diverse ethnically as the population of the city. March Fong of Oakland has served several terms in the state legislature, and is now one of two women in that eighty-member body. William Soo Hoo was the mayor of Oxnard. Chinese-Americans as well as Nisei sit on the city councils of various California communities and are serving on local government boards and as judges throughout the state. Norman Mineta is the mayor of San Jose, the fourth largest city in the state, located in a rapidly expanding area with a large Chicano population.

Political participation should be checked against numbers. In the listing of racial minorities in the state in the 1970 census, the largest number are Negroes, followed in order by Japanese, Chinese, Filipinos, Indians, and "all others." [50] In this last blanket category are over fifteen thousand Koreans and over fourteen thousand Hawaiians, who are concentrated mainly in the urban areas of the state. [51] Also included are between fifteen and twenty thousand immigrants from American Samoa, who have arrived in California within the last two decades and are living in Los Angeles, San Diego, Oceanside, and in the San Francisco Bay Area. As natives of an American protectorate, they immigrate and become naturalized without the delays and difficulties sometimes experienced by people from foreign countries. Many of the men work in the shipyards or in heavy industry, and the women in hospitals as nurses' aides. Their adjustment to mainland life is eased by a strong attachment to family and church. Some are Roman Catholics, others are Mormons, but the majority are Congregationalists, whose forebears were converted on their home island by preachers from the London Missionary Society. Other dark-skinned immigrants in California come from Indonesia and from the smaller Asian countries, and about five hundred people are from Pakistan and over five thousand from India.

The First Americans

Of the total number of American Indians, or Native Americans, in California, a great many have come from other parts of the United States. Some were brought from reservations by the Bureau of Indian Affairs to take part in training programs in cities on the West Coast. [52] Of the

91,000 Indians recorded in the state in the 1970 census, almost 70,000 were in urban areas, the largest number in Los Angeles.

Most of the eighty-four small reservations in California, which occupy 1200 square miles in all and house only 10 percent of the state's Native Americans, are in obscure places reached by unpaved back roads, the sites unknown to most whites and not desired by them. An exception was some land near Palm Springs, owned by about one hundred members of the Aqua Caliente band, which was appraised at fifty million dollars. The group was victimized by court-appointed guardians for the minors and for those adults who the Secretary of the Interior decided were "in need of assistance in handling their affairs." Local businessmen bilked the Indians for exorbitant fees until an exposé by a reporter from the Riverside *Press-Enterprise* brought about an investigation by the state attorney general's office. One man whose "conservator" demanded over twenty thousand dollars, said, "You know what the Indians would like? They'd like to be free for just a spell without having to fight somebody off." [53]

Indians in California have recently found a particularly effective means of dramatizing their grievances by establishing claims to federal land, thus reversing the process of white expropriation of their original lands. In November 1969 a small landing party invaded Alcatraz Island in San Francisco Bay, which housed a former federal prison. They were soon joined by Native Americans from all over the country, who claimed the site under an 1863 treaty that promised to restore to Indians land relinquished by the federal government. They offered to buy Alcatraz for twenty-four dollars and some red cloth, drawing up a treaty which was a parody of all the documents that the white man had negotiated with Indians over the years. The proclamation stated: "We will give to the inhabitants of this island a portion of the land for their own to be held in trust by the Bureau of American Indian Affairs and by the Bureau of Caucasian Affairs to hold in perpetuity—for as long as the sun shall rise and the rivers go down to the sea. We will further guide the inhabitants in the proper way of living. We will offer them our religion, our education, our life-ways, in order to help them achieve our level of civilization and thus raise them and all their white brothers up from their savage and unhappy state." [54]

The Alcatraz occupation developed into a pan-Indian movement, generating a pride and an ethnic consciousness that was transplanted to other places long before the Coast Guard removed the last members of the occupation force in 1971. Indians occupied an abandoned Air Force telephone communication center near the Davis campus of the University of California in November 1970, and there founded Deganawidah-Quetzalcoatl University for Native American and Chicano studies. In March 1972 some Indians occupied land at the Mission of San Antonio de Padua, north of Paso Robles, and claimed ownership of the twenty-one California missions. In September 1972 representatives of more than a dozen tribes appropriated land in Ventura County for a halfway house for reservation Indians. The invasion of Catalina Island by a group of Brown Berets, who claimed it for Mexico, also occurred in 1972.

Whites have shown mixed reactions to these incidents, which are usually handled by negotiation and arbitration. When a band of Pit River Indians invaded land in Shasta County belonging to the federal government and the Pacific Gas and Electric Company, many of their white neighbors complained that local Indians were being stirred up by radical outsiders. Since Indians are the only racial minority group of any size in parts of Northern California, Indian-white relationships there are apt to be more emotionally charged than in other parts of the state.

A good many whites in this area think of Indians in negative terms, citing automobile accidents caused by drunkenness, and Indian children in classes for the mentally retarded. Approval is awarded to those who live according to white standards. When a member of the Pit River tribe who helped Indian children in the Burney school was tragically killed when his car was struck on the highway, he was elected posthumously to the school's board of trustees as a tribute to his moral character; he was a Christian and a non-drinker, as well as a spokesman for cooperation between the races.

White interest in conservation has led to approval of the red men's relationship with nature. "The Indians knew how to handle a forest," said a resident of Davis Creek in Modoc County, contrasting their management with that of the U. S. Forest Service.[55] "Everyone is on this big ecology kick," said John Trudall, a Sioux who was a leader on Alcatraz. "We've always been on it." [56]

Indians have not been too pleased at some of the whites' imitations of their garb or misinterpretations of their legends and beliefs. Native American women attending a local history course at Shasta College offered authentic resource material as well as a corrected Indian view of local pioneer heroes among the white settlers.

In other places Indian elders are coming into classrooms to share reminiscences and to convert oral traditions into a permanent record. Language is being transcribed into textbooks. "I think we have about five years left," said the white coordinator who is bringing in elderly members of the Yurok, Hupa, and Tolowa bands to write down their legends in their own languages.[57] There is also a race against time for the archaeologists who are digging for Indian artifacts in areas threatened by development of new waterways.

Indian concerns are being listened to. California's senators have espoused the rights of the Paiute Indians living on Pyramid Lake in Nevada whose livelihood from fishing has been threatened by the diversion of Truckee River water by California and Nevada. A quarter-of-a-million-dollar Ford Foundation grant was awarded to Deganawidah-Quetzalcoatl University at Davis, and a three-million-dollar grant from the U. S. Department of Labor subsidizes its program for migrant workers in four agricultural centers in the state.

In spite of these new developments, however, the majority of Indians in California are, by their own estimation, the most deprived racial minority in the state in terms of income and employment. Alcoholism and suicide attest to their difficulty in moving between two contradictory cultures. Though the oldest people in the state have been Indians—two Los Angeles residents of 112 and 120 were discovered at the time of the Bicentennial Exhibition—Indians have a higher mortality rate than any other racial group.

Other Pioneer Descendents

The oldest "native son" was a 111-year-old *Californio*.[58] Some of the descendents of the *rancheros* are still living on small pieces of the vast estates their families once owned where they were discovered recently by a team of Los Angeles writers. One man was employed as a caretaker on his ancestral acres now owned by someone else. Another was converting what remained of the family's 100,000-acre *rancho* into a housing tract. A third, who has no connection with the family land, is intensely interested in its past history, but also became involved in the Chicano movement a few years back as a member of MAPA.[59]

Descendents of families who played an important role in early California history may or may not speak fluent Spanish or reveal their ancestry in their faces, dress, or lifestyles. But many are proud of their heritage and keep vivid family memories and a few, like the descendents of the Dominguez family, have held onto enough land to have benefited from its appreciation in the present market.[60] The Society of Californianos, whose members are descendents of pioneers who arrived before 1836, meets to discuss genealogy and to plan for the erection of historical landmarks to commemorate the Hispanic period.

Some of the older European immigrant groups have been in California long enough to take stock of their history. The landing of Columbus is re-enacted every October 12 in San Francisco by members of the Italian colony, but in 1970 the Genoa-born Joseph Cervetto, who had taken the principal role for eleven years, lost his supporting cast of real Indians. The Native Americans boycotted the ceremony.[61] On the other side of the coin, some of the long-established ethnic groups complain that they are being left out of the special programs and services that benefit racial minorities.[62] Two reporters speculated before the 1972 elections as to whether there would be a "backlash vote" resulting from racial tensions in Los Angeles and elsewhere by the city's half-million Jews, who have been traditionally strong voters and financial supporters of liberal candidates and causes. They concluded that the group that voted against Proposition 14 in 1964 would not change their orientation. In fact, a number of Jewish as well as black and Chicano voters in the city switched from Democratic to Republican affiliation in their choice of a presidential candidate, though the majority did not change.[63]

The ferment in black-white, brown-white relationships may, however, have contributed to the popularity of many of the new European immigrants who, despite language differences, are ideologically in tune with older, and to many whites, more comfortable American traditions. These newcomers introduce a novelty, with the surface aspects of their foreignness in food, costumes, dance, and music—for example, the long-established Danish colony at Solvang in the Santa Ynez Valley, which has become a tourist attraction. This is the more acceptable because at a deeper level many of the immigrants, old and new, reinforce certain values to which Americans pay lip service but which are being challenged by critics within the society and among racial minorities.

How far the attitude toward foreigners has changed in California from the nativist prejudice of fifty years ago can be seen in more recent studies of the transplanted life of Europeans. In 1942 Holland-Dutch dairymen and their families who had settled in communities near Los Angeles were generally respected by their neighbors.[64] Members of a Portuguese colony of 12,500 people living in a city in the San Francisco Bay Area were praised by their Anglo fellow townsmen in the late sixties for their "high standards." One outsider called them "the best people" in town. The security and closeness of the Portuguese family life were envied by outsiders who compared it with the hurried, fragmented existence of Americans.[65] It should be noted that both the Dutch and the Portuguese who were studied had fixed occupations which satisfied them. They were not competing with others in the community for jobs or political office. They themselves were satisfied with their lives in California.

Some of the earlier immigrants have had Horatio Alger careers. An Armenian, Jack Danielian, who arrived in the United States with five dollars and a suit of clothes and who became the millionaire owner of a Los Angeles carpet company, said, "I wish I could stand at the dock and tell every immigrant: 'Have faith, and work, and all of this can be yours!' "[66] The hero of another Armenian success story, George Mardikian, the proprietor of San Francisco's Omar Khayyam restaurant, spoke of his great pride in America and said of his years in Fresno, "I cannot tell you how beautiful it seemed to me—all this life, this movement and color."[67]

We are now hearing more often the stories of people with a professional background in their home countries who have to work in menial jobs on their arrival in California;

one such was a district judge from Poland who spoke five languages, but who was employed as a janitor in a post office in Mountain View.[68] Yet a young Croatian couple, who escaped from Yugoslavia in the early sixties by hiding in the woods and eluding the border guard near Trieste, enjoy a standard of living in San Jose that they said they could never have hoped to attain in the land of their birth.[69] A Cuban exile in Los Angeles, who got a job as a cook through a union five days after he applied, noted that in his country one often had to bribe people to obtain a certain kind of employment.[70]

Political refugees speak in wonder of the freedom they find here. Included in the refugee category are Armenians, Indonesians, Cubans, Yugoslavians, and Hungarians who have contributed to the foreign population of California, which is the largest in the United States. The alien registration of 1971 noted the various nationalities, which are listed according to their numbers in the state, as coming from Mexico, Canada, the United Kingdom, the Philippines, China and Taiwan, Germany, Japan, Cuba, Portugal, Italy, Colombia, Yugoslavia, Greece, Poland, Jamaica, and the Dominican Republic.[71] Among the large group from the United Kingdom are a good number of Australians, longtime residents of California, whose accents as overheard in San Francisco were noted in Bancroft's history.[72] A recent study was made of the "rhyming slang" spoken by the men from "Down Under," particularly those connected with prize-fighting, in the San Francisco Bay Area.[73] The large number of Canadians in California have become so completely assimilated that it is difficult to distinguish them from Americans. The Canadian who made the most important contribution to the economy of the state was George Chaffey, who designed the canal that brought Colorado River water to the Imperial Valley.

There are many foreign language newspapers in California as well as radio programs for different ethnic groups.

In addition to the programming for the most numerous language groups, there are radio hours in Greek, Polish, Swedish, Hebrew and Yiddish, Dutch, Hungarian, Serbian, Russian, Arabic, Korean, and the language of Thailand. A weekly two-hour program for the East Indians of the Yuba City–Marysville area is given in Hindi, Punjabi, and Urdu. There are regular broadcasts for the Scottish and Irish immigrants. Several stations have all-black and all-Mexican-American programming.

Some of the people who come to California are of immigrant stock that had an intermediate residence in other parts of the country, such as the Dutch from Michigan who joined the Holland-Dutch. A group of Dakotans of German descent began migrating to Lodi in the San Joaquin Valley around the turn of the century after a pathfinder, "Columbus" Hieb, had investigated the possibilities for agriculture. The Dakotans, who had been wheat farmers in the Midwest, switched to almond- and grape-growing in Lodi. The migration still continues, inspired by the weather and the presence of the folks from home.[74] "Lodi is to the Dakotas what Long Beach is to Kansas and Iowa," wrote a recent investigator.[75]

The investigator found large numbers of people from Oklahoma and Arkansas in San Diego. Though many of the original Dust Bowl migrants settled down in the San Joaquin Valley to become substantial citizens, new migrants from the south central states are continually coming into California—a small continuation of the vast influx of the thirties. Some who work in the lumber business in Shasta County go back and forth every year. Most of them settle in small towns or on the outskirts of larger towns located in rural areas. Parts of Marysville so resemble the rural South in its mixed composition of poor black and white families that Hollywood movies with a southern locale are filmed there, using the townsfolk as extras. Racial tensions are much less acute there than in large metropolitan centers like Oakland. By the same token, the assimilation of new foreign immigrants is eased in small towns where bilingual neighbors act as interpreters.[76]

Some changes are occurring in California. The momentum of growth is slowing, due in part to a recession, particularly in the aerospace industry. It has been suggested that a turning point may have been reached.[77] Though in the decade 1960 to 1970 California still recorded the largest numerical growth—as distinguished from percentage growth—of any state in the nation, in the year 1970 it was estimated that more people left the state than came into it.

San Francisco and Los Angeles have recorded a small decline in population in the last year or two. It appears that though minorities are increasing, whites are leaving in greater numbers, going to outlying areas. Demographers have predicted that if this trend continues, by 1980 black, Spanish-surnamed, Asian, and Indian citizens could conceivably outnumber whites in Los Angeles.[78]

Recent talk of setting limits to the size of Los Angeles and San Francisco suggests that in these cities there will be a clash between environmentalists who want to curb growth and low-income families for whom services and housing may be priced out of existence. Though California has abolished most of the early discriminatory laws, the economic constraints upon individuals in the coming decade may be far more stringent than those which governed settlement in the early years of statehood. There is increasing recognition that California has ceased to be a frontier, a place of limitless possibilities. Carey McWilliams recently suggested that the "last West" has moved across the Pacific to Australia, where racial restrictions were lifted in 1966 and where Californians have found a new locale for agriculture and new sources of mineral wealth.[79]

Will California continue to be a social frontier? The turbulence of the sixties was connected with the migrations of youth and the conflict between generations, as well as with ethnic rivalry. A historian recently called the state "an avant-garde showcase of the brave new world," but he noted that its people were "ill at ease in Zion." [80]

1. Douglas Graham Glasgow, "The Sons of Watts Improvement Association: Analysis of Mobility Aspirations and Life-Styles in the Aftermath of the Watts Riot, 1965" (Ph.D. thesis, University of Southern California, Los Angeles, 1968), p. 26.

2. Franklin Williams, "The Keepers of the Wall," *Frontier*, April 1960.

3. Glasgow, "Sons of Watts Improvement Association," pp. 57-58.

4. J. K. Obatala, "The Sons of Watts: Off the Streets and into the System," *Los Angeles Times West*, August 13, 1972.

5. Glasgow, "Sons of Watts Improvement Association," pp. 4-5.

6. Obatala, "Sons of Watts."

7. Glasgow, "Sons of Watts Improvement Association," p. 156.

8. Robert M. Fogelson, "White on Black: A Critique of the McCone Commission Report on the Los Angeles Riots," *Political Science Quarterly*, September 1967.

9. *Violence in the City—An End or a Beginning?* A report by the Governor's Commission on the Los Angeles Riots, December 2, 1965, p. 1.

10. Obatala, "Sons of Watts."

11. *Ibid.*

12. Ben Williams, "Pulse of the Ghetto," *San Francisco Examiner & Chronicle*, September 19, 1965.

13. *San Francisco Examiner*, November 12, 1972.

14. Celeste Durant, "Affluent Blacks Responding to GOP'S Call," *Los Angeles Times*, October 29, 1972.

15. Jack McCurdy, "Minority Students Rise in Segregated Schools," *Los Angeles Times*, September 15, 1972.

16. *Los Angeles Times*, October 14, 1972.

17. William Gardiner Hutson, "Voting Attitudes of Mexican-American Residents of Belvedere-East Los Angeles" (M.A. thesis, University of Southern California, Los Angeles, 1960), p. 72.

18. Stanley Levy, Marvin Gelfand, Michael D. Saphier, and Stanton L. Stein, "Putting Chicanos on the Political Map," *Los Angeles Times*, May 21, 1972.

19. Interviews with Donna and Thomas Ambrogi, Palo Alto, Calif., and Dario Marenco, San Francisco, November-December 1972.

20. Doug Willis, "Reign of Terror Paralyzes Old Farming Town," *Palo Alto Times*, September 14, 1971.

21. Jack Jones, "San Joaquin Valley Latins Turn to Elections to Upset Status Quo," *Los Angeles Times*, May 8, 1972.

22. Interview with Feliciano Urrutia, Livingston, Calif., February 23, 1970.

23. Cesar Chavez speech in San Jose, September 26, 1972.

24. Quoted in W. Evan Golder, "Delano—Revisited," *San Francisco Examiner & Chronicle*, October 11, 1970.

25. Frank del Olme, "Cesar Chavez—Out of Sight but Still in Fight," *Los Angeles Times*, February 14, 1972.

26. *Ibid.*

27. Dexter Waugh, "Nisei Farmers Assail Chavez' Methods," *San Francisco Sunday Examiner & Chronicle*, June 18, 1972.

28. Interview with Gus Stamenson, Livingston, Calif., September 6, 1972.

29. Gus Stamenson testimony presented to the Migratory Labor Subcommittee of the U. S. Senate at Fresno, January 12, 1972.

30. *The Open Forum*, publication of the Northern California American Civil Liberties Union, May 30, 1936; June 13, 1936.

31. Interview with Harbhajan Johl, Yuba City, Calif., June 24, 1970.

32. Del Olme, "Cesar Chavez—Out of Sight but Still in Fight."

33. Chavez speech in San Jose, September 26, 1972.

34. When twenty-six grape growers signed contracts with UFWOF, Governor Reagan issued a statement: "It is tragic that the workers who are most affected by this have no choice in determining whether or not they want to join the union." *The New York Times*, July 30, 1970.

35. The Legislative Investigative Committee of the State of Illinois in 1971 published a detailed study of the problem of illegal Mexican aliens and their effect on the economy of the state.

36. Text of Assembly Bill 528 as amended February 16, 1971.

37. Kenneth J. Fanucchi, "Sweep of Aliens Spurs Investigation by Tunney," *Los Angeles Times*, April 26, 1972.

38. They were permitted if they had been married before May 26, 1924.

39. Not all of the quota was permitted in the first years after repeal of the exclusion laws.

40. See the 1970 census. In 1960 there were 95,600 Chinese in California. In 1970 there were 170,131.

41. George Chu, "Chinatown," *San Francisco*, June 1969.

42. Charles Howe and Rose Pak, "Anger in Chinatown," *San Francisco Chronicle*, July 8, 1972.

43. Peter Beagle and Michael Bry, *The California Feeling: A Personal View* (Garden City, N. Y.: Doubleday & Co., 1969), pp. 131-132.

44. George Shima's testimony before the Committee on Immigration and Naturalization, San Francisco, Calif., July 12, 1920, House of Representatives, 66th Congress, 2nd Sess., Part I, p. 66.

45. Wen-Hui Chung Chen, "Changing Socio-Cultural Patterns of the Chinese Community in Los Angeles," p. 156.

46. Glenn Omatsu, from *Hokubei Mainichi,* reprinted in *Pacific Citizen,* January 28, 1972. The male-female ratio of all races in California is now more nearly in balance. See census figures for 1970. The Chinese list some 87,000 males to approximately 82,000 females. Among the Filipinos there are almost 79,000 males compared with 61,000 females.

47. A suggestion that there were Issei living below the poverty level in San Francisco led to an investigation which showed that elderly Japanese were reluctant to accept extra old-age security benefits, *Pacific Citizen,* August 11, 1972. A significant number of elderly Jewish people in Los Angeles were also discovered to be in want, as were many senior citizens on fixed incomes from all backgrounds throughout the state.

48. Lawson Inada, "West Side Songs," in *Down at the Santa Fe Depot,* 20 *Fresno Poets,* pp. 47-53.

49. "India Native Goes to Congress," *San Francisco Chronicle,* November 8, 1956.

50. The figures are: 213,180 Japanese; 170,131 Chinese; 138,859 Filipinos; 91,018 Indians; and all others, 178,671.

51. *California Manpower Indicators from the 1970 Census,* State of California Department of Human Resources Development, Employment Data and Research, February 1972.

52. Recently the Bureau of Indian Affairs is conducting more training programs on the reservations instead of transplanting Indians to an alien environment.

53. *Agua Caliente Indians and Their Guardians.* Selections from Pulitzer Prize-winning entry for meritorious service, published in *The Press-Enterprise,* Riverside, Calif., 1968.

54. The Alcatraz Proclamation is reproduced in Daniels and Olin, *Racism in California.* pp. 51-53.

55. Interview with Mrs. Perry O. Clark, Davis Creek, Calif., October 19, 1970.

56. "The Reasons for the Take-over of Alcatraz Island." Speech by John Trudall in Palo Alto, Calif., April 1970.

57. *San Francisco Chronicle,* November 29, 1971.

58. *Ibid.,* August 31, 1969.

59. Elaine and Art Berman, "This Land Was Their Land," *Los Angeles Times West,* April 2, 1972.

60. Interview with Mrs. Royce Skow, Saratoga, Calif., *Los Angeles Times,* April 7, 1967.

61. *San Francisco Chronicle,* October 8, 1970.

62. A representative of the Slavic Community in Los Angeles said, "We seem to be a non-people." *Los Angeles Times,* November 24, 1971.

63. Bill and Nancy Boyarsky, "A Report on Jews and Politics in Los Angeles," *Los Angeles Times West*, May 21, 1972; Richard Bergholz, "California Gives President his Biggest Victory," *Los Angeles Times*, November 8, 1972.

64. William Driver Spencer, "Problems of Assimilation of the Holland-Dutch People in a Selected Area in Southern California" (M.A. thesis, University of Southern California, Los Angeles, 1942).

65. Hans Howard Leder, "Cultural Persistence in a Portuguese-American Community" (Ph.D. disseration, Stanford University, 1968), pp. 56, 70.

66. *Victory*, June 1950, pamphlet in the Bancroft Library of the University of California at Berkeley.

67. George Mardikian, *Song of America* (New York: McGraw-Hill, 1956), p. 148.

68. *Palo Alto Times*, June 24, 1972.

69. Interview with Dinka and Rudolf Spajic, San Jose, Calif., May 6, 1970.

70. Father Laurence E. Clark, "The Social Adjustment of Cuban Refugee Families" (M.A. thesis, University of Southern California, Los Angeles, 1963), p. 23.

71. Aliens who reported under the Alien Address Program by Selected Nationalities and State of Residence. California had the largest total.

72. "Australian slang floated freely upon the infected atmosphere," Bancroft, *History of California*, vol. 6, pp. 178-179.

73. Luba Blumberg, "Rhyming Slang" (M.A. thesis, University of California, Berkeley, 1968).

74. Interview with Ed Preszler, Lodi, Calif.

75. Douglas E. Kneeland, "Lodi, Calif.: A Home for Ex-Dakotans Without the Snow," *The New York Times*, February 19, 1971.

76. Interview with Mrs. John Sequeira, Livingston, Calif., February 24, 1970; interview with Dr. and Mrs. C. H. Loehlin, East Marysville, Calif., June 24, 1970.

77. Carey McWilliams, "Australia: America's New Frontier," *World*, October 10, 1972.

78. Ray Herbert, "L. A. County's Minorities Could Become Majority by 1980," *Los Angeles Times*, October 1, 1972.

79. McWilliams, "Australia."

80. Prof. Moses Rischin of California State University, San Francisco, at a California History symposium at Stanford University, February 28, 1970.

Index

Frémont, John Charles, in Mexican War, 53-54, 56-60; Mariposa Grant, 61, 69; meets mission Indian, 14; opinion of *Californios* on, 57, 58, 73

French, at Gold Rush, 88-89, 107, 109, 110, 111; characterized, 100, 111, 148; in Los Angeles, 136, 148; numbers, 89, 224 fn. 27; occupations, 110-111, 136, 148; in San Francisco, 100, 101, 110-111, 112, 136; in Spanish California, 21, 45, 47, 51

Fresno, California, 139-140, 143-144, 149-150, 151, 200, 214, 239

Fresno County, 138, 250

Fuhrman, Alfred, 153

Furuseth, Andrew, 153

Galarza, Ernesto, 205-207

Gallo, Ernest and Julio, 144

Garcia, Jack (three-fingered), 112

Geary, John W., Mayor of San Francisco, 99

Gentlemen's Agreement, 184, 189

George, Henry, 174

Germans, as Democrats, 132-133; at Anaheim, 132; characterized, 100; early settlers, 131; numbers, 89, 130, 224 fn. 27, 260; occupations, 132; refugees of 1848, 89, 90; success of, 131-132, 136-137; traders, 45, 47; vintners, 132; during World War II, 218

Ghirardelli, Domingo, 146

Giannini, A. P., 145-146, 218

Gillespie, Archibald H., Lieutenant, 59

Gilroy, California, 137

Goldwyn, Samuel, 149

Graham, Isaac, 49, 50

Grant, Ulysses S., U. S. President, 170

"Greaser Law," 72-73

Greeks, arrival, 89; in agriculture, 243; in dairying, 139; marry late, 140-141; numbers, 224, 260

Greeley, Horace, 88

Green, Thomas Jefferson, Colonel, 108

Griffith, D. W., 222

Guadalupe Hidalgo, Treaty of, 27, 60, 68, 238

Guimarra, John, Jr., 242

Gwin, William M., California Senator, 62-63, 69, 70-71, 135

Hall, Calvin, 34

Halladie, Andrew S., 130

Hanford, California, 216

Haraszthy, Agoston, 132

Harte, Bret, 18, 32, 101, 106, 121-122, 170-171

Hartnell, William E. P., 48

Hastings, Lansford W., 54-55, 62

Hawaiians, 86, 90, 253

Hawkins, Augustus, California Assemblyman, 234

Hayakawa, S. I., Dr., 251

Henley, Thomas J., 26

Hieb, "Columbus," 261

Hindus, *see* East Indians

Hittell, Theodore, 90

Homesteaders, and Bear Flag revolt, 57-58; conflict over land grants, 67-72; conflict with *Californios*, 55-56; conflict with Indians, 17-24; dispersal to different areas, 123-124; legislature awards land, 119

Hoopa Valley Indian Reservation, 26

Hoosiers in California, 125

Hopkins, Mark, 138, 166, 172

Hornitos, California, 146, 176

Hot Creek Indians, 31-32, 33

"Hounds," or "Regulators," 107

Hudson's Bay Company, 42, 46, 50